Additional Praise for *The Oath and the Office*

"No office in American government is more studied than the presidency, and no figure in American politics is more closely watched than the president. Brettschneider provides the judgment of a renowned constitutional scholar, dramatic cases, historical sweep, a gift for clarity, and a sense of moral urgency. This is a foothold from which we can survey the dangerous course the presidency has taken and our responsibility as citizens to defend the constitution."

—*Nancy Rosenblum, Senator Joseph Clark Professor of Ethics in Politics and Government, Harvard University*

"Those who one day may find themselves behind the Big Desk in the Oval Office need to understand the limits of their power as well as its potential. Brettschneider's cogent and comprehensive user's manual—grounded in sophisticated legal and political analysis—is exactly the right place to start."

—*Gordon Silverstein, assistant dean for graduate programs, Yale Law School*

"'When the President does it, that means it is not illegal.' So said Richard Nixon. What then are the limits on presidential action? Can the president of the United States pardon himself, fire anyone in the Executive Branch, or wage war without Congressional approval? Can California develop a foreign policy on immigration and sign international climate treaties? In an era of rising executive power, Corey Brettschneider provides an essential guide for citizens and aspiring office holders on the powers of the president and how the U.S. Constitution constrains that power."

—*Rob Reich, professor of political science, Stanford University*

THE OATH
AND
THE OFFICE

THE OATH
AND
THE OFFICE

A Guide to the Constitution
for Future Presidents

Corey Brettschneider

W. W. Norton & Company

INDEPENDENT PUBLISHERS SINCE 1923

NEW YORK • LONDON

For information about permission to reproduce selections
from this book, write to Permissions, W. W. Norton & Company, Inc.,
500 Fifth Avenue, New York, NY 10110

For information about special discounts for bulk purchases,
please contact W. W. Norton Special Sales
at specialsales@wwnorton.com or 800-233-4830

Manufacturing by Quad Graphics Fairfield
Book design by Brooke Koven
Production manager: Lauren Abbate

Library of Congress Cataloging-in-Publication Data

Names: Brettschneider, Corey Lang, author.
Title: The oath and the office : a guide to the Constitution for future
    presidents / Corey Brettschneider.
Description: First edition. | New York : W.W. Norton & Company,
    2018. | Includes bibliographical references and index.
Identifiers: LCCN 2018016664 | ISBN 9780393652123 (hardcover)
Subjects: LCSH: Presidents—Legal status, laws, etc.—United States. |
Executive power—United States. | Constitutional law—United States.
Classification: LCC KF5051 .B74 2018 | DDC 342.73/0628—dc23 LC
    record available at https://lccn.loc.gov/2018016664

W. W. Norton & Company, Inc.
500 Fifth Avenue, New York, N.Y. 10110
www.wwnorton.com

W. W. Norton & Company Ltd.
15 Carlisle Street, London W1D 3BS

1 2 3 4 5 6 7 8 9 0

For my daughter, Sophie Brettschneider

Contents

SECTION III · *Checks on the President*

Introduction: The Oath

You want to serve your country. You aspire to run for office—and not just any office. You want to be president of the United States.

If you succeed, you will control the most advanced technology ever conceived, much of it secret. You will be able to authorize missile strikes, negotiate treaties, and spy on people around the world. And with a vast payroll, you will now run the largest employer in the country—the federal government.

For a moment, say that you win. You might hope to use this power to achieve great things such as ending poverty, providing affordable health care, or eliminating violent crime. You will have the ability to influence legislation and shape decisions about how to use the enormous federal budget. Lives, jobs, and trillions of dollars hang in the balance—and you have the ability to tip it. As you wave to your inauguration crowd through a blizzard of confetti, nothing seems out of reach.

Be careful: History might judge your presidency harshly. You don't want to be lumped in with Andrew Johnson, a president who opposed and undermined the core values of the country. Surveys of historians from 2002 and 2010 each ranked Johnson as one of the worst presidents in American history.[1] He was impeached by the House of Representatives (but not removed from office by the Senate) for firing his secretary of war Edwin Stanton, an ally of many in Congress at the time. Far worse, he fiercely opposed the Fourteenth Amendment— the monumental civil rights achievement of Congress after the Civil War. The amendment guaranteed equal protection of the law and extended citizenship to African Americans and all people born or naturalized in the United States. That amendment was necessary in part because Johnson essentially refused to execute the Thirteenth Amendment, which banned slavery—a violation of his sworn duty to carry out the law of the land.[2]

On the other hand, Abraham Lincoln, who directly preceded Johnson, is seen as one of our greatest presidents. Among his many achievements, he kept the country together by winning the Civil War and shepherded the passage of the Thirteenth Amendment, which abolished slavery.[3] Why was Lincoln able to be so great? He had a diligent fascination with the Constitution, the core principles that upheld the nation and the presidency, and the history of the Framers (the collective term we use for the storied people who crafted the Constitution, such as James Madison and Alexander Hamilton). As the political theorist George Kateb writes, "Lincoln revered the principle of human equality and believed that he therefore should revere the US Constitution, the system of government created under it . . . making real the abstract principle of human equality."[4] For Lincoln, that meant standing up for the fundamental values of the oath and the Constitution while working within the constraints that limited his office. To end the evil of slavery nationwide, he didn't rule by dictate; instead, he used the Constitution's legal procedure to pass an amendment accomplishing his goal. Lincoln was a great president because he understood how the office of the presidency—used as the Framers had created it—could preserve, protect, and defend constitutional values.

As we shall see, the oath requires that the president uphold the Constitution—even parts with which he or she disagrees. If you fail to do so, you'll end up with Johnson on the list of worst presidents. If you succeed, you can be remembered with Lincoln among the greats.

All presidents, from George Washington to Donald Trump, began their terms with dreams of accomplishing great things. But whether your presidency is monumental or disastrous will hinge largely on a simple thing: that you, a future president, understand how the responsibilities of the Constitution apply to your job.

WHAT DO you need to know to be president? Most of all, you need to know the US Constitution. As president, your first task is to recite the oath of office. You'll stand in front of your inauguration crowd, guided by the chief justice of the Supreme Court, and recite the following words: "I do solemnly swear that I will faithfully execute the Office of the President of the United States, and will to the best of my Ability, preserve, protect and defend the Constitution of the United States."[5]

This oath is your public contract with the American people, and reciting it is your first constitutional responsibility. Before you recite it, you must know what it means and where it comes from. The oath is found in Article II of the Constitution, which established the presidency and defined its powers and limits. Ratified in 1788 and amended three years later in 1791 with a Bill of Rights, the Constitution contains a series of principles that limit the power of all federal officials, including the president, and defines the powers that those officials do have.[6] The Constitution will serve as your blueprint for how to do the president's job, helping you to anticipate the pitfalls that all presidents should avoid.

The oath itself is a reminder that your powers are conditionally granted and come with limits. The Constitution, in literally dictating your first instant in office, signals clearly that you are not free to act however you wish. Article II goes on to provide directions for what you must do and avoid. The oath is thus not merely a ritual—it is a recognition that you temporarily occupy an immensely powerful office, and that you must internalize the demands and responsibilities that come with it. Notice that you are promising to "preserve, protect and defend" the Constitution—not just to avoid violating it. In pledging to "faithfully execute" the office of the president, you promise to put aside your private interests to occupy a public and limited role on behalf of the American people.[7] If you are not willing to work within these limits and take initiative to promote the document, the Oval Office isn't for you.

It was George Washington's second inaugural address—which at 135 words remains the shortest in history—that gave voice to the ideas underlying the oath and the office. Today, we tend to think of inaugurations as grand affairs, with modern presidents using them to draw widespread attention to their agendas. But Washington's 1793 inauguration was much more subdued—fitting, since his address emphasized the limits of the presidential office. He held the inaugural ceremony in the relatively modest Senate Chamber of Congress Hall, located just steps from Independence Hall, where he had presided over the Constitutional Convention six years earlier.[8] This choice of venue signified his respect for the legislative branch as a coequal to his own executive branch. In his speech, Washington challenged Americans to stop him should he fail to live up to his duties:

> Previous to the execution of any official act of the President, the Constitution requires an oath of office. This oath I am now about to take, and in your presence: That if it shall be found during my administration of the Government I have in any instance violated willingly or knowingly the injunctions thereof, I may (besides incurring constitutional punishment) be subject to the upbraidings of all who are now witnesses of the present solemn ceremony. [9]

In emphasizing the solemnity of the oath, Washington here was speaking to future presidents and the future Americans charged with holding them accountable. Washington is asking you, a future president, to respect the obligations and the limits of your new office. And to those of us who won't be president, Washington is reminding us that we, too, must ensure that a president carries out the duties of the office.

Washington's words here provide the impetus for our focus on what the Constitution demands of a president. This guide will detail what you need to know—how to take the oath seriously, and how to understand both the obligations and the limits that it places on you. It is not enough merely to avoid constitutional punishment, although that punishment—in the form of impeachment, censure, or losing an election—is still something you should worry about. You should go beyond this bare minimum requirement of the office, and defend the values that the Constitution enshrines. Unlike President Johnson, and like President Lincoln, you must recognize what the Constitution requires: read it, study it, and through your speech and actions, promote it.

It's crucial that you see the Constitution's rules as legitimate constraints, not obstacles to get around. But the Constitution is more than just these rules: it stands for a wider morality of limited government and respect for people's rights. You must find a way for your actions and words to honor and expound those values, while abiding by the limits that your office places upon you. You might be tempted to see the Supreme Court as the sole authority to tell you when you've strayed from constitutional values. Sometimes, it does play this role: courts have often limited the president by declaring his actions unconstitutional. But as you will see, the court's role in American history has often been limited. The Supreme Court has sometimes protected civil liberties that presidents have put under threat, but at other times it has failed to do so. As president, you have an obligation to go beyond what courts require of you, taking it upon yourself to defend the principles and rules of the Constitution. In order to do that, you must first understand what those principles and rules are.

As A professor of constitutional law, my job is to introduce students to the core tenets of the Constitution. My students are often amazed by the scope and foresight of this document. It does more than create our entire system of government. It also provides tools that can limit those who try to abuse that system to violate the rights of the people.

The Constitution creates and defines the duties of the three branches of government: legislative, judicial, and executive—the last of which contains the office of the presidency. The Constitution strictly limits the president's powers in Article

II, but it also limits the president in other creative ways: by granting certain powers to the other two branches, letting states retain certain privileges, and enshrining the rights of the people. Each of the three branches interprets the Constitution and encourages the others to act in ways that are consistent with its requirements.

This includes you, no matter where you live or what you do. The Constitution is not magically self-enforcing, and there is no "Constitution police." Not even the Supreme Court will always succeed in defending the Constitution's values and enforcing the proper limits it places on you. Fortunately, you will not be alone in defending the Constitution. In the end, it is essential for all citizens to recognize that there is no guarantee that presidents or courts respect the Constitution. By demanding that elected representatives—whether senators or town council members—read, understand, and comply with the Constitution, the people can make sure that the requirements of the Constitution do not become, as Madison worried, mere "parchment barriers."[10] Ultimately, the president is checked not by the Constitution itself, but by the American people demanding that it be respected.

To uphold this duty, though, you need to understand the principles of the Constitution for yourself. Together, we'll be taking a deep dive into our country's founding document.

——•——

THE CONSTITUTION isn't the first thing most people think about when they vote for a presidential candidate. My own interest in politics certainly didn't start with the Constitution.

When I was growing up in Queens, my father worked for a local politician. I sometimes tagged along for political events. And in Queens, the political event of the year was the Queens

Day Celebration—a parade that transformed Flushing Meadows Park, a faded gem that had twice held the World's Fair, into the center of the world—in my young eyes, at least.[11] It was the sort of grand event that all the major figures from Queens would attend—and perhaps among them, a certain future president. It was there, at age nine, that I first saw my boyhood hero at the front of the parade: Edward Koch, the mayor of New York City.

At the time, Koch was larger than life. Some even mused that he might become the first Jewish president. Now I was walking directly behind him, right under Koch's enormous arms, which he threw open every few seconds as he bellowed to the crowd, "How am I doin'?" The crowd of onlookers screamed their approval.

Just then, Koch whispered to a local politician next to him, "I'd love some ice cream. Vanilla." The politician turned behind, pointed to a man next to me, and snapped, "Get the mayor some ice cream. Vanilla!" The aide turned and sprinted across the field next to the parade route, and returned about ten minutes later with a vanilla ice cream cone.

That was the day I decided I wanted to be mayor. To the mind of a nine-year-old boy, being mayor meant having the power to seemingly get anything—even ice cream—and get it on demand.

What can a nine-year-old boy intuit about politics? A lot, actually. For many adults, it's moments just like these that draw them to politics in the first place. For them, the presidency is shorthand for fame and power. They want to live in the White House. They want access to the staff. The helicopters. Air Force One.

When they wrote the Constitution, the Framers were well aware of the trappings of power. That is why the Constitution's oath is meant to take a private citizen, whose focus lies with his or her own beliefs and desires—whether ice cream or the nuclear football—and transform that person into a public "officeholder," whose job is to safeguard the Constitution and the country it governs. Presidents, of course, are required to recite the oath. But reciting it is not enough; they should read the oath carefully, internalizing its fundamental principles and the constraints it creates on the office. When you've just been elected by millions of people, you might feel as if you're authorized to do as you wish—or whatever your supporters want you to do. But the constraints on your office are critically important. In fact, they are a defining feature of our system of government.

IN THIS guide, we will examine the difficult balance between respecting the wishes of the people who elected you and respecting the limits the Constitution places on your power. These limits constrain presidents who cater to the worst prejudices of the people who elected them. But such safeguards, which operate by slowing down the pace of government, can also contribute to government gridlock.

President Harry Truman observed this conundrum first-hand. In 1952, as he was preparing to leave office, Truman turned to an aide and predicted what would happen to his successor, former general Dwight Eisenhower, who was accustomed to the military's famous efficiency. "He'll sit here and he'll say, 'Do this! Do that!' And nothing will happen," Truman mused. "Poor Ike." [12]

Truman's words indicate a central irony of the American presidency: yes, the office is immensely powerful. Yet it is so often constrained and thwarted—by Congress, the courts, the press, the states, ordinary citizens, and even by its own executive bureaucracy. This limited role in the constitutional system is no doubt frustrating for presidents, but it serves the wider goal of the Framers: respecting individual rights and the rule of law—the notion that we are not governed by individuals' whims but by standards common to all. The constraints are a feature, not a bug. They ensure that the oath is not a set of mere words, but that there are mechanisms for constraining a president.

The "Poor Ike" story is often told by scholars of the presidency. It was reported in Richard Neustadt's influential book *Presidential Power and the Modern Presidents*.[13] Neustadt's book taught future presidents and their aides how to use the power of persuasion to lead the country. With its focus on power, the book was so popular in the 1960s that President Richard Nixon's chief of staff, H. R. Haldeman, made it required reading for all staffers in the White House. Later, as we'll see, after Nixon was impeached for his role in the break-in at the Watergate Hotel and the subsequent cover-up of the event, one Nixon staffer told Neustadt that "you have to share the responsibility" for the illegal actions because of the ideas in his book.[14]

Neustadt took this accusation seriously. He had learned to understand the Constitution when he was a student in civics class and assumed that his readers had done the same. But during Watergate, he realized that the decline of civics education meant that Nixon's staffers had not developed an appreciation for the limits of the Constitution, instead focusing more on presidential *power*. Our guide makes clear what Neustadt's book did not: that the Constitution is not a mere obstacle to get around, and trying to do so would be a disservice to the Framers' ideas.[15] To understand the Constitution, you need to see that the powers it grants are of a particular kind—loaded with tripwires, trapdoors, and springboards that protect the rights of the people and the rule of law. Presidents should celebrate, not bemoan, this complex design.

The best guide we have to the Constitution is the *Federalist Papers*. Written anonymously during the course of a single year between 1787 and 1788, the *Federalist Papers* were the project of three Framers—James Madison, Alexander Hamilton, and John Jay—and were an effort to persuade New York and other states to ratify the Constitution.[16] Like many of their fellow Framers, Madison, Hamilton, and Jay were concerned about the tyranny of Great Britain, against which they had just revolted. As a result, the *Federalist Papers* focused a great deal on how the governmental structure outlined in the Constitution would protect citizens from a flawed government—including a despotic president. They emphasized what it meant to be a legitimate leader.

James Madison, an author of the *Federalist Papers* and a primary writer of the Constitution, will serve as our guide throughout this book. Madison is a good guide in large part because he was the Framer who most consistently stressed the limits on the president, writing, "the ultimate authority . . . resides in the people alone."[17] He was also the most influential proponent of a Bill of Rights.[18] And as president, Madison went beyond what he believed he was required to do by the courts, using his own veto power to strike down laws he viewed as violations against the Constitution. This guide may not always agree with Madison: for instance, in matters concerning hiring and firing, where he wrongly ascribed too much power to a president.[19] But overall, it is Madison's vision of a limited presidency that inspires the ideas of this book.

Madison's vision of the presidency was just one of many debated at the time. Another Framer, Alexander Hamilton, stood for a markedly different vision. These days, Hamilton, a famous delegate to the Constitutional Convention from New York who later became secretary of the treasury, receives a good deal more popular attention than his fellow Framers.[20] (Let's just say there is no *Madison: The Musical.*) At times, Hamilton was Madison's ally—recall that they wrote the *Federalist Papers* together. But they often clashed, especially on where presidential limits ought to lie.

Hamilton referred to the need for "energy in the executive," by which he meant the president's ability to make great things happen quickly.[21] In a Hamiltonian view, the president is not a king—but does retain some kinglike powers. He argued that the president should have broad powers in war and foreign policy, even though the Constitution didn't say so explicitly. Madison disagreed. These debates still resonate long after the Founding. For example, some legal precedent has suggested that the president is not required to uphold the equal protection of the laws in certain areas, such as immigration. Other thinkers have suggested the Constitution's ban on "cruel and unusual punishment" may not prevent the president from using or sanctioning torture. President Nixon even famously claimed the president couldn't be indicted while in office. However, with Madison as our guide, we will push back against this strain of Hamiltonian constitutional thinking that emphasizes the powers of the president over the constraints on the office.

A president who takes the oath seriously needs to consider these Framers' competing visions. But the Framers aren't the only thing that needs to be considered: the president also needs to consider the text of the document, case law, and the meaning of later amendments such as the Fourteenth Amendment and its Equal Protection Clause. The Framers' ideas should be honored—particularly Madison's vision of a limited presidency—but only as a guide, not as the final word on what the Constitution means.

Madison designed the Constitution to ensure that those of us who will not be president—"the people"—could protect the office from a president who failed to carry out the oath. He and the Framers gave us a Bill of Rights and institutions such as the judiciary, the Congress, and state governments to protect those rights if a president failed to do so.

In modern-day politics, we often try to understand what "We the People" want through polls and policy preferences. But the Constitution means something different by "We the People." These words don't just refer to voters and their preferences of the moment. And they don't mean that a populist president who claims that his personality reflects the desires of the people has a mandate to ignore the requirements of the law.[22] Rather, "We the People" is an ideal of a "constitutional" people—citizens not only versed in the Constitution, but who demand that public officials, especially the president, comply with it.

Lincoln explained this constitutional ideal when he distinguished between people's base instincts and their "better angels." Later, eulogizing the war dead at Gettysburg, Lincoln explained that ours was a government "of the people, by the people, [and] for the people."[23] That phrase best explains the Constitution's meaning and how it treats the ideal of a constitutional people. We are a government "of" the people, because ultimately all government officials work for and are accountable to "We the People"—an idea expressed in the Constitution's first three words. We are a government "by" the people, in that we participate in elections and in lawmaking. Finally, we are a government "for" the people, because we recognize in our founding document that each of our fellow citizens is a rights holder. Without the right to free speech, we could not conceive of the ideas necessary to make democratic decisions. If we were denied religious freedom, we could not truly develop our own beliefs.

The Constitution protects this higher ideal of "the people" most obviously through the Bill of Rights—the first ten amendments to the Constitution. But the structure of the original Constitution itself also protects the rights of the people. Madison gave the best early explanation of the Constitution's ideal of "the people." To him, the Constitution protected not just against kingly domination, but also against the "tyranny of the majority."[24] A president might become a tyrant by catering to the worst prejudices of the populace, but Madison argued that the people could never be stripped of their rights—even if a large majority of people favored such a move.[25] Those rights allow the people to be the Constitution's best protector. Sometimes, the people can exact punishment on an errant president indirectly, by working through the other branches: for example, by demanding vigilance from Congress. But the people can also take action directly, using rights like the First Amendment's free speech protection to criticize a president.

As president, you will be constrained by these legal dynamics of the Constitution. But far more integral to your presidency is something else: the Constitution's political morality. By this, I mean the values of freedom and equality that inform the document beyond its judicially enforceable requirements. We can tell whether presidents embrace the Constitution's values not just by their executive orders or official appointments, but by how they speak to the American people. No court can tell you what to say. But you still must be guided by the Constitution in this crucial endeavor. As president, you should speak for all of us—and more, you should speak for what our country stands for, and aspires to be.

The Constitution's morality transcends any one administration—and this guide won't be tailored to defend or attack any particular president. It is essential that we think about the office independent of its holder. This means that while you, a future president, might have the best intentions and grand ambitions, this guide will not cater to your personal agenda. Neither is it a strategy guide, designed to help you maximize your influence. (For that, read Machiavelli's famous guide, *The Prince*.[26]) Instead, this guide will discuss your primary duty as a presidential officeholder: to execute the office of the president in line with the Constitution's text and its political morality. It will not teach you how to avoid constitutional constraints, but rather how to embrace them, working within the Constitution to do what is best for the country. Some presidents might see their constitutional advisors as employees whose job it is to help them get around the obstacles the document presents. In this guide, however, my role as your constitutional advisor is not to figure out how to defend all of your actions. Rather, I will give you advice on behalf of the Constitution, trying to ensure that you stay true to your oath.

Disagreements about the meaning of the Constitution are commonplace today, and they are as old as the rivalry between Madison and Hamilton. Throughout this book, you will see historical and contemporary examples of presidents, members of Congress, Supreme Court justices, scholars, and "We the People" each debating the best applications of the Constitution. Rather than shy away from this disagreement, I will try to make it transparent, providing you with opposing views and my own interpretations, all the while giving you the tools to sift through the debates yourself.

Some people may tell you that you have to choose between the words and the principles of the Constitution when interpreting the document, or that you should just listen to the Supreme Court. None of these approaches is complete. Looking to the Constitution's text, the history of Supreme Court rulings, *and* the broader values underlying the Constitution gives us the best method to resolve constitutional disputes and discover the document's meaning. I refer to this approach as value-based reading.[27]

So what are constitutional values? They are best understood as principles of constitutional self-government—principles that realize the ideal of an American populace with all citizens regarded as equal, always retaining their right to rule and influence public life. Although the text of the Constitution is the first place to look for signs of these values, they have also been argued over and worked out through Supreme Court cases throughout American history. We will look to these cases as an important guide to the Constitution, sometimes invoking the conclusions of the court's justices and, where necessary, pointing to how the case law should evolve to better reflect the Constitution's deeper values. And throughout, we will come back to the architect of the Constitution itself: James Madison. In the *Federalist Papers*, his public speeches, and other writings, Madison is essentially speaking to us across the ages.

We should listen.

———————

THIS GUIDE is organized into three sections.

In the first section, we examine Article II of the Constitution, which outlines the powers and responsibilities you will have as president. We start with Article II's creation of the powers of the president as well as the duties that arise from them. We next discuss the bully pulpit—the term for presidential communication—where you still face constitutional duties and constraints. Then we examine the Constitution's demand to respect the powers of the other branches—avoiding the temptation to make laws, like a king, instead of executing them. Relatedly, we consider your nominations to the Supreme Court, where your reading of the Constitution will inform your choice of judicial nominees. Finally, we explore the vast power of the president as commander in chief in times of war—a power that has grown exponentially in the last century, but should be returned to a more limited scope.

In the second section, we move from your powers to your limits—in particular, those imposed by the Bill of Rights, the cluster of amendments most crucial to your job description—and the Fourteenth Amendment. As we'll see, the Bill of Rights has its own history—one we need to learn in order to truly understand the Constitution. We begin with the First Amendment, which includes the right to criticize the government. It also includes strong protections for religion—and, simultaneously, important limits too, which together guard against theocracy and prevent the imposition of one set of religious beliefs on the American people. Then we jump to the Eighth Amendment, which bars cruel and unusual punishment. Lastly, we turn to the Fourteenth Amendment, where we address your immigration powers and the question of whether even noncitizens should enjoy equal protection of the laws.

In the third and final section, we examine what happens if you disregard your oath. We begin with the myriad ways that "We the People" and the other branches can stop you—starting with the question of whether you can be indicted for a crime in office. Next, we consider how a president who disregards the oath can be met with resistance from state and local officials. Finally, we study the ultimate check on your authority as president: impeachment and removal from office. Distinct from punishment for a criminal act, impeachment is the last resort to stop a president who has disregarded the oath.

I urge you to use your new knowledge to interpret the Constitution for yourself, whether or not you aim to become president. If the people are ultimately responsible for enforcing the Constitution—and voting out officeholders who violate it— then we cannot leave that task solely to courts and politicians. So, this book will also serve as a guide for everyday citizens.

But let's say you do want to be president. Do you want to be among the revered, like George Washington or Abraham Lincoln, or the notorious, like Andrew Johnson or Richard Nixon? The choice is yours, and it begins with a simple task: understanding the Constitution. Luckily that's exactly what this book is designed to help you do. Okay, Madam or Mister President: let's get started.

SECTION I

THE POWERS OF THE PRESIDENT

1

Article II and the Limited Presidency

PRINCIPLE: The president is not a king or dictator. See yourself as a public servant whose powers are limited by the Constitution.

"When you get to be President, there are all those things—the honors, the twenty-one gun salutes . . . you have to remember it isn't for you. It's for the Presidency."
—HARRY S. TRUMAN[1]

O nly about one thousand words long, Article II of the Constitution creates the presidency and describes its duties. Understanding the authors who wrote it is essential for you to uncover what the presidency is. So, before taking office, you'll need to study up on Article II. Of course, understanding the entire Constitution is important, too. Like a company-wide office manual, you should read all of it, not just the parts that pertain directly to your position. And, like any such manual, it tells you where to find the CEO's office. In literally the first

3

three words—"We the People"—the Constitution makes very clear who your supervisors are. But for now, we'll focus on Article II, which has the specific details of your job description. The powers you will be granted, the duties you have in carrying them out, and the limits of the office are all laid out clearly in this section.

Monday, September 17, 1787, was the last day of the Constitutional Convention. That morning, George Washington, who had presided over the debates, sat at a small table in front of a narrow room. From there, he invited each delegate to sign the outline of the young country's proposed government. If it was approved by the drafters at the convention, the Constitution would next be presented to the states, and could come into effect only once nine of the states had ratified it.[2]

When it came time for Washington to call on George Mason, a Virginia delegate, Mason refused to sign. He worried that the Constitution was missing a list of rights, one that could reasonably limit Congress and the president from oppressing the people. More generally, Mason thought the Constitution did not do enough to protect against monarchy.[3]

Madison and Hamilton offered the strongest rebuke to Mason. To them, it was the structure of Article II itself that prevented monarchy: the president could only exercise those powers granted to the office by the Constitution. That meant a president had no constitutional ability to violate rights. Most of the delegates knew that Washington would be president—and they crafted the presidency with him in mind.[4] Nevertheless, they included protections against a future president—like yourself—who might not share Washington's virtues.

Today, many American history books (and plenty of politicians) talk about the Framers in reverent and hushed tones. In fact, the Framers themselves were skeptical of this kind of reverence, since it reminded them of the way many people regarded the English monarchy they despised. The Constitutional Convention, the gathering where the Constitution was drafted, was itself a modest affair. Delegates gathered on the ground floor of a building owned by the state of Pennsylvania, which today is known as Independence Hall. That summer, the heat was so torturous that even delegates from the South such as Pierce Butler of South Carolina found it difficult to withstand. To make things worse, George Washington ordered that the towering windows be shut to ward away eavesdroppers. Needless to say, wool frock coats and powdered wigs aren't exactly summer attire, and let's just note that deodorant had yet to be invented. This was not a royal court, or anything like it.[5]

The delegates sat in simple wooden chairs. From the front, Washington presided from behind a table draped in a plain green cloth. To the surprise of many, he spoke little. (Madison, who was the unofficial note taker of the Convention, recorded almost no statements by Washington during the four-month duration.) In this way, although the presidency had not yet been invented, Washington was beginning to create its norms: even when the Convention exploded in raucous debate, Washington presided rather than ruled.[6] Like any good leader, he understood intuitively that his power lay in the respect of others. Although you occupy an immensely powerful office, you should take heed to model this humble behavior.

The Framers came from many different backgrounds, but they shared certain characteristics. Many were lawyers and had been formally trained at institutions like Harvard and Princeton. One, George Wythe of Virginia, was the first law professor in the United States. Still others were doctors or merchants. And those who had served in the Revolutionary War shared an intimate understanding of the blood already spilled for this new country.[7] Above all, the Framers were marked by a common commitment to deliberation—reasoned and respectful debate—and to subsuming themselves to the rule of law. Theirs would be "a government of laws, not of men," in John Adams's phrase, meaning that no official would enjoy status above the law, not even the president.[8] The Framers' task at the Convention was to develop principles that would apply to everyone in the nation, including themselves.

The format of the Convention, too, set the tone for the new government. A Constitution developed through careful deliberation stood as a symbol against the enemy that most concerned the Framers: a demagogue who enables and manipulates an irrational, impassioned citizenry. Hamilton warned against the danger of demagoguery in the very first *Federalist Paper*: "Of those men who have overturned the liberties of republics, the greatest number have begun their career by paying an obsequious court to the people; commencing demagogues, and ending tyrants."[9] They feared a leader who would simply act on hot instinct—as well as citizens who, in their lack of deliberation, might allow him to do so. Perhaps this is what Washington meant when he later said, "It is on great occasions only, and after time has been given for cool and deliberate reflection, that the real voice of the people can be known."[10]

After Washington finished calling on the signatories to sign, the national deliberation began—launched when the first public copies of the Constitution were printed in *The Pennsylvania Packet and Daily Advertiser* on September 19, 1787.[11] Formally, the document was presented to the people for approval at the state level. This happened through a series of state ratification assemblies that resembled the Constitutional Convention on a smaller scale. While the Convention itself was attended only by a select few elite men, the ratification debates involved more people than had ever before participated in founding a country around a written document. The Convention and the debates were still exclusionary, as women and minorities had little input. But for its time and era, the widespread participation they inspired was historic. During the debates over ratification, local leaders understood the importance of addressing the concerns of all citizens who would be bound by the future Constitution; thus, they instructed their electors to base their judgment on the "welfare and dignity of the union as well as that of [the state]."[12]

When the state conventions began reading aloud the proposed Constitution, delegates found signs in the document of the Framers' obsession with their primary villain: King George III, the chief antagonist at the heart of the Declaration of Independence and its myriad complaints[13] about his "train of abuses."[14] Each of his abuses shared a theme: failing to respect the rule of law. For instance, King George dissolved the colonial assemblies of Massachusetts, South Carolina, Maryland, Georgia, and Virginia for their criticism of taxation without consent.[15]

The Constitution also reflected the Framers' fear of another kind of oppression: the "tyranny of the majority." Direct democracies—in which voters decide issues by voting on laws themselves, without representatives—were particularly vulnerable to the passions of enflamed mobs. A passionate electorate might enact policies that disregard the rights of political minorities. Madison wrote in *Federalist* 10 that "such democracies have ever been spectacles of turbulence and contention;

have ever been found incompatible with personal security or the rights of property; and have in general been as short in their lives as they have been violent in their deaths."[16] Instead, Madison and the other Framers chose a republic, or what we call today a representative democracy, in which laws are made by elected representatives.

Finally, the Framers were concerned about another threat: chaos. This was the opposite extreme of a strong-handed ruler like King George. The Articles of Confederation, which was the governing document of the United States before the Constitution was ratified, had no chief executive like a president. Although there was a "President of Congress," he served only as a moderator for debates within Congress. He had no control over the military, no ability to set a legislative agenda, no right to meet with foreign leaders, and no power to make appointments. The federal government under the Articles of Confederation also lacked the power to tax, forcing it to rely on voluntary, and often inadequate, funding from the states. This shortcoming felt particularly egregious to veterans of the Revolution: framers who had fought in the war had first-hand knowledge of the lives lost and the inadequate funding of continental troops. And even those who hadn't fought remembered when Continental Army veterans showed up at the Congress of the Confederation with guns on June 20, 1783, demanding their payment for prior war service. A government that could not help its own veterans was clearly a government that was too weak.[17]

During the Constitutional Convention, a great deal of time was devoted to drafting Article I, which created a legislative branch with two chambers: a House of Representatives and a Senate. Delegates gave this Congress enormous powers. It could tax and spend, raise and support an army, declare war, and make budgets. It could also regulate interstate commerce. Presidential appointments to the Supreme Court and the executive branch, as well as international treaties, were subject to confirmation by the Senate. Congress could even turn bills into law without the president's signature by overriding a presidential veto. Such a Congress would be far more powerful than the congress of the Articles of Confederation.[18]

The House was conceived of as a body that would be highly responsive to the demands of voters, held to reelection by the people every two years. The Senate—evidenced by its role in giving advice and consent on presidential appointments, the staggered terms of its members, and its smaller size and higher age requirement than the House— was designed as a deliberative body, where passions would be mediated through thoughtful discussion. This would avoid the danger of rash decision making that Madison described in *Federalist* 62: "The necessity of a senate is not less indicated by the propensity of all single and numerous assemblies to yield to the impulse of sudden and violent passions, and to be seduced by factious leaders into intemperate and pernicious resolutions."[19]

Article I was the first indication that the Framers were serious about limiting a chief executive who might become far too powerful. But the tools of Article I only limit a president if they are used actively by those in Congress. The Framers would be severely disappointed in a Congress that delegates its core powers to the president. Throughout this book, I will urge you as president to demand that Congress play its constitutionally designated role. As president, you can affirm that Congress must take responsibility in limiting your presidential power by scrutinizing your nominations, passing laws establishing independent prosecutors, and having the last word on whether the country goes to war.

But what about the opposite problem—a chief executive who is far too weak? During the first weeks that the Framers discussed the executive branch in Article II, a fierce debate broke out inside the convention hall. Should the presidency consist of one person, or more than one? Edmund Randolph, a delegate from Virginia, opposed having a single president. What use was it to replace King George with this so-called president, a man who might attempt to usurp kingly powers for himself?[20] Randolph instead suggested a plural executive, one with three presidents. Another delegate, William Paterson, endorsed the idea of a plural executive in his "New Jersey plan" for the Convention.[21]

Alexander Hamilton disagreed. The country needed a strong presidency, he said, citing the example of the maddening inefficiency of the Articles of Confederation. Hamilton believed Americans could enjoy the decisiveness that came with a single person as president—rather than a committee— and still be free of the dangers of a king. He went further: the president, Hamilton said, should be elected for *life*.[22] This struck some of the delegates as a good idea, in large measure because of Washington, who it was widely assumed would become the first president.

Madison, our advisor throughout this guide, agreed in part with Hamilton: the country needed a single president. But he argued forcefully that the president must be limited—both in the term of office and the powers granted. While Madison trusted and admired Washington, he thought "the people" needed to feature more prominently in the Constitution. The people's rights, Madison argued, would best be served by limiting the president—indeed, the entire federal government—within specifically defined powers. The powers of a president would begin and end with those granted in the document. In Madison's proposal, a divided government would prevent a president from behaving like a monarch.

Madison's vision ultimately won out.[23] Fearing another King George or worse, the delegates imposed significant limits on the presidential office—limits that you will still face today as president. The main power they granted to the Oval Office also limited it: the power to "execute" the law. Only Congress could propose bills, leaving the president with only two choices: veto a bill or sign it. And even the veto power was limited: Congress could overturn a president's veto with a two-thirds majority. The final language of Article II states that the president's job is not to write laws, but to "take care that the laws be faithfully executed."[24] This may mean enforcing laws signed by an earlier president—or a current Congress—that the sitting president might disagree with entirely.

Article II also lays out the qualifications for being president: you must be a natural-born citizen of the United States, be at least thirty-five years old, and have lived in the United States for at least fourteen years.[25] But we know from Madison's Convention notes and from the *Federalist Papers* that the Framers also had two other important qualifications for the president in mind: wisdom and civic virtue. Madison put it best in *Federalist* 57 when he wrote, "The aim of every political constitution is, or ought to be, first to obtain for rulers men who possess most wisdom to discern, and most virtue to pursue, the common good of the society."[26] Madison and his colleagues knew that presidents needed the wisdom to determine what policies were best for the people and the virtue to fight for those policies.

The Constitution relied on this idea to prevent the collapse of the system. Madison put the concept well when he wrote, "Is there no virtue among us? If there be not, we are in a wretched situation. No theoretical checks—no form of government can render us secure."[27] Virtue was essential for stability. Even with Madison's stipulation that the president be granted only the powers on the physical document, the Framers understood that the concerns of the day might raise new questions about which actions are within presidential purview. The discretion of a president meant that a chief executive without regard for—or worse yet, with contempt for—the common good, could cause the system to collapse.

When it came to civic virtues, the Framers held up one virtue higher than most others: deliberation. You must be cool-headed, careful, reasoned, and collaborative in your decision making. They hoped deliberation would guide the presidency in a few ways. They imagined a soft-spoken Washington, quietly encouraging the debates within Congress to pass legislation, or discussing the merits of executive actions within his own office. Deliberation is almost always slow, and that was fine with Washington, because "the people will be right at last."[28] We often complain today about the pace of change in the federal government, but that is how the Framers wanted it.

This deliberative approach is not a written requirement in Article II, but it's just as important as any explicit text. It provides the president with the ability not just to think carefully about official matters but also to internalize the principles of the Constitution so that they can guide his or her actions. We'll be discussing more of these informal principles and the judicially enforceable norms required of the job in the remaining chapters of this book.

WHY SHOULD you care about the Constitution? The idea of being bound by a document written over two hundred years ago—and entirely by white men—can seem absurd at first glance. If they met today, this group would have been disparaged as elite, secretive, and "out of touch" with the average American. (Imagine the headline: "Rich white lawyers gather to write the rules of society for us.") Indeed, many of them attended the same Ivy League colleges that still define the northeastern elites today. Others were born to a southern aristocracy, including slaveholding families.

The evil of slavery marred the legacies of two of the Framers whose words and actions informed the principles discussed in this book—James Madison and George Washington—as well as the legacy of the document itself. In politics, they sought to combat tyranny, but on their slave plantations, they practiced it. For all their talk of virtue, Madison and Washington together owned around four hundred enslaved people, several of whom tried to escape their lives of bondage.[29] Both Madison and Washington acknowledged misgivings about the morality of slavery, but only Washington had a provision in his will to free his slaves, and only then after his wife's death.[30] There should be no hiding from the Founders' massive personal shortcomings.

Neither should we overlook the evil condoned by the original Constitution. It did not abolish slavery, despite the protestations of Hamilton and others during the convention. It did not even allow Congress to consider abolishing the slave trade until 1808, and even then, there was no guarantee Congress would act. Moreover, for purposes of representation in Congress, the Constitution egregiously counted African Americans as only three-fifths of a person. This not only undercut the humanity of enslaved persons, but was also mathematically designed to increase the electoral power of southern slaveholders.

There is no avoiding the inconsistency of many of the Framers. Any story of the Founding must start with the paradox that the Constitution embedded high ideals along with the evil compromise of slavery. But we should acknowledge the Framers' prescience in embedding broad values into the Constitution and creating a process for amending the document. That process would allow later generations to better realize its ideals—such as equality before the law and freedom from tyranny.

Frederick Douglass, a leading African American abolitionist in the nineteenth century, approached the Constitution in a way that teaches us its value, despite its shortcomings. Douglass, who was born a slave, became one of the most important interpreters of the Constitution because he delved deeply into the contradiction between the Constitution's appeal to equal rights and the fact of slavery. Addressing Americans who were not slaves, he said, "The rich inheritance of justice, liberty, prosperity and independence, bequeathed by your fathers, is shared by you, not by me. The sunlight that brought life and healing to you, has brought stripes and death to me."[31]

But Douglass's conclusion was never that we should reject the Constitution or the flawed Framers who wrote it. Rather, Douglass tells us that the task at hand is to use the principles in the document to think about how to expand rights as we move forward. His words to fellow abolitionists who gathered to hear him speak in Rochester, New York, in 1852 are ones you should keep in mind when deciding what to do as president: "We have to do with the past only as we can make it useful to the present and to the future," Douglass said.[32]

To that end, the notion of who "We the People" includes has changed with history to become more inclusive. The same people who were excluded from the convention itself—African Americans, like Douglass, and women—did not yet have many of the rights that had to be recognized by the president or the federal government. Later, rights were expanded to these and other groups, and today, a primary duty of a president is to continue that progress. Refusing this duty warrants the most severe constitutional punishment.

It is true that Article II uses male pronouns to discuss the presidency.[33] But after the passage of the Fourteenth Amendment, and later the Nineteenth Amendment, which granted the vote to women, being a woman is no longer a formal barrier to the office. Still, *informal* barriers, such as sexism, persist. To better realize the ideal of equal protection, and to once and for all move past the time when, as suffragette Elizabeth Cady Stanton put it in 1888, "women have been the mere echoes of men," these too must be removed.[34] But today, no matter what group you come from, as long as you are thirty-five years old and a natural-born citizen and fourteen-year resident of the United States, you can run for president.[35] Even if you do not see yourself represented among the figures at Philadelphia, it's thanks to a Civil War, an ongoing civil rights movement, and, ultimately, important amendments to the Constitution that today you can become president.

———•———

FLAWED THOUGH they were, the Constitution and its Framers not only shaped our own system of governance but also shaped governments abroad. Some estimates suggest that 160 countries have based their Constitution on ours,[36] showing the global reach of the Framers' ideas.[37] But simply adopting some tenets of our Constitution does not guarantee a country freedom from demagogues. Take the Venezuelan Constitution, written explicitly to protect civil and political rights and adopted in 1999. Like the US Constitution, it places similar institutional checks on its president. But as Venezuelan president from 1999 to 2013, Hugo Chavez undermined those checks. For example, he harassed political opponents and weakened the free press.[38] Though he was the legal president under the Constitution, to Chavez, the document was mere "parchment," as Madison might say.

Could a scenario like this happen in the United States? What's to prevent it? In one sense, examples like Venezuela vindicate the wisdom of many ideas discussed in Philadelphia in 1787—namely, that a single-person presidency is particularly vulnerable to a hot-tempered individual with authoritarian ambitions. Perhaps Edmund Randolph, William Paterson, and the other proponents of a plural presidency were not worried enough—and should have fought harder to prevent such dangers from becoming reality. The seriousness of this question has grown in proportion to the modern powers of the president, capabilities literally unimaginable in 1787. When George Washington became president, the United States was a backwater nation with little economic or military might to speak of. It was a world in which the president had weeks to respond to a crisis. Today, as president, you could launch a nuclear weapon in minutes without getting permission from anyone.

There are some scholars who defend massive presidential powers.[39] They believe the Vesting Clause of Article II gives the president kingly powers to act beyond the law, arguing that presidents, like kings, can exercise the power of "prerogative"—a kind of legal discretion that puts them above ordinary statutory law or other constitutional constraints. According to these scholars, the president retains prerogative in some areas that are not subject to the constraints of either the other branches or the Bill of Rights. They say this prerogative is inherent in what it means to be granted the executive power.

But other scholars remain doubtful that the Constitution supports this expansive view of presidential power. This guide agrees with them. As constitutional scholar Martin Flaherty has argued, that reading of the Vesting Clause has little historical support, since almost no one at the Founding argued for it.[40] Stanford law professor Michael McConnell, a former federal judge, believes the traditional prerogative powers of the king of England were broken up by the American Constitution.[41] The power to declare war was taken from the executive and given to the Congress, as was the power to raise and support armed forces. This eliminates, rather than preserves, the prerogative power.[42] Even where remnants of prerogative were retained—for instance, the power to pardon those convicted of crimes—these remnants were kept because they were thought to be "benign."[43] Most importantly, as I will argue in the second section of our guide, the Bill of Rights restrains the supposed prerogative or absolute powers of the president.

Further, as scholars Joseph Bessette and Gary Schmitt argue,[44] we can see the limits in the presidency by paying attention to the text of Article II. The *duties* of the president are the core of the office, and the *powers* granted to the president only exist to carry out those duties. Consider the president's primary duty: to "take Care that the Laws be faithfully executed."[45] That duty is realizable because of the "executive power" vested in the presidency. In order to accomplish the tasks that you "shall" do as president, you must look to the powers that you "may" use. This distinction serves to limit your power, as the actions you take must be to serve a constitutional duty, and you can only do so using specific, constitutionally granted provisions.

In this section, we'll explore key powers that Article II grants to the president and work through the constitutional dilemmas that have accompanied these powers. Past presidents have faced wars, civil rights battles, and fierce public disagreements about their roles. As president, you may encounter events like these too, so you have to know how Article II relates to them. In public speeches, executive orders, hiring and firing, judicial nominations, and war-making, Article II empowers the president while also providing constraints. Understanding each of these powers is crucial for you to do the job of president well.

Be warned: Article II isn't foolproof. Despite the constraints it presents, a president who simply sets aside the oath could potentially become a tyrannical pseudo-monarch or a rubber stamp for the will of a tyrannical majority, just as the Framers feared. We cannot trust any one individual, or assume that the good faith exercised by many previous presidents will always prevail. Fortunately, should we ever find ourselves with the kind of president the Framers feared, our system is not powerless—and we will discuss in later sections the recourse "We the People" have against presidential tyranny. As you read through this guide and consider what the Constitution requires of you, remember Washington and his audience in the second inaugural. Your audience, the American people, are watching to see that you understand the limits of Article II. They need to know that when you recite the oath, you really mean the words you say.

2

The Bully Pulpit

PRINCIPLE: The presidency comes with a bully pulpit from which to speak to the people. Use it to explain and defend the Constitution's core values, never to undermine them.

> *"Most of us enjoy preaching, and I've got such a bully pulpit!"*
>
> —THEODORE ROOSEVELT[1]

I t is your second day in office. CNN is blaring through the West Wing of the White House. An extremist evangelical minister in Michigan has burned the Koran live on his Facebook feed. Millions have now seen the footage, and outrage has erupted across the world.

You cannot imprison the minister: even he has free speech rights. But you also want to assure Muslims in our country that they are safe—a message just as important to Mormons or Jews, since defending religious minorities is one of the bases on which this country was founded. But your advisors suggest that you not get caught up in contentious issues with limited political payoff. Keep your approval rating high, they say, so you can achieve your policy goals. Battles over symbolic issues, such as the burning of the Koran, are a distraction from things that matter more, like infrastructure and taxes. Keep the focus on your agenda, and don't get distracted.

There's some truth in that. But here's the thing. You just took an oath to uphold the Constitution. If you do not defend it and promote it—not in the abstract, but in the moment— your oath will become an empty exercise. To solemnly swear to uphold the Constitution doesn't simply mean to avoid transgressions. It means that from day one onward, you always stand up for the values of the Constitution—in your actions and your speech.

So, what to do about the Koran-burning incident? Should you address the nation from the Oval Office? Take to your newly assigned @POTUS Twitter account? Use your communications department to distribute a press release with your official statement? Moreover, what should you say?

Whatever you do, it's crucial that you speak out—and in a way consistent with constitutional ideals. In fact, speaking to the country is one of the president's most important jobs. Your first two tasks as president involve speaking: first, taking the oath, and second, giving your inaugural address, which signals your aspirations for your presidency and the country. What's more, Article II requires that the president "shall from time to time give to the Congress Information on the State of the Union."[2] Though for much of our early history presidents delivered a written address to Congress, every president since FDR has turned this requirement into an annual speech to the country: the State of the Union Address.[3]

Despite all these references to speech in the Constitution, the document never mentions whether or how the president's words might reach a broader audience beyond Congress. In 1909, President Theodore Roosevelt coined his own term for the platform the presidency gave him: the "bully pulpit"—with "bully" meaning "excellent" or "wonderful" in the slang of his time.[4] He was referring to the president's ability to bring a message directly to the people, just as a minister might speak to a congregation.

This "bully pulpit," while not found in the Constitution, is one of the implied powers of the office—crucial to your job, but not laid out explicitly in Article II. If a president can give a State of the Union address and generally is responsible for executing the law, it follows that he or she should be able to speak directly to the American people. Like all the powers that Article II grants, this implied power of speech comes with constraints and responsibilities. Given that technology now allows the president to speak to millions of people at a moment's notice, the lines of communication between the president and the people are more open and relevant than ever—making your choice of words ever more important.

This open line of communication comes with limits on how you should use it. There are things Americans should hear from their president, and also things they should not. You should use the bully pulpit to outline a vision of policy and to discuss national issues like security. Also remember that your oath requires you to defend and promote the values of the Constitution. You should never use the bully pulpit to speak in a way that is contrary to the values of the Constitution. The constitutional constraints govern more than just actions; they guide and limit how you should speak. The fact that this role is not explicit in Article II does not take away from the president's obligation to speak on behalf of, and never against, the values of the Constitution.

That means speaking on behalf of equality under the law. And it means condemning its nemesis: discrimination.[5]

————

WHEN TEDDY Roosevelt coined the term "bully pulpit," he was comparing himself to a minister speaking to a congregation. Few in history can rival Roosevelt's talent for using speech to rally support for his agenda. Roosevelt's critics, though, thought it unseemly that the president would speak directly to the masses, and in a casual, freewheeling style, no less. Earlier presidents had rarely spoken to the people. As political scientist Jeffrey Tulis explains in his book *The Rhetorical Presidency*, presidents in the eighteenth and nineteenth centuries delivered their State of the Union (often in writing) to Congress, not to the people. They also tailored their *messages* to Congress, sometimes using language and concepts that would have been unfamiliar to the public.[6]

Roosevelt's presidency brought a radical change in how the president spoke to the people. In 1902, Roosevelt was the first president to establish a modern-day White House press office, in which reporters could gather and write their stories. It was only a few years earlier that the press had even started to cover the White House regularly. Reporters went where the political power was; before the twentieth century, that was with Congress, since it largely dictated the agenda that presidents could support or oppose. Roosevelt understood the power of the press, and he used this increased access to try to influence stories about him and pressure Congress to enact his agenda.[7]

Throughout his presidency, Roosevelt pursued an important policy goal—mitigating the influence of monopoly power on the nation's economy—and he decided this goal was crucial enough to warrant some unconventional tactics. In 1906, Roosevelt found himself battling aggressively for food safety regulations—a major national issue, thanks in large measure to the era's "muckraking" journalists like Upton Sinclair, who exposed the sordid (and less than appetizing) process by which food products were manufactured.[8]

But Congress was reluctant to regulate the powerful food industry. So, Roosevelt appealed directly to the American people, hoping that they would then pressure Congress to fall into line. Addressing Congress in June of 1906, Roosevelt chose language that would grab a wider audience's attention when it was reported by the press. Referring to stockyards in Chicago, he said, "The conditions . . . are revolting. It is imperatively necessary in the interest of health and of decency that they should be radically changed."[9] Within the month, Roosevelt signed the Meat Inspection Act and the Pure Food and Drug Act that Congress had put on his desk.[10] Later, scholars like Richard Neustadt attributed this legislative victory to Roosevelt's "power to persuade" the people.[11]

WHAT WOULD the Framers have thought of Roosevelt's use of the bully pulpit? They might have been concerned.[12] They certainly weren't interested in re-creating King George's style of communication: issuing dictates and ignoring tough questions raised by his subjects. But they also didn't want to swing too far in the other direction. Many of the Framers worried about a president who pandered to the lowest instincts of the majority. They would have likely thought it too risky for presidents to speak directly and regularly to the public. One of their worst nightmares was a president who, in an attempt to win popular support, actually undermined the values of the Constitution.[13]

In Washington's speeches, he consistently showed his deference to the Constitution by stressing the limits on presidential power created by Article II, as we saw in his second inaugural address. Similarly, Jefferson's first inaugural address showed that the Constitution could be used to heal national wounds. In 1800, the country had just emerged from a contentious election. The election was a face-off between Jefferson and John Adams—but a quirk in the electoral system resulted in a tie between Jefferson and his running mate, Aaron Burr. The tie had to be broken by Congress, a process that took thirty-six rounds of white-knuckle votes. On the thirty-sixth try, Jefferson won.[14]

The nail-biting victory was only the half of it. Jefferson's party, the Democratic-Republicans, had defeated the Federalists, the party of the sitting president, John Adams, after campaigning against the Federalists' assault on free speech in the Alien and Sedition Acts. The Federalists' imprisonment of newspaper editors and even a congressman for criticizing the Federalist president John Adams stoked public outrage. The two parties seemed like mortal political enemies, dripping with animosity toward each other: How would the new party, and President Jefferson, address the still-fragile, infant republic?

The anxious country awaited Jefferson's words. Although Jefferson's speech was delivered mainly to Congress, it was the first inaugural address published in a newspaper on the same day the president gave the speech.[15] Jefferson did not rail against Congress for taking so long to vote him in. He did not inflate his margin of victory to convince the nation that he won by a landslide. Instead, Jefferson used his address to speak of the people's rights, especially those of political minorities. In his administration, Jefferson said, Congress would be obligated to respect religious freedom, freedom of the press, and the right to a trial by jury. Those rights mattered to his political opponents, who had just lost their first national election and must have feared legal reprisals for their opposition. Jefferson assuaged these worries, asserting that those who had opposed him in his bid for office "possess their equal rights, which equal law must protect, and to violate would be oppression. . . . We have called by different names brethren of the same principle. We are all Republicans, we are all Federalists."[16]

Jefferson's words worked. Historians have described the election of 1800 as a bloodless revolution.[17] Jefferson had set an example of a peaceful transition of power after a heated and contested election. Jefferson's first inaugural is a testament to the importance of appealing to the core values of the Constitution. In times of deep division, doing so can bring the country together.

———•———

We have already seen how Teddy Roosevelt invented the bully pulpit. Woodrow Wilson, who served as president only a few years later, turned it into a fundamental part of the structure of the presidency.[18] As a professor who taught constitutional law at Princeton, Wilson was one of the first to develop a theory that became known as "living constitutionalism"—the notion that the Constitution should be interpreted more flexibly to adapt to the challenges of current times.[19]

As part of this theory, Professor Wilson argued that presidential power should not be limited to Article II. He believed that it should be vastly increased to match the scope of modern problems, such as complex global conflicts and consolidated corporate power. That meant a president who derived his or her authority directly from the people, not solely from the Constitution. As political scientist Jeffrey Tulis puts it, the word *leadership* became fundamental to Wilson's conception of the presidency: whereas before, Congress was seen as coequal with the president, Wilson wanted the president to step out in front of the other branches as the only leader who could be said to represent all the American people.[20]

When he took office in 1913, Wilson tried to put his theory to the test. Although the legislative and judicial branches checked his ambitions, they couldn't prevent him from rousing public support. During his presidency, Wilson appealed to the population directly to lobby for a "League of Nations" that would cooperate to end war, and, somewhat reluctantly, lobbied for a constitutional amendment to grant the vote to women.[21]

But Wilson made a grave error. The constitutional law professor failed the most fundamental test of the presidency: Wilson used his bully pulpit to undermine the values of the Constitution by failing to speak out against racial discrimination and even defending segregation.

By 1913, the Constitution had changed immensely since the Framers' time. In particular, a large-scale shift in legal thinking was occurring, based on the new importance of the Fourteenth Amendment. That amendment, passed after the Civil War, granted "the equal protection of the laws" to persons regardless of race.[22] The Supreme Court ruled in 1896, in the infamous case *Plessy v. Ferguson*, that the amendment was compatible with segregation, on the grounds that "separate" facilities could still be "equal."[23]

At the time Wilson took office, the ruling in *Plessy* was contested. Supreme Court justice John Marshall Harlan had argued in a now-famous dissent that segregation was white supremacy, not equality, and that it reinstituted a form of domination akin to slavery through a different legal mechanism.[24] Wilson knew Harlan's argument, and had likely taught it, since he was teaching constitutional law at Princeton and New York Law School in 1896. But he chose to reject it, instead endorsing the "separate but equal" ruling and implementing segregationist policies in the federal government, perhaps to appease his constituency of southern Democrats, many of whom held racist views.[25]

In 1914, Wilson agreed to meet in the Oval Office with African American civil rights activist and newspaper owner William Monroe Trotter to discuss his segregation policies. When Trotter questioned him, Wilson defended segregation on grounds that it was only insulting in the minds of African Americans: "If you take [segregation] as a humiliation, which it is not intended as, and sow the seed of that impression all over the country, why the consequence will be very serious." When Trotter said he and his colleagues were "sorely disappointed" by Wilson's position, the president retorted, "Your tone, sir, offends me."[26] Wilson then asked Trotter to leave the Oval Office. Trotter got the better of Wilson, though, when he shared the details of the meeting with reporters at the White House.[27]

The story quickly spread across the country. Wilson looked like a petty racist, indifferent to the suffering of African Americans under segregation. He immediately saw his public relations mistake, calling himself a "damn fool" for the way he handled the encounter, although he still held fast to his racist views.[28] In this case, the press had proved more powerful than the president's bully pulpit—something you should keep in mind when speaking to the press as president today.[29]

Wilson even used his bully pulpit more actively to promote

the *Plessy* ruling and the racist ideology it signified. The 1915 silent film *The Birth of a Nation* is one of the most notorious and noxious films in American history. It celebrates the founding of the Ku Klux Klan, a racist organization that supported segregation and terrorized African Americans who tried to exercise their rights.[30] The film portrayed the KKK as heroes who defend southern whites against aggressive African Americans, including one black man who is lynched after attacking a white woman. Chillingly, the film adapts a quote from one of Woodrow Wilson's books, plastered in large type across the screen: "The white men were roused by a mere instinct of self-preservation . . . until at last there had sprung into existence a great Ku Klux Klan, a veritable empire of the South, to protect the Southern country."[31]

Did Wilson publicly disavow these words? Did he criticize the film? No. Instead, he held a special screening of *The Birth of a Nation*—the first film to be shown inside the White House— honoring its makers and the KKK.[32] Trotter, in contrast, organized a protest against this film for its racist views, demonstrating how a public figure can use his or her position to promote, rather than undermine, the spirit of the Constitution.[33]

The Equal Protection Clause marked a new chapter in American history, a transition from a slavery-era Constitution to one that mandated equality regardless of race. But it took effect in 1868, when the original Framers were long since dead. We shouldn't then look first to Framers like Washington or Jefferson—who owned hundreds of enslaved people—to defend the concept of equal protection. Wilson should have used the new bully pulpit to defend the protections that African Americans were entitled to under the law. But he didn't merely fail to do so; he actively undermined the protections it should have granted. He went to pains to defend segregation and white supremacy, even segregating the federal workforce in a step away from equality. You should be sure to correct Wilson's mistake when given the chance today. Give voice to the abstract ideal of equal protection, and renounce, through both your words and your actions, the white supremacy that the Fourteenth Amendment deems illegitimate.

Years after Wilson's presidency, President John F. Kennedy showed how the bully pulpit can be used to do just that. In June of 1963, after a federal court had ordered the University of Alabama to integrate, the governor promised to defy the ruling. Kennedy then deployed federal troops to enforce the order—a decision he would have to explain to the country. On prime-time television, Kennedy addressed the country.[34] He spoke of the need to respect the courts and the law. But he also articulated a new vision, beyond what the courts were already doing. Civil rights was a "moral issue," Kennedy said— one so important that it required a new civil rights bill that would bring about the integration of "public accommodations" such as hotels[35] and restaurants.[36] He asked white Americans to imagine what it would be like to be African American, enduring the indignity of being denied a seat at a lunch counter because of white supremacy: "If an American, because his skin is dark, cannot eat lunch in a restaurant open to the public, if he cannot send his children to the best public school available . . . if, in short, he cannot enjoy the full and free life which all of us want, then who among us would be content to have the color of his skin changed and stand in his place?"[37]

As we will see, some forms of public segregation were outlawed by the Supreme Court in the 1950s. But the segregation of hotels and restaurants would continue into the 1960s. It would take much political wrangling by President Kennedy's successor, Lyndon Johnson, to pass that bill outlawing discrimination in public accommodations: the Civil Rights Act of 1964. Johnson went further, the next year signing the Voting Rights Act of 1965, which finally enforced the voting rights that were promised in the Fifteenth Amendment, ratified in 1870. Johnson capitalized on the public civil rights struggle led by Martin Luther King Jr. and other activists, which won national attention through television images of brutal southern sheriffs ordering the beatings of protestors. With the nation primed to stop the injustice, Johnson used the bully pulpit to garner public support for legislation that would better guarantee the promise of the Constitution's commitment to equal protection than had ever previously been accomplished.

Modern presidents have not always lived up to Kennedy's and Johnson's examples, at least during the campaign phase. In 1980, Ronald Reagan's infamous Neshoba County Fair campaign speech in Mississippi was criticized for emphasizing "states' rights" in a part of the country that had long used that phrase as code for segregationist policies. In fact, he delivered the speech just miles from where three civil rights workers had been brutally murdered in 1964.[38] In his 1988 campaign for president against Michael Dukakis, George H. W. Bush, then the vice president, ran a TV ad about Willie Horton, a black man who, under a program Dukakis had supported, was temporarily released from prison and then raped a woman after stabbing her fiancé. The ad, approved by Bush's campaign manager Lee Atwater, was part of a larger campaign strategy to feed on white Americans' racial anxieties and make Dukakis seem soft on crime.[39] If you're skeptical of the campaign's motivations just ask Atwater himself. He later bluntly explained how the campaign had used race implicitly to win votes: "By 1968 you can't say 'n***'—that hurts you. Backfires. So you say stuff like forced busing, states' rights and all that stuff."[40]

As these examples make clear, nothing about the bully pulpit—whether for candidates or for sitting presidents—guarantees that it will be used for good, or that it will support, rather than undermine, our constitutional values. Yet we need the bully pulpit. It is crucial for a president to explain decisions that have a direct impact on the lives of Americans, such as going to war, and to calm the nation during tumultuous times, such as in the wake of an unpopular court verdict that has spurred violent protests.

EVER SINCE the days of Teddy Roosevelt, presidents have tried to speak to the people, with the ultimate aim of influencing Congress to enact their agendas. Some were masters of the press, such as Ronald Reagan.[41] Others found a way to take their message directly to the people in an ongoing conversation, such as Franklin Roosevelt, whose "fireside chats" were one of the first successful presidential uses of the radio to speak to the American people. Kennedy was the first to use television regularly: he used unedited press conferences, broadcast live, to contrast the United States' "free society" with the secretive Soviet government.[42]

TODAY, PRESIDENTS and their communications staffs can even bypass the press, communicating directly with the people by using tools like Twitter or Facebook. President Donald Trump has already reinvented the bully pulpit through his use of social media. His Twitter feed—spelling and grammar mistakes included—was the star of the 2016 campaign, reducing the influence of traditional media outlets.[43] And because Twitter still allows him instant and direct access to the people, without the filter of the press, he has a unique ability to influence public opinion relative to other presidents who used more formal means of communication.

The speed and global reach of social media also mean that silence about constitutional values can speak greater volumes than before. We don't always realize how great a modern president's duty to issue moral condemnation of hate is—that is, until that duty is flouted. President Trump's failure to unequivocally condemn a violent 2017 rally in Charlottesville by gun-toting white supremacists, which resulted in the death of a counter-protestor, must be understood in the context of the bully pulpit. He equated the white supremacists and their counter-protestors by saying "there's blame on both sides," and claimed that there are "very fine people" among a group that carried Nazi symbols and chanted anti-Semitic slogans. This was a failure to use the presidential bully pulpit to defend constitutional values.[44] No court can require you to speak out, but it is an essential part of your constitutional duty to defend the basic values of equal protection. Failing to do so is a part of Woodrow Wilson's legacy that we can all do without.

The Trump Twitter phenomenon also illustrates how important the press is in the era of social media. As president, you can now speak directly to the American people first, without the media there to filter your message. But the press needs to follow up, checking facts and providing a platform for others to condemn racism when you are silent.

In the absence of a president committed to using the contemporary bully pulpit to defend the Constitution, other actors need to step up and use their own direct influence on the American people to speak in favor of constitutional values. In Wilson's time, a man named Trotter could use the press to draw attention to a president's racism. In our time, it might be done by individual public figures, either through traditional news sources or through their own use of social media. Like Trotter, these people should speak on behalf of the Constitution to counteract a president who has failed in his or her duty to do so.

———•———

You're BACK in the Oval Office on day two as president. Reactions to the Koran burning have intensified. A group claiming allegiance to ISIS has issued a death threat for the minister. Meanwhile, an imam in Illinois is reporting vandalism of his mosque. What do you do?

You know now that you have a responsibility to speak to the people—and the Constitution can help you find the right words. You might follow the example of President George W. Bush. On September 20, 2001, nine days after the worst terrorist attack in US history was perpetrated by Al Qaeda, President Bush gave a televised address to Congress and the nation, praising the American people for their courage, strength, and support. And, in the face of increased hostility toward Muslims across the country, Bush denounced American citizens who would equate Islam and terrorism. After describing Al Qaeda as "a fringe movement that perverts the peaceful teachings of Islam," he said Islam is practiced "freely by many millions of Americans and by millions more in countries that America counts as friends." He called the terrorists "traitors to their own faith, trying, in effect, to hijack Islam itself."[45] At that moment, Bush taught the American people about the meaning of the Equal Protection Clause: the Constitution protects people from collective punishments based on religion or ethnicity, and it is a president's role to voice respect for these protections—and for the values of religious freedom and tolerance upon which they rest.

You might also follow the example of President Barack Obama. On June 23, 2012, an anti-Islamic video called *The*

Innocence of Muslims was released by a radical Coptic Christian resident of California. The video depicted Muslims killing Christians and suggested the Prophet Muhammad was a child molester. It quickly went viral, spurring angry reactions around the world. Riots broke out in Pakistan. President Obama's State Department responded by paying for advertisements in Pakistan criticizing the video. In these TV spots, Obama appeared, explaining that the United States respected Islam, and he condemned the video. Secretary of State Hillary Clinton also appeared to say that the video did not represent the views of the United States. The ads reached as many as 90 million Pakistani people in an effort to quell the violence.[46]

As president, you can look to the Constitution for rules about the powers you have and the limits on those powers. But the Constitution doesn't just provide you with a set of rules; it also encompasses principles and values that you must figure out how to articulate. You will often need to do so in the midst of a crisis. Don't be fooled by the technological ease of communicating directly to the people using the social media tools of the modern bully pulpit; using the bully pulpit well is not an easy task, nor one to take lightly. Twitter has revolutionized the way a president can speak to the American people, but it hasn't changed the solemn commitment that the Framers laid out for you: always speak on behalf of the Constitution. Never speak against it.

3

The Power to Execute the Laws

PRINCIPLE: Kings and dictators rule by decree, but a president's job is to execute the law, not to make it. Respect Congress by leaving lawmaking to the legislative branch.

> *"Men have discovered no technique for long preserving free government except that the Executive be under the law, and that the law be made by parliamentary deliberations."*
> —JUSTICE ROBERT H. JACKSON[1]

Y ou've campaigned hard to make it to the White House, and you want to get to work right away. The economy is in a recession, and unemployment is skyrocketing. Your economic advisors tell you to take emergency action. In the storm of ideas and argument, staffers from the White House's Council of Economic Advisers argue for a radical solution: provide every American with a minimum annual income of thirty thousand dollars. Use the bully pulpit to put this solution on the agenda, they say. Push your allies in Congress to propose a new program to guarantee the income and fund it through a new national sales tax. Such a law would never get through Congress, your deputy tells you. He's right. But your political advisor offers a devilish grin. "No matter," he says. "We'll just use an executive order."

Executive orders allow you to act alone and immediately. With executive orders, you can command the vast executive bureaucracy at your disposal—more than 2 million civilians and 1.3 million active duty military personnel—to implement policy in a way that is consistent with your ideals.[2] These people work for you in various agencies, ranging from Education, to Housing and Urban Development, to the State Department. In the past, executive orders have been a great tool for progress and also a powerful force for harm: the desegregation of the military, for example, was implemented via executive order.[3] Unfortunately, so was the internment of Japanese Americans during World War II in Executive Order 9066.[4]

So, to be blunt, here is what you need to know about executive orders. As president, you lack the authority to simply disregard or act contrary to legislation because you don't agree with it. Your constitutional mandate is to "take care that the laws be faithfully executed"—to implement the laws Congress passes, not to enact the ones you prefer. To make an executive order, you need to root it in your role as an executor of the law or as manager of the executive branch. That means your power comes from legislation itself—or from Article II of the Constitution. For instance, sometimes you can act on your inherent executive authority in determining how you want your branch of government organized, including the armed forces. But contrary to what some suggest and what many presidents have tried, you cannot just assume legislative powers in any scenario you deem to be an "emergency."

THERE HAS been a large increase in executive orders since the birth of our country. George Washington, for example, issued about one executive order every year, and they were simple in nature.[5] In the first executive order ever issued, several months into his first term, Washington asked for a report on the work under way in the various departments of the executive branch.[6] In contrast, presidents from Kennedy to Obama have issued, on average, almost two hundred executive orders per term. These are vastly more complex than those issued in Washington's time.[7]

Today's executive orders are also increasingly ambitious in scope. Sometimes, the orders look a lot like laws. For example, after a series of failed attempts to urge Congress to pass gun control legislation, President Obama presented a more limited plan of his own that relied on executive orders to place tighter controls on gun sales.[8] Predictably, this delighted his allies and enraged his detractors.

The actors on the television comedy show *Saturday Night Live*, which often pokes fun at contemporary political issues, offered their own take on Obama's executive orders. In a sketch during his second term, they reimagined the 1970s "Schoolhouse Rock" cartoon "I'm Just a Bill," in which a friendly, personified cartoon bill walks children through the steps of becoming a law—from passing both houses of Congress to being signed by the president.[9] But in *SNL's* modern send-up, the personified bill is instead violently pushed down the marble steps outside Congress and replaced by a new character: a brawny, cartoon executive order. The executive order sings, "I'm an executive order and I pretty much just happen."

To be clear, presidents can use executive orders to serve important functions that don't trample on legislative turf. As we saw earlier, the first executive order by George Washington fit this description: it simply asked for a report on ongoing work in the executive branch. Other times, by changing how the executive branch is organized and managed, presidents can use executive orders to realize constitutional ideals. When President Lyndon Johnson used an executive order to make the federal government an equal opportunity employer, this means of advancing the constitutional value of equal protection was well within his purview as rule-maker for the federal workforce.[10] When President Truman desegregated the American military, he used his power as commander in chief to support constitutional equality.[11] In these examples, we see that executive orders can be used for good—as long as they are made within the limits of the Constitution and promote the document's values.

When do executive orders usurp the lawmaking power of Congress? The key lies in the difference between "making" law, which Congress does, and executing it, which the president does. Remember, the Constitution calls for the president to "take care that the laws be faithfully executed"—not to write the laws him- or herself.[12]

One famous Supreme Court decision helped to define this difference. In 1952, President Harry Truman was leading the United States in the Korean War, a military intervention on the Korean peninsula in the early years of the Cold War. The Americans were struggling and badly in need of munitions when President Truman received bad news: the country's steelworkers were going on strike. Truman's secretary of defense,

Robert Lovett, warned him that "any curtailment of steel production would endanger the lives of our fighting men."[13] Invoking his duties as commander in chief to ensure success in Korea,
Truman issued Executive Order 10340, ordering his secretary
of commerce to take control of the steel mills.[14] With the stroke
of President Truman's pen, the federal government took over
ownership of eighty-six steel companies, ousting the former
owners and requiring the striking union members to get back
to work. The war effort, Truman reasoned, demanded it.

Within hours of Truman's executive order, representatives
of the steel industry arrived at federal court with a lawsuit to
stop the president. In this case, *Youngstown v. Sawyer*, the court
asked whether Truman's executive power under Article II
allowed him to seize the steel mills, or whether this executive
order went beyond the president's powers.[15] On June 2, 1952,
the court ruled that Truman didn't have the power, delivering
him a major rebuke. The court pointed out that there was no
law passed by Congress that authorized Truman's seizure of
the steel mills. In fact, the Labor Management Relations Act of
1947 had prohibited such a presidential act years before. When
Congress was debating that legislation, it rejected the idea that
the president should be granted the power to seize property
to prevent a work stoppage, but did grant the power to issue
an injunction to stop a strike when health and safety were at
stake. According to Justice Robert H. Jackson, who wrote the
concurrence's oft-cited explanation, the legislation should be
read as prohibiting Truman's seizure.

In other words, the president's requirement to "take care
that the laws be faithfully executed" meant that the president
has little power to contradict an existing statute. The case had
three dissenters, led by Chief Justice Fred Vinson. Vinson
wrote that in times of emergency, the president has the ability

to act even if not authorized by Congress to do so, and even the ability to act against the express wishes of Congress. It is the president, Vinson argued, who has the power to determine what actions are necessary in critical times such as wartime.[16]

But Vinson was outmatched by Justice Jackson, whose concurring opinion still defines the law today. At stake, Jackson wrote, was the principle stressed at the founding to reassure those who worried about the president becoming a king: only the Congress, and not the president, could make laws—even if a wartime emergency demanded otherwise. Jackson contrasted the president's powers with those of the English monarchs who had "powers of legislation by proclamation."[17] The president's powers were at their "lowest ebb," Jackson wrote, when they contradicted an act of Congress.[18] To Jackson, people have "discovered no technique for long preserving free government except that the Executive be under the law, and that the law be made by parliamentary deliberations."[19]

If Congress had never passed the 1947 Labor Management Relations Act, the *Youngstown* case would have been more difficult to decide, because the president's power would have been in an ambiguous "zone of twilight," as Jackson put it in his concurrence.[20] But Congress had explicitly prohibited seizures, putting the president at the lowest ebb of his or her power. The only thing that could save Truman was a Supreme Court that reasoned that the president had "emergency" constitutional powers. But Jackson rejected that view, arguing that there was no "plenary," or absolute, power of the president during an emergency. He went further, criticizing the lack of precision in the appeals to such a proposed emergency power: " '[inherent]' powers, 'implied' powers, 'incidental' powers, 'plenary' powers, 'war' powers and 'emergency' powers are used, often interchangeably and without fixed or ascertainable meanings."[21]

Justice Jackson's own life probably influenced his decision. In 1945, seven years before *Youngstown* was decided, Jackson had been asked by President Truman to serve as the chief United States prosecutor at the Nuremberg war crimes trials of Nazis that followed World War II. In that role, he saw firsthand the fallout from the Nazis' rule. On February 27, 1933, the building housing the Reichstag, Weimar Germany's lower legislature, burned to the ground under mysterious circumstances. Adolf Hitler, who had been appointed chancellor by President Paul von Hindenburg in January of that year, blamed the Communist Party and various other political enemies. Acting on Hitler's advice, President Hindenburg promptly issued an executive decree suspending many fundamental civil liberties, "The Decree of the Reich President for the Protection of People and State," later known notoriously as the "Reichstag Fire Decree."

The two chambers of the German legislature, the Reichstag and the Reichstrat, soon passed the Enabling Act on March 24, 1933. This Act reinforced Chancellor Adolf Hitler's power to make laws without the legislature, a power already codified in Article 48 of the Weimar Constitution, which allowed the president to take emergency measures, such as suspending fundamental rights or using the armed forces to restore public order, without legislative approval. Hitler also used the Act to essentially outlaw opposition parties.[22] These actions helped spur Hitler's rapid ascension to total power, though they appeared to be within his constitutional prerogative due to the emergency powers granted in Article 48.[23]

In one memorable moment during the Nuremberg Trials, Jackson brilliantly questioned Hermann Goering, the Nazi leader and president of the Reichstag. Jackson pressed Goering over the use of the Reichstag fire as a pretext to suspend civil liberties via decree. He was able to prove that Goering "had lists of Communists already prepared at the time of the Reichstag fire of persons who should be arrested" and that "[they] were immediately put into execution . . . after the Reichstag fire."[24]

After the Reichstag fire, Hitler's Germany was often ruled by decree—a fact made manifest in the unspeakable wartime atrocities the Nazis perpetrated against their own fellow citizens and those they conquered.[25] But it was also present in subtler forms of oppression. Hitler issued special decrees aimed at punishing political opponents and even issued decrees that punished citizens for acts that were not crimes when they were committed. Jackson would have recognized these as "bills of attainder"—laws that single out individuals for punishment—and "ex post facto" laws, which punish people for actions that were not illegal at the time they were committed. Both are explicitly forbidden by our Constitution.[26] Rule by decree threatens a constitutional democracy's requirement to make generalized laws, debated and enacted by a deliberative body, that respect and protect the people's rights. The end of the Reichstag marked the end of the rule of law. After his experience in Germany, Jackson had seen firsthand how quickly democracy and the rule of law can vanish due to overly broad executive power.[27]

To be clear, issuing an executive order to take over a steel mill is a far cry from ordering the murder of millions of innocent people. But Jackson's opinion in *Youngstown* was no doubt shaped by a concern to keep America far from the destructive path of Nazi Germany, which he had just witnessed firsthand. All aspiring presidents should take the lessons of *Youngstown* to heart: presidents cannot make laws or ignore them—they can only enforce them.

TODAY, JUSTICE Jackson's opinion is not as revered as it once was. Throughout his two-term administration in the 2000s, President George W. Bush tried to undermine congressional legislation that would have limited his administration's practice of using "enhanced interrogation" techniques—which many saw as akin to torture—to extract information. In the aftermath of the September 11th attacks, two of Bush's appointees to the Office of Legal Counsel, John Yoo and Jay Bybee, wrote memos examining whether "enhanced interrogation" techniques, such as waterboarding or locking people in coffins, were legal.

Yoo and Bybee concluded that they were legal, and Bush's lawyers, somewhat like Truman during the Youngstown controversy, decided that the president's war powers granted him wide latitude in taking action to stop a potential terrorist attack.[28] Bybee and Yoo knew that a US statute and an international convention ratified by the United States both banned torture. But they argued that these did not apply to "enhanced interrogation" techniques because the techniques did not cause enough prolonged pain to qualify as torture. Even further, their memos suggested that such domestic and international restrictions unconstitutionally interfere with the president's commander-in-chief power.[29] In making this claim, though, Yoo and Bybee neglected to address the most important Supreme Court case about presidential powers. As law professor Jack Balkin put it, "you just don't begin a discussion of presidential power without mentioning Youngstown."[30]

Congress disagreed with the conclusions of the memos and took action to show it. In 2005, it passed a bill, the

Detainee Treatment Act of 2005, banning torture by requiring the Department of Defense to abide by the army field manual, which prohibits torture.[31] The legislation had been introduced by Senator John McCain, himself a victim of torture when he was a prisoner of war in Vietnam. McCain said, "We've sent a message to the world that the United States is not like the terrorists. We have no grief for them, but what we are is a nation that upholds values and standards of behavior and treatment of all people, no matter how evil or bad they are."[32]

Bush resisted the bill but hesitated to veto it. He and his advisors knew it would look bad to veto a bill banning torture, especially if that veto was then overturned. (Congress had passed the bill with a veto-proof majority.) In the end, Bush did sign the bill, but he got out of the dilemma by issuing a "signing statement."

Like executive orders, signing statements are not inherently good or bad. In benign form, these statements are used by presidents to give their own gloss on the meaning of laws they have just signed. But in malignant form, they can undermine Congress's authority by signaling a refusal to carry out certain aspects of legislation.

In this case, Bush's signing statement limited the bill's ability to stop "enhanced interrogation." In the statement, Bush agreed that, yes, "torture" would be banned. But he also claimed that he reserved the right to "construe [the law] in a manner consistent with the constitutional authority to the president."[33] Essentially, he decided that the executive would determine what torture was, instead of submitting to an outside definition—effectively keeping Yoo and Bybee's interpretation in his back pocket. Moreover, he implicitly invoked Justice Vinson's dissent by saying the president could, in an emergency that threatened national security, engage in torture, even if it was outlawed by the legislature. But that is exactly what the majority ruling in *Youngstown* prohibited.

Regardless of your opinion of "enhanced interrogation," it's clear that Bush's signing statement blurred the distinction between making the law and executing it, a distinction defended passionately by Justice Jackson. If Bush wanted to voice his opposition to the bill, he could have vetoed it.[34] Used in the way Bush did, the signing statement was an act of constitutional defiance, an official and public rebuke of the constitutional principles the law intended to affirm. Bush may have thought—like Chief Justice Vinson—that limits on the president's authority would have hindered his practical ability to carry out his role as commander in chief. But a president cannot simply claim more authority when he or she decides it is convenient. In the end, Bush circumvented his duty to "take care" that the laws be executed faithfully.

Presidents are not the only ones guilty of trying to blur this line. To enforce the distinction between making laws and executing them, Congress has to be willing to challenge the president's overreach. In recent years, Congress hasn't flexed this muscle enough, especially in areas of national security. Since the 1930s, Congress has delegated a great deal of power to the president. Even though the president is required to execute laws, and the Constitution states "all legislative Powers herein granted shall be vested in a Congress of the United States," there are times when Congress grants the president vast powers.[35] In areas like food safety in the early 20th century and environmental protection standards in the 2000s, the Supreme Court has allowed such delegations of power.[36] This has meant that Congress has often taken a backseat in its role as lawmaker, instead granting broad powers to the president and his agencies.

The delegations of power have also extended to issues of national security, with Congress passing off hard decisions to the president. For instance, through the 2001 Authorization for Use of Military Force, Congress gave the president broad powers to fight a war against a vaguely defined enemy with no time line.[37] In the same year, Congress also granted vast powers of surveillance to the executive branch through the Patriot Act.[38] Recently, members of Congress from both parties have complained that the grants of power in the AUMF were too vast.[39] But they have failed to muster enough political capital to pass legislation that might change this arrangement.

The concern in questions of delegation isn't about whether the end result is good or bad. It's what the Framers would think of a Congress that shrinks from its authority to check presidential power.[40] I suspect they would be none too pleased. The Framers' emphasis on deliberation demanded transparent and robust debate, especially on matters as important as national security.

Some argue that in the modern era, delegation is inevitable.[41] The executive branch has over 2 million civilian employees. Congress, on the other hand, is anemic by comparison. It has a tiny staff and budget, and can't possibly do the work of the executive branch. For example, staff numbers for key Congressional support agencies decreased by 45 percent between 1975 and 2015.[42] But Congress does possess advantages that the executive branch does not. First, in Congress, the risk of bad decision making is lessened by the wisdom generated by the body's size and diversity. A president is just one person. His or her decisions might be influenced by a short temper, a personal crisis, or just a bad night's sleep. Second, because the president requires no consensus, he or she is less likely to deliberate carefully over decisions. On the other hand, Congress has no choice but to deliberate. To pass a bill, Congress must first build consensus within one chamber (either the Senate or the House of Representatives) and then arrive at a compromise bill with the other chamber. Finally, while the president is technically accountable to the entire country, he or she can be limited by the scope and perspective of the White House bubble. Members of Congress, on the other hand, are more responsive to their constituents because they see them regularly, on visits to their home districts on weekends and in between congressional sessions. They are closely connected to the people and can act as their voice when the executive overreaches.

Essentially, the lawmaking power should rest with Congress, because, as an institution, it can better preserve the rule of law that is essential to constitutional democracy—and keep us from the rule by decree and disrespect for rights that often mark dictatorship. The steel seizure case is illustrative here. The president needed to act fast in an emergency and was willing to violate rights to do so—in this case, the mill owners' right to property and the workers' right to strike. Congress, with its deliberative process and accountability to constituents, would likely have been less willing to sacrifice these rights, even considering the military's need for steel. Our rights are best protected, and the democratic process best respected, when debates on legislation and declarations of war are handled by Congress.

One reason for Congress's excessive deference to the president is that increased executive power suddenly becomes popular when you like the current president. As partisanship reaches record levels, senators and representatives increasingly see their loyalty as being to their parties, not to the legislative branch as a whole.[43] Many of President Obama's supporters applauded his use of executive orders yet criticized Bush for his. Likewise, many Bush supporters were quick to accuse President Obama of executive overreach, overlooking the liberties Bush had taken with presidential power.

For example, Obama critics charged that he overstepped his bounds by creating the Deferred Action for Childhood Arrivals program, commonly called DACA, which granted work permits and deportation deferrals to young people who were brought into the United States illegally as children.[44] Only after Congress had failed to pass a bill, the DREAM Act,[45] that would have accomplished a similar goal by allowing undocumented minors to be granted permanent residency in the United States, did Obama take his more limited action. Critics charged that, as the *SNL* skit suggested, Obama was making laws cloaked as executive orders. Defenders of the order argued that Obama was only changing the priorities of immigration enforcement officials—not writing a new law. A rancorous battle would ensue.[46] In September 2017, President Trump announced he would rescind the DACA policy, throwing the fate of hundreds of thousands of immigrants into question.

Whether you support the program or not, DACA is a good example of why legislation cannot be replaced by executive action. Important protections for immigrants should not be subject to disappearance at the stroke of a pen; laws, not executive orders, are what best protect people's rights. Regardless of your party, you should be concerned about executive over-reach from any president. Even if an executive action doesn't violate *Youngstown* directly, executive overreach usurps Congress's lawmaking power and undermines the constitutional value of deliberation.

As PRESIDENT, what can you do to stop this silly cycle of hypocrisy? Instead of lamenting the decline or intransigence of Congress while enacting still more executive orders that usurp legislative power, you can challenge Congress to reinvigorate itself.

As president, one way to challenge Congress to act is to use your increasingly forgotten veto power. The veto power has fallen into disuse. President Obama, for example, used it only twelve times, much less often than most other contemporary presidents.[47] It is, however, the proper constitutional avenue for rejecting legislation you oppose. Using it, or even threatening to do so, will make Congress work together to produce a better bill, restoring its obligation to deliberate about the hard issues facing the American people rather than simply deferring to the executive. Further, using the veto to stop legislation that you think unconstitutional or unwise allows you to avoid the problem of President Bush's signing statement on torture, which pretended to honor the legislative-executive distinction but really undermined it. You should also veto legislation that grants "emergency" powers to a president to make decisions that should really be made by Congress after serious consideration. Finally, you can also refuse to accept broad authorizations from Congress like the AUMF and require more detailed authorizations of war.

We have focused so far on the danger of aggressive presidential actions that overreach into the territory of lawmaking. But another threat to the *Youngstown* principle has emerged not from presidential action but from inaction. During the 2017 Conservative Political Action Conference, Steve Bannon, then the chief White House strategist, stated that the "deconstruction of the administrative state" was one of three goals President Trump seeks to achieve during his term.[48] But a president cannot simply abolish the Department of Education or the Environmental Protection Agency. Neither can a president undermine these agencies by refusing to carry out their missions. The governing statutes of these agencies were created by Congress, and it is a president's Article II duty to "take care" that these laws be executed—even if he or she disagrees with their missions.[49] It would be a violation of this duty and the principles of *Youngstown* to engage in a passive strategy to undermine these statutes by failing to carry out the duties ascribed to them.

Justice Jackson was clearly worried by his firsthand examination of the Nazi rise to absolute power. But there was another dimension to that tragic chapter of world history that we should study in order to better understand the difference between making laws and executing them. As we saw, Hitler's path to dictatorship started by invoking emergency powers granted in the German constitution. Thus, he could justify his actions as being legal—even though they led to the collapse of democracy. We are a long way from such a moment in the United States, and there is no single part of the Constitution or piece of federal legislation that is anything like Weimar's Article 48. But small delegations of power add up, and over time they might amount to giving too much deference to the executive. We aren't likely to have a Reichstag fire on our hands. But if we line enough slow-burning fuses together—emergency powers, signing statements, deliberate undermining of government agencies—we could eventually find ourselves with a president who is enabled to act more like a dictator than a constitutionally limited officeholder. If congressional delegation to the executive is even at the initial stages of that slow burn, it is best to stamp out those little fires right now.

So, SHOULD you use an executive order to do what Congress will not? In most cases, no. The notion that the president executes law and does not make it means that you cannot simply do through an executive order what you and Congress have failed to do through legislation. The legislative process requires a bill to be passed by the Senate and the House. You can certainly advocate for your policy proposals—such as the universal income that was suggested by your economic advisor—but you can't pass them on your own. You can, however, share ideas with legislators and encourage them to develop them into bills, ones that you could later sign. The work of legislating is Congress's work.

Of course, it will be tempting to use executive orders to make good things happen. You might even find yourself in an emergency situation that makes my advice seem off the mark. For example, during the Civil War, President Lincoln bypassed Congress when he issued the Emancipation Proclamation, an executive order granting freedom to enslaved persons in the states that were in rebellion. Lincoln justified his action on the grounds that the country was at war and faced a grave emergency, though the order clearly exceeded the normal scope of presidential authority.[50] However, by taking this action of questionable constitutionality, Lincoln helped herald the birth of a new constitutional era—one with a stronger commitment to equal protection.

I mention Lincoln's example to acknowledge that in truly extraordinary times, the limits may need to bend. But those limits should never fully break; otherwise, every political difficulty would offer an excuse to abandon the Constitution whenever it gets in the way of your agenda. It's dangerous to compare yourself to Lincoln, perhaps our greatest president ever. Whatever crisis faces the country during your presidency will not be as severe as the Civil War. You may believe deeply in your policy positions, but your sincere desire to enact them does not entail a constitutional crisis. In practically all cases, it is best to respect that our system of government is purposefully designed for legislation to be debated and transparent—and that must be accomplished in Congress.

In other words, don't just use your executive power to push that cartoon congressional bill from "Schoolhouse Rock" down the stairs of the Capitol because you are anxious to win a legislative victory. Avoid the temptation of speed offered by an executive order that can "pretty much just happen."[51] The slow and deliberate process of legislating is by design. It distinguishes laws from dictates. The division between making and executing the law defines the limits of your office. The president is not elected to make the laws, but rather to carry them out on behalf of the American people.

4

The Power to Hire and Fire

PRINCIPLE: Presidents might want to fire any executive branch employee they don't like, but some employees are rightly protected by law from being fired at will. Understand the need for the independence of some executive employees, including those who might prosecute you.

"When the president does it, that means it is not illegal."
—RICHARD NIXON[1]

Imagine you've been in office for a while now. You're trying to implement your agenda by working with Congress to pass legislation and by signing executive orders when appropriate. To garner support, you've been speaking to the people about the ideals of the Constitution and how your policy agenda would advance those ideals. But then the phone rings with terrible news: your chief of staff, who was also a campaign advisor when you ran for president, has been accused of participating in a bribery scheme. It is possible that you, too, will be implicated.

The *New York Times* has reported that the chief of staff took money from a construction company in exchange for helping that company win a federal contract underwritten by the Pentagon. You trust the chief of staff, and he is doing important work for you. It occurs to you that this claim could have been engineered by one of your political opponents to interfere with your agenda.

Your attorney general plans to appoint a special prosecutor to investigate the accusation, given that you (as your chief of staff's boss) might have a conflict of interest and want to let him off the hook. It seems likely that the prosecutor will bring charges against him. You want to avoid the political turmoil that could result from an investigation, so you lean on the attorney general to drop the case and ask her to conveniently "forget" about appointing a special prosecutor.

She refuses, and you consider firing her. After all, because she is a member of the executive branch, she works for you. Doesn't that mean you can fire her?

———

THE PRESIDENT has broad power over most members of the executive branch, including the power to hire and fire. But what is the constitutional purpose of presidential control over the many employees who work in this branch? These employees aid the president in executing the laws, and any manager requires some control over employees for them to do their jobs well.

Article II of the Constitution only references the executive departments once: "[The president] may require the Opinion, in writing, of the principal Officer in each of the executive

Departments, upon any Subject relating to the Duties of their respective Offices." The Constitution also has a clause allowing the president to appoint executive officers if the majority of the Senate approves.[2] Other than that, there is no constitutional guidance on how to organize the executive branch. Even the president's cabinet is never mentioned in the original Constitution.

At the time of the country's founding, this lack of guidance probably didn't seem to matter much: the federal government was so small that there wasn't much there to structure.

But by the late 1860s, the federal government had grown dramatically, reflecting an increasingly diverse economy and the profound social problems that emerged after the Civil War.[3] In this era, the jobs within various agencies were often treated as "spoils" to the victor of an election. Political allies were rewarded with plum positions, which often meant that important federal jobs were occupied by incompetent people. Civil service jobs were all about who you knew, rather than what you knew.

It was an assassination, oddly, that woke the public up to the rot in the executive branch. During the 1880 presidential election, a mentally ill man, Charles Guiteau, campaigned for James Garfield, speaking in his favor to several small groups of people. Despite his minor role, Guiteau still credited himself with Garfield's electoral victory. In return, he expected a diplomatic appointment in Paris or Vienna.[4] As many nineteenth-century politicos had done before him, Guiteau lobbied for an appointment, first with letters to the president and, after the inauguration, with in-person visits to the State Department and White House. Few took Guiteau seriously, but he would not take no for an answer and became increasingly aggressive. In May 1881, White House ushers permanently banned him from the building. Infuriated, the next day Guiteau accosted the secretary of state (who shouted to him, "Never speak to me again on the Paris consulship as long as you live!").[5]

Frustrated and angry, Guiteau began plotting Garfield's assassination, a relatively easy task in the days before the Secret Service was so heavily focused on protecting the president. Finally, in July 1881, as Garfield was walking through a Washington train station, Guiteau shot him twice. Garfield died seventy-nine days later, after a painful infection from the gunshots was made worse by his doctors' unsanitary attempts to remove the bullets. Upon hearing the news, Guiteau blamed Garfield's bad doctors: "The doctors killed Garfield. I just shot him."[6]

Guiteau had finally gotten the attention of the nation's capital—and of the wider public. Americans were enraged, incredulous that someone who played such a small role on a campaign would think he were entitled to such a position. Guiteau became a metaphor for the civil service system: both, as it happened, were insane. One popular cartoon depicted Guiteau as a representative of the spoils system, demanding of Garfield: "An office or your life!"[7] It was a rare triumph in American history in which the public was able to look beyond the immediate symptom (mental illness) and identify the root disease: a corrupt civil service.

Congress channeled the public outrage over Garfield's murder into modern civil service reform. The Pendleton Civil Service Reform Act of 1883 changed the way workers in the executive branch were hired, establishing that civil service positions should be awarded based on merit—including performance on a civil service exam—not as a spoil for political loyalty.[8] The Act did something else, too, especially important to your job as president: it forbade presidents from firing a civil service employee using a purely political rationale. In the spoils era, civil servants were expected to kick back part of their salary to those who helped appoint them—and those who didn't comply were fired. The Pendleton Act changed all that.[9]

The result is a fascinating artifact of American democracy: presidents, the most powerful people on Earth, have pretty much never been happy with the expansive protections afforded to the employees working directly under them in their own branch of government. This has led to more than a few showdowns, pitting ordinary people against the head of their government.

The Myers affair is a great example. In 1920, President Wilson fired a federal postmaster in Oregon named Frank Myers. Myers was a Wilson supporter, but had become involved in a local political controversy that earned him negative attention from the Wilson administration. After being fired, Myers sued Wilson for back pay, citing the law that protected him from capricious firing. By law, Wilson was required to obtain the consent of the Senate before firing him.[10] But the White House argued that the president was the sole boss of his employees: After all, are you really the boss if you can't fire a bad employee? The White House maintained that Congress could only set standards for when such a firing was permissible. In 1926, the Supreme Court went even further: if the postmaster worked under the president, the president should have total authority to fire him. In upholding the firing, the Supreme Court cited the president's power, implied under Article II of the Constitution, to staff his or her administration. A president needed the power to fire, not just the power to hire, in order to fulfill his or her constitutional duty to execute the law.[11] *Myers* made it clear that in at least some executive appointments central to the president's power to execute the law, Congress could not limit the president's power to fire.

For Wilson, more was at stake than just this one employee.

He envisioned the presidency as strongest when it broke free of control from the Congress. He saw the right to fire an employee as one battle in his larger efforts to expand the role of the president.

Franklin Delano Roosevelt didn't have the same luck that Wilson did. In 1935, President Roosevelt tried to fire William Humphrey, a commissioner on the Federal Trade Commission. Humphrey was a conservative and a holdover from a previous Republican administration. Roosevelt ordered Humphrey to resign, but Humphrey refused. Roosevelt then fired him, writing, "Effective as of this date, you are hereby removed from the office of Commissioner of the Federal Trade Commission."[12]

However, as if in a civil service rendition of the cult comedy *Office Space*, Humphrey kept showing up to work, and insisted he was still owed his salary. The law said he could only be fired for "inefficiency, neglect of duty, or malfeasance," and nobody had shown he had exhibited any of them.[13] In a landmark ruling in *Humphrey's Executor v. United States*, the Supreme Court agreed. If Congress wants to limit how the president hires and fires (as it had by passing the Pendleton Act), then the president is not above the law and must respect the protection of an agency's officer. The court distinguished between officers of agencies created by Congress for legislative or judicial purposes, like the Federal Trade Commission, and executive officers fully under the control of the president, such as Postmaster Frank Myers. Yes, Article II gave the president complete firing power in regard to executive officers in "units in the executive department."[14] But the court clarified that some agencies were created by Congress with the intent of protecting the leaders of those agencies from being fired without good cause. Congress sought to insulate such agencies from political retaliation by a president, and the officers of these entities were there to carry out legislative will, not executive function.[15] According to the Supreme Court, Humphrey could not be fired by the executive, since he was fulfilling a task mandated by Congress and therefore expressly protected by that branch.[16]

If a government employee is a White House staffer or a political appointee in a purely executive agency, he or she is an at-will employee. This means the president need not give reasons for firing him or her. For example, the Department of Justice is a purely executive agency, so you can fire the attorney general. But if the employee is a civil servant or the head of an administrative agency created by Congress, such as the Federal Trade Commission, a clunkier rule applies. It's something more like, "I can't be fired by the president, unless I really am incompetent at my job." *Humphrey's Executor*, therefore, left the president complete control over hiring and firing of top officials in his or her own purely executive agencies, such as Postmaster Frank Myers. But it said that this control did not necessarily extend to heads of other agencies created by Congress to carry out its will. The case solidified the place in our Constitution for an administrative state charged with carrying out the law, while not fully at the disposal of the president.[17]

The full picture is a bit more complicated, but the bottom line is this: today, civil service laws protect a vast amount of the federal bureaucracy that has become known as the administrative state.[18] But the modern bureaucracy has presented all kinds of new challenges to the Constitution. For one, the Framers could not have imagined an executive bureaucracy of more than two million employees, plus a plethora of federal contractors.[19] They could not imagine, for instance, that an NSA contractor named Edward Snowden could imperil the country's security apparatus by walking out of a building carrying a USB stick filled with secrets about government surveillance.

Just think of how many potential Snowdens there are: if civilian executive branch employees were a city, they would be the fifth-largest in the country.[20]

The enormous size of the executive branch means that some of your employees will see the mission of their agencies as more important than your agenda. The Federal Communications Commission, for instance, was created by a statute, and its employees will likely care more about the mission articulated in that statute than about your goals for the Commission.[21] Indeed, these civil servants, like the president, take an oath to uphold the Constitution.[22] Many see their devotion to the law—both the Constitution and the law that established their agency—as their primary mission, over and above service to specific individuals. That creates a tension between a president and his or her employees. Inevitably, when you are president, your employees will not always do as you wish. How should you manage this responsibly?

———————

THESE VERY old debates are hot topics once again. The year 2017 saw a deluge of internal leaks from executive branch agencies to the press. Are these leaks examples of civil servants upholding their own oath to protect the Constitution? Or are they acts that undermine the president's rightful authority and privacy? Several commentators argue that the torrent of leaks amounts to a "deep state"—unelected government officials with their own agenda—working to undermine the duly elected president.[23] No matter what your party affiliation, they argue, everyone should be concerned when executive agents are unmoored from any loyalty to the president and his or her agenda.

There is some legitimacy to this view: presidents hate leaks, and they would love to fire the people who are responsible. In fact, some leaks can truly be harmful—and the president could be justified in firing executive branch workers who threaten national security. However, the fact that some leaks have threatened national security doesn't mean that every leak is from members of a "deep state." Civil servants provide a crucial constitutional service: they ensure that the laws passed by Congress will actually be carried out. If the president could hire and fire on a whim, that would make it easier for workers to simply refuse to execute the laws on the books whenever the president pressures them into ignoring those laws. It is worthless, for instance, to pass an environmental protection act without an Environmental Protection Agency to carry out its mission. If employees of the agency, such as climate scientists, had no civil service protection, a president who didn't believe in climate change could simply fire them. Scientists charged with protecting the environment would be beholden to the political ambitions of a president who has no interest in this mission.

Furthermore, the president still retains plenty of power to dole out jobs to political allies, such as the members of the cabinet or ambassadorships for those who supported the presidential campaign. In fact, today, the booklet of executive appointees that the incoming president can choose—a total of nine thousand—is still known as the "plum book."[24] Among these appointees are some of the most sensitive positions in the government, including the attorney general, who is in charge of prosecuting federal crimes, and the FBI director, who investigates them. Both can be fired at will.

This fact has led to one of the biggest "bugs" in the software of the Constitution: What happens if the president, as the Framers feared, is caught violating the law? Couldn't he or she fire anyone who tried to thwart him or her? We would likely have a constitutional crisis. In 1973, that's exactly what happened. Looking closely at that episode makes it clear why the president should not have the complete authority to hire and fire executive branch employees at will.

At 2:30 a.m. on June 17, 1972, five men were arrested for breaking into and trying to install wiretaps in the Democratic National Committee's headquarters at the Watergate Hotel in Washington, DC. The burglars were convicted on January 30, 1973, and the Senate Watergate Committee was established in February to investigate links between the burglars and the Nixon administration. Facing public pressure as evidence mounted, Nixon accepted the resignation of his attorney general, Richard Kleindienst. He appointed Elliot Richardson, who had a strong reputation for integrity, as the new attorney general. Before approving Richardson's appointment, the Senate made him commit to appointing a special prosecutor to investigate the Watergate scandal. After Richardson's appointment, he selected Archibald Cox, a respected professor of federal labor law at Harvard and former solicitor general of the United States.

In a dramatic hearing on July 16th, the Senate Watergate Committee discovered that Nixon had made tape recordings of private conversations held in the Oval Office. Cox subpoenaed these tapes, filing a court order for the president to turn them over. Nixon tried to evade the subpoena, claiming executive privilege. On October 20, 1973, Nixon ordered Richardson to fire Cox as the special prosecutor.

Richardson refused and instead resigned in protest. When Nixon then gave the same order to the deputy attorney general, William Ruckelshaus, he too refused and resigned in protest. The next in line was the solicitor general, Robert

Bork. When Bork suddenly became attorney general and Nixon ordered him to fire Cox, Bork complied.

In this "Saturday Night Massacre," as it came to be known, Nixon demonstrated the central problem in this chain of command: a president who wants control over an investigation can simply fire those conducting it.[25] Later, when he was asked about the massacre, Nixon was unapologetic and even said the firings stemmed from his authority under the Constitution. "When the president does it," Nixon later said bluntly, "that means it is not illegal."[26] Whatever you think of him, Nixon sure didn't mince words. Importantly, Nixon was partly right. At the time, no legislation had been passed by Congress to protect Special Prosecutor Cox from being fired. Moreover, the attorney general was an executive officer. So, Nixon really *could* fire him at will.

What checks do we have against another Saturday Night Massacre? Not many. One partial check is the Office of Legal Counsel. The OLC, formed in 1934, is a part of the executive branch within the Department of Justice that is made up of lawyers who work for the president. The OLC functions a bit like a Supreme Court just for presidents. It is an office that examines pending executive orders and policy to ensure they are constitutional, although unlike the real Supreme Court, it cannot compel the president to do anything. A cynical take on the office is that it is meant to avoid lawsuits. But as a virtuous president, you can use it as an essential tool in helping you to uphold the Constitution. Even if an actual court doesn't stop a White House policy, you should not implement it if that policy is unconstitutional. The OLC can help you make these determinations.

However, since its purpose is advisory, the OLC is not a fully robust check. In the past, it has succeeded in constraining the president merely on the merits of its persuasiveness. In the 2000s, while the Bush administration tried to prosecute the War on Terror, some advisors wanted to disregard limits on executive power in the name of security. Alberto Gonzales, who served as President Bush's White House counsel, wanted to continue a top-secret program at the National Security Agency that obtained, without a warrant, the international email and telephone metadata of US citizens if one party on the call was foreign or allegedly linked to terrorists.[27] Gonzales found himself opposed by the Office of Legal Counsel, led at the time by a lawyer named Jack Goldsmith. Together, Goldsmith and Acting Attorney General James Comey, who would later head the FBI, expressed their concern that the policy violated the law. The NSA program had been authorized to collect metadata about international calls and emails, but the OLC had discovered that the NSA was bulk-collecting purely domestic metadata also.[28] If an American citizen had no direct link to terrorism, the OLC thought that this kind of program operating domestically would constitute an unreasonable search, potentially violating the Fourth Amendment.

This internal conflict led to one of the most dramatic moments of the Bush administration. As the OLC and Gonzales clashed, the fate of the program fell to Attorney General John Ashcroft to decide. But Ashcroft had fallen severely ill in the hospital, recovering from a pancreas problem, meaning Comey was serving as the acting attorney general in his absence. Gonzales raced to the George Washington University Hospital in northwest Washington, hoping to convince Ashcroft to preserve the program. Gonzales entered the hospital room where Ashcroft lay in bed, clasping a sheaf of documents that needed Ashcroft's signature. When Gonzales looked across the room, he saw Goldsmith and Comey, who had beaten him there. As Ashcroft listened to Gonzales's request, color returned to the attorney general's face. With tubes and wires protruding from his body, Ashcroft rose up in his bed and told Gonzales that he would not sign the authorization.[29] Even in his weakened state, Ashcroft was worried about the constitutionality of the program. He deferred the decision to his healthy deputy, Comey.

The White House thought that the NSA program was necessary. The OLC disagreed, however, and they enlisted the Department of Justice to act as an internal constitutional check on the president. Even though the attorney general can be fired at will by the president, the OLC and the DOJ were able to resist what they viewed as an unconstitutional act. But the check only works in our system if the president is motivated to deliberate about the Constitution, even at the expense of prized policy goals. The OLC can advise a president not to fire the attorney general, but he might do it anyway. The president also might simply fire the head of the OLC if he gets tired of having his policies questioned. This weakness of the OLC will often mean that the office just affirms what the president would have done anyway.

In 1978, Congress passed a law, the Ethics in Government Act, to prevent future Saturday Night Massacres. It constrained the president's power to fire the person charged with prosecuting him by establishing a new office: the Office of Independent Counsel.[30] Under this statute, which has since expired, in the event of suspected wrongdoing by a president or other high official, the attorney general would recommend that a panel of judges appoint a special prosecutor (called an "independent counsel" after 1983) to investigate. The independent counsel could only be fired by the attorney general if the attorney general could show that the prosecutor had flouted his or her job duties or was mentally or physically incapable of fulfilling them.

Ironically, Bill Clinton signed a reauthorization of the law in 1994, and it was then used to launch an investigation into his own potential financial crimes. This investigation, led by independent counsel Kenneth Starr, mushroomed into a massive inquiry into Clinton's sexual relationship with a White House intern—and his misrepresentation of that relationship while under oath. The House impeached him for perjury and obstruction of justice charges related to this misrepresentation, but the Senate voted not to remove him. Not surprisingly, Clinton wasn't thrilled with the law he had previously reauthorized. He and Congress—motivated by concerns about prosecutorial overreach by Starr—let it expire in 1999.[31]

The current system allows the attorney general to appoint a "special counsel" instead of an "independent counsel." The policy of the attorney general's office is to protect that special counsel from arbitrary firing by the president. However, since this is an internal regulation and not a law passed by Congress, the president can more easily repeal or disregard it. In that case, the ultimate check is public opinion—outrage over the president's abuse of power to hide his or her own political crimes. But this is an uncertain check, one that depends on the popularity of the sitting president.

So, should Congress reinstate the 1978 independent counsel law? One objection—bolstered by concerns about prosecutorial overreach raised by Kenneth Starr's investigation—is that an independent counsel insulated from firing by the president would be unconstitutional. That argument, though, is contested. In the most recent case on the matter, *Morrison v. Olson*, the Supreme Court upheld the independent counsel law.[32] But a different court may well agree with the dissent in that case, that criminal prosecution is a "purely executive power,"[33] meaning the executive must retain the power to fire at will. I, however, agree with the court's majority in *Morrison*. It affirms the reasoning of *Humphrey's Executor*, which stands for the broad proposition that Congress can make laws that protect against firing by a president at will.[34] That principle is especially important when the law in question is designed to make sure that a corrupt president does not evade the same criminal standards to which all are rightly subject in a constitutional democracy.

If the independent counsel law were reinstated, a president could still try to convince the attorney general to fire an independent council for purely political reasons by merely claiming that it was done for cause. But this would be a violation of the law, and courts would be enabled to stop it. A requirement to show cause would at minimum give a president pause in firing a prosecutor. It would be a disincentive to such a raw use of power.

———————

WHAT CAN you do as president to ensure that your successors don't declare themselves above the law? For one, don't give in to the temptation to intimidate civil servants who cross you, so long as their actions reflect a reasonable reading of the Constitution or the law. And do take seriously the advice of the OLC.

But you can do even more to help better codify a limited presidency, working with Congress to limit your hiring and firing power. To do this, you should seek the renewal of the now-expired independent counsel statute. To me, there is something wrong with a system that allows a president to fire those charged with investigating him or her. If the civil service, the Federal Trade Commission, and other agencies are insulated from that kind of retribution, the prosecutor charged with looking into wrongdoing by the president and his or her aides needs it even more. If you become president, you should support efforts to establish an independent counsel and protect his or her office against politically motivated firings.

But you could go further still. An independent counsel law could also extend protection to federal civil servants across the board—not just independent counsels—who report on illegal activities within the executive branch. Federal employees are protected by a 1989 law called the Whistleblower Protection Act, which ensures that a federal employee who discloses government illegality, waste, or corruption cannot be fired.[35] But now they report this information to a watchdog agency called the Office of Special Counsel—a different agency than the special counsel that investigates the president—and the head of that office is ultimately subject to firing for cause by the president. If leaks could be reported instead to the new independent counsel, whistleblowers would have more protection from the president.

James Madison thought a president should have complete control over hiring and firing members of the executive branch; he did note, however, that Congress could impeach a president over an arbitrary or irresponsible use of the president's firing power.[36] But some of the Founding Fathers had other ideas. If you take a walk down a steep hill from my office in Providence, Rhode Island, in less than a mile you will arrive at Providence Harbor. There, in 1777, the patriot marine captain John Grannis witnessed his colleague Commodore Esek Hopkins torturing British soldiers who had been captured.[37] He reported what he saw to the Continental Congress. Hopkins was suspended, and when he tried to retaliate, the Congress responded by passing a resolution protecting those who reported on illegal actions.[38] This policy was passed before the Constitution had even been written, but today's Whistleblower Protection Act captures its spirit. An even stronger version of the Whistleblower Protection Act linked to an independent counsel would provide greater assurances to civil servants that if they report illegal activities of a superior—even if that superior is the president—they'll be protected, just as Grannis was in 1777.

Civil servants who work in the executive branch put their right hand up—just as Washington did over two hundred years ago—and take an oath to the Constitution, not to a particular person. That's what it means to be a nation of laws, not men. When a leak from a civil servant reveals an unconstitutional act by a superior, this is not a shadowy act of the "deep state." It is a patriotic act that helps to keep our democracy strong.

So, SHOULD you fire an attorney general who appoints a special counsel to avoid a conflict of interest to look into wrongdoing by your staff? Definitely not. Your oath demands that you broadly respect the values and ideals of the Constitution. That means you should not subvert the core value of the rule of law, making sure that all officials—even the president—are responsible for criminal wrongdoing. Article II's requirement that you "take care that the laws be faithfully executed" means that you should respect the chief law enforcement officer's decision to allow crimes to be investigated, regardless of who perpetrates them.

But the truth is that nothing in the Constitution currently gives courts the power to prevent you from firing your attorney general. And that's a problem. While we should expect a president to uphold the oath of office, we shouldn't, as a matter of course, rely on it. Madison put this best in the *Federalist Papers*: "If angels were to govern men, neither external nor internal controls on government would be necessary."[39] The Framers didn't provide for a sufficient mechanism to ensure that the president is not above the law. We need Congress for that. It has already protected the civil service and independent federal agencies. Now it needs to extend those protections by passing a law that will make it impossible for you to fire an independent or special counsel without good cause—or, as in the case of the Saturday Night Massacre, to pressure your attorney general, under threat of firing, to do so. Even well-intentioned presidents need legal checks to ensure they stay faithful to their oath.

5

The Power to Nominate
Supreme Court Justices

PRINCIPLE: The president has a responsibility to nominate justices to the Supreme Court. Choose those who respect the Constitution's text and its wider political morality.

> *"The mere fact that a law is outrageous is not enough to make it unconstitutional."*
>
> —ROBERT BORK[1]

A few months into your term, you receive word that an ailing Supreme Court justice has died. You knew this moment was coming, so you've already asked your advisors to prepare a list of possible replacements. After all, Article II does give you the power to nominate justices to the Supreme Court, with the "advice and consent" of the Senate. The list they drew up includes brilliant law professors, well-respected federal circuit judges, legislators with legal backgrounds, state attorneys general, and even a few governors. How do you begin to narrow down the list and decide on your nominee?

71

Among other things, you'll need to think deeply about how courts should interpret the Constitution. This is no minor task: as we have seen, your nominee might one day be charged with stopping you from enacting an executive order or firing an employee. In order for you to choose the best nominee you can, you will need to look to the Constitution, influential Supreme Court justices, and past nominees to the court.

———•———

ONE FEBRUARY morning in 2016, a private hunting camp in the Texas desert became the most famous place in America. There, Justice Antonin Scalia, one of the most influential Supreme Court justices in history, died in his bed during a hunting trip.[2]

The reaction was swift. Flags around the country were lowered to half-mast, as Scalia's seat was draped in black. Scalia's funeral was held in the Basilica of the National Shrine of the Immaculate Conception and attended by hundreds of the most prominent people in the country, including Vice President Joe Biden and Chief Justice John Roberts. According to the *Washington Post*, the archbishop presiding over the ceremony remarked that it was "a simple parish family Mass," drawing laughter from the audience who knew that it was anything but simple.[3]

What takes place after a justice dies is familiar: a period of public mourning is followed by an intense debate about who will be next to put on the robes. The president then nominates a candidate to fill a vacancy among the court's nine members. Justices are appointed for life (unless they are impeached and removed), so this opportunity is rare. It grants a term-limited president a kind of influence that can last for decades: Supreme

Court justices can decide the most important matters in society long after the president has left office.

In the wake of Scalia's death, President Obama began preparing to make his appointment to fill Scalia's seat. The power to confirm or reject such appointments rests with the Senate. There, the Senate Judiciary Committee holds multiday hearings with the nominee. If the Judiciary Committee approves the nomination, it goes to the entire Senate for a vote. In the vast majority of cases, the nominee is confirmed.

But this time, the rancor around the nominee was different. For one thing, Scalia was no ordinary justice. He helped pioneer a judicial philosophy called "originalism," which sparked a still-ongoing debate about how the court, presidents, and citizens should approach the Constitution. Scalia helped to spark something else, too: the court had become significantly more polarized between the time that Scalia was appointed in 1986 and when he died in 2016. Hot button issues like abortion, gay rights, and religious freedom produced multiple five-to-four votes on the nine-member court. The loss of Scalia meant that the swing vote on these close cases might now go to a more moderate or left-leaning justice appointed by President Obama.[4]

Obama offered his nominee: Judge Merrick Garland. But the Republican-controlled Senate refused to hold a hearing on Garland. This was an unprecedented tactic in the modern age, meaning Obama would not get to appoint a new justice. The court functioned with a vacant seat for over a year. When Trump was elected and nominated Neil Gorsuch for the vacant seat, Senate Democrats tried to filibuster Gorsuch's confirmation vote, which under existing rules needed 60 votes to be approved. In turn, Republicans changed the Senate rules to lower the number of votes needed to allow a vote on a Supreme Court appointment. In the end, Gorsuch was confirmed to Scalia's seat. Justice

Gorsuch was confirmed when he was only forty-nine years old. He could sit on the court for more than thirty years.[5]

The incendiary battle over Scalia's replacement captures the extraordinary stakes of one of your sacred duties as president: appointing justices to fill vacancies on the Supreme Court. This court is the arbiter of how society thinks about our Constitution. As president, you are responsible for filling vacancies throughout the federal judiciary, not just the Supreme Court. You nominate judges, and the Senate either confirms or rejects your nominees. Modern presidents typically have the opportunity to appoint over three hundred judges to federal courts at the district and circuit level in two four-year terms.[6] Much of the judicial branch is made up of these lower court judges. But when some of those cases are appealed, or when states themselves clash, the cases go to the Supreme Court. The Supreme Court can strike down laws passed at any level of government, and it can also stop a president who violates the Constitution. These appointments are by far the most important you can make.

So, HOW do you decide whom to choose? First, you should keep in mind that you're looking for someone who can be trusted with the power of judicial review—the ability to determine the constitutionality of laws and to strike down those that are deemed unconstitutional. Article III of the Constitution establishes the judiciary.[7] Mysteriously terse, it never even mentions that the courts have the power of judicial review. Many of the Framers, though, clearly believed that they did: in *Federalist* 78, Alexander Hamilton outlined the rationale for this check on legislative and executive power. It is the duty of the courts, Hamilton wrote, to strike down laws that violate citizens' constitutional rights.

"Without this," he warned, "all the reservations of particular rights or privileges would amount to nothing."[8]

The power of the Supreme Court to strike down legislation was most famously defended in *Marbury v. Madison*, a case from 1803 in which the court clearly claimed its power of judicial review. Thomas Jefferson was president, and he sought to block a series of so-called "midnight appointments" to the bench made by his predecessor, John Adams, between the time Adams lost the election and Jefferson took office. Chief Justice John Marshall handed Jefferson a victory—granting him the power to deny the judges their seats—but he did so on the grounds that the law, which would have otherwise forced Jefferson's hand, was itself unconstitutional. Marshall wrote, "It is emphatically the province and duty of the Judicial Department to say what the law is."[9] From that premise, Marshall argued that because the Constitution was itself law, the court had the right to say what it meant and to strike down legislation that violates the Constitution. Although Marshall didn't stop a president in this instance, he gave courts the power to do so in the future.

Because the power of judicial review is now widely accepted and utilized, appointments to the court have become increasingly contentious. The recent history of the court's use of the judicial review power explains why its appointments provoke such heated debate. The middle of the twentieth century was a historically tumultuous time, and the Supreme Court played a memorable role. Led by Chief Justice Earl Warren, the court began to weigh in on the most divisive issues of the day. The court banned racial segregation in all public schools, and it upheld the segregation ban Congress had passed in all public accommodations, including hotels and restaurants.[10] The Warren Court also expanded the rights of accused criminals, mandating that they be told what their rights are when arrested,[11] and expanding the right to counsel to those who could not pay for it.[12] In response to these decisions, conservatives launched a campaign to impeach Earl Warren, which is allowable under the Constitution. Across the country, especially in the Deep South, billboards declared, "Save our Republic! Impeach Earl Warren."[13]

Many of the decisions of the Warren Court are rightly celebrated today, and the Impeach Warren movement is seen as a vestige of the racism of the Jim Crow era. But part of the controversy behind the Warren Court's rulings was based on an important difference over how to interpret the Constitution. Are the rights that citizens have under the Constitution limited to those that are explicitly spelled out in the text, as it was understood at the time it was written over two hundred years ago? Or do citizens have broader constitutional rights, based on our best modern understanding of what the Constitution's moral principles require? The first approach is a version of originalism—the philosophy Scalia helped to popularize.[14] The second is what I call value-based reading, which is an attempt to understand the values enshrined within the Constitution's text. It is an account of the Constitution's morality, and should not be confused with an individual's beliefs. So, should we follow originalism and take the text of the Constitution as the final word in adjudicating constitutional questions? Or should we use value-based reading, considering the text as well as the deeper values to which it refers to understand the Constitution's meaning?

Consider one of the most significant decisions of the Warren Court, *Griswold v. Connecticut*. In this 1965 case, the court struck down a Connecticut law that had prohibited married couples from using contraception, even in their own bedroom. Writing for the court, Justice William O. Douglas argued that the law violated the right to privacy.[15] A justice who is an originalist would differ from Douglas, interpreting the Constitution according to the meaning of the text when it was written. On this approach, there is no right to privacy, since the words *right to privacy* do not appear explicitly in the Constitution. But a justice who uses value-based reading would point out that the Constitution also has no explicit guarantee of such fundamental rights as those concerning interracial marriage and one-person-one-vote—yet they are crucial rights that we understand the Constitution to protect. Instead, a value-based reader would ask if the right to privacy is connected to any of the core principles of the Constitution.

In this way, Justice Douglas found in *Griswold* that the principle of freedom to conduct family and intimate life is a theme that runs throughout the Bill of Rights. As Douglas wrote, the First Amendment protects freedom of association for citizens to meet in groups, including family, without government intervention. The Third Amendment prohibits the government from housing troops during peacetime in people's houses without consent. The Fourth Amendment safeguards the "right of the people to be secure in their persons, houses, papers, and effects, against unreasonable searches and seizures."[16] Implicit in these parts of the Constitution, Douglas said, is the thought that there is a zone, such as the home, where citizens should have the freedom to pursue their intimate and family relations outside of the control and monitoring of the government, as long as there is no abuse. The right to privacy is a right that is implied by the explicitly named rights of the Constitution, and it is a requirement of the moral principle of freedom found in the Constitution to pursue family and intimate life. By recognizing the right to privacy, Douglas argued, we give explicit constitutional rights "life and substance," making them more secure.[17]

In the decades since *Griswold*, the right to privacy has been central to the court's decisions to extend constitutional protections to women who seek abortions and to gay and lesbian citizens.[18] But at the time, *Griswold* provoked a conservative backlash. The protestors had a point behind their anger: Why should nine unelected justices get to decide the country's direction on crucial matters? For this reason, some scholars have argued that judicial review is undemocratic. And some democratic countries agree. In New Zealand, for instance, courts cannot strike down laws passed by the legislature. Unelected judges cannot decide issues of fundamental rights, like abortion. Instead, abortion is an issue that is left to the legislature.[19]

Our Framers, though, made it clear that they disagreed with this kind of unchecked legislative power. In the *Federalist Papers* and elsewhere, Madison and Hamilton emphasized the danger of the legislative and executive branches violating the Constitution. Hamilton describes this danger in *Federalist* 78: "The Executive not only dispenses the honors, but holds the sword of the community. The legislature not only commands the purse, but prescribes the rules by which the duties and rights of every citizen are to be regulated."[20] Given the vast powers of the executive and legislative branches, it was all the more important to ensure that they were checked by one another and by the judiciary.

The Framers saw judges as having a special role in defending the Constitution against Congress and the president: striking down laws or executive orders that violate the Constitution. As Hamilton argued, the limits that the Constitution places on government power "can be preserved in practice no other way than through the medium of courts of justice, whose duty it must be to declare all acts contrary to the manifest tenor of the Constitution void."[21] In other words, if a law violates the general principles of the Constitution, the courts should strike down that law.

This is an immense power to give to a handful of justices appointed *for life*. How can we trust that justices will not simply invalidate laws with which they disagree? The basic answer is that when justices make an argument in favor of striking down a law, they must frame that argument in the context of the Constitution. However, sometimes the Constitution isn't perfectly clear. For example, what does a phrase like "cruel and unusual punishment," which is banned by the Constitution, actually mean? Is the death penalty "unusual"? Is solitary confinement "cruel"?[22]

These are deep disagreements not just about the outcome of the law, but about how to read the words themselves. In the midst of these disagreements, Scalia's originalism made its mark. According to this view, most words and phrases in the Constitution—even broad terms like "cruel" or "unusual"— should be interpreted not the way we conceive of them today, but as they were understood at the time the Constitution was ratified in 1788 (or, if they appear in an amendment, at the time the amendment was passed). For Scalia, the Constitution is a people's method of restraining and binding their future selves. Since, to him, the people who approved the Constitution in 1788 are its source of authority, that people's understanding of the document is what binds us today. For Scalia, historical dictionaries, not theories of morality, are what matter most in interpreting the Constitution. Scalia was a fierce critic of the court's decision in *Griswold* to guarantee a right of privacy and its subsequent ruling in *Roe v. Wade* expanding that right to abortion. In Scalia's view, privacy and abortion were never mentioned in the text, so those rights should never have been recognized by the court.[23]

The fundamental problem with Scalia's originalism, however, is that it does not account for some of the most widely recognized and crucial rights that we have today. It is true that the Constitution's text is sometimes narrow and clear—for instance, when it specifies that the president must be thirty-five years old to take office. But much of the Constitution is written more broadly, inviting an inquiry about the document's political morality.

Consider the Fourteenth Amendment's requirement of equal protection under the law. The Fourteenth Amendment—passed in the aftermath of the Civil War—states that no state shall "deny to any person within its jurisdiction the equal protection of the laws."[24] An originalist reads the Constitution and its amendments according to the historical meaning of the words at the time of their passage. When the Fourteenth Amendment was passed in 1868, the legal meaning of this clause was not yet widely understood to include women. If justices relied on Scalia's originalism, then women would have no legal protection of their right to be free from government discrimination on issues like admission to public universities or receipt of public benefits.

A value-based reading of the Constitution, by contrast, would not be confined to the meaning of words from 1868, when the Fourteenth Amendment was passed. Instead, it would ask: What is our best understanding of the moral principles of the Constitution enshrined in its text and in our case law? If we interpret the Constitution this way, the moral principle of equality requires that equal protection of the law be extended to women.

The divide between originalism and value-based reading exploded onto the national scene when it was put on trial in one of the most acrimonious confirmation hearings in history.

In 1987, Justice Lewis Powell retired from the Supreme Court, and President Ronald Reagan had to find a replacement for him. Reagan wanted intellectual firepower on the bench, so he chose as his nominee former Yale Law professor Robert Bork, who was then a federal judge. (This is the same Bork who played a pivotal role in the Saturday Night Massacre described in Chapter 4.) Bork was also a revered scholar of originalism, and he assumed he would sail through the hearings. When he appeared before the Senate Judiciary Committee, Bork seemed a bit rumpled; his gray beard was styled to exuberant effect, giving him the appearance of having dropped in from a previous century. A chain smoker, Bork was famous for his prickliness. This may not have caused him much of a problem in academia, but it was a dangerous trait for a Senate hearing.[25]

Supreme Court confirmation hearings are usually dry affairs. But Bork was seen as a talkative and combative professor. Critics called him arrogant. And the hearing represented more than just one person's nomination: originalism itself would have its time in the public spotlight. Underlying the tension of the hearings was the question of whether the court was correct to protect a right to an abortion, which has its legal basis in the right to privacy found in *Griswold*.[26] In a new age of televised hearings (C-SPAN had just started televising Senate debates in 1986), senators were eager to leave a mark. The Senate Judiciary Committee was led by a young chairman, Joe Biden, then a dashing senator from Delaware. Biden opened the hearings, saying somewhat mischievously, "I do not want to get into a debate with a professor." He then proceeded to do exactly that.[27]

In front of TV cameras and a gallery packed with onlookers, Biden played prosecutor, seeking to convict Bork and the theory of originalism and to defend a value-based reading. First, he pressed Bork on *Griswold*, which Bork opposed. If Bork opposed a decision in which married couples had a right to use contraception in their own bedroom, Biden asked, wouldn't that mean Bork also would have upheld the forced sterilization laws? Those, too, had been passed by states and similarly regulated people's sexuality.

Sure enough, Bork's famous temper came out. In a heated exchange, Bork called one of Biden's examples "wholly bizarre and imaginary,"[28] suggesting that Biden's worries about privacy violations were unfounded. Biden kept prodding. Why, exactly, would he not strike down a terrible law, like the one that banned married couples from using contraception in their own bedroom? Surely even the Framers would find such a law outrageous. Senator Patrick Leahy from Vermont, a Democrat and ally of Biden on the judiciary committee, continued the line of questioning about *Griswold*. How could Bork not agree with the court that the law banning married couples from using contraception was "crazy"? Bork took the bait. "The mere fact that a law is outrageous," Bork sniped back, "is not enough to make it unconstitutional."[29]

The hearings went on like this. Senators asked direct questions about the nominee's judicial philosophy, and Bork was brutally honest in response. In the end, Biden's ploy worked: Bork, seen as too extreme, was rejected by the Senate. The legacy of the Bork hearing was enormous. First, it exposed Americans, many of whom were watching confirmation hearings on TV for the first time, to the raw emotion in the debate over the court. Second, it left a clear precedent for nominees: never again would judicial appointees be so utterly honest about what they actually believed. In every hearing since, justices have answered questions about their judicial philosophies with generalities about upholding the Constitution.[30]

Some lamented the Bork hearings for bringing a circus-like atmosphere to the court's traditionally stoical proceedings. But for many Americans, the increased access to the hearings through C-SPAN was not only a new window into the process, but also a new motivation to develop their opinions about constitutional interpretation—and to share those opinions with their senators.[31] In India, justices are appointed by the president on the advice of a group of judges meeting behind closed doors and outside of public view. But in the American system, we reject that secretive approach as undemocratic.[32] While the people do not directly choose a justice, their senators speak for them in open hearings, battling it out on behalf of their vision of the Constitution.

Scalia—who had been appointed by Reagan the year before Bork's contentious hearing in a much less dramatic confirmation process—had a different version of originalism than Bork did. Bork often admitted the Constitution's meaning was ambiguous. But Scalia sought and found clarity in its words.[33] He appealed to originalism when he attempted to reverse Warren-era decisions about the rights to abortion, affirmative action, and gay rights—none of which were explicitly endorsed by the Constitution at the time of the founding.[34] For instance, in a dissent in the 2003 case of *Lawrence v. Texas*, which dealt with a Texas law criminalizing homosexual sex, Scalia rejected the view that the constitutional right to privacy includes a right of gay or straight couples to have consensual sex. "What Texas has chosen to do is well within the range of traditional democratic action," he wrote, "and its hand should not be stayed through the invention of a brand-new 'constitutional right' by a Court that is impatient of democratic change."[35]

As this quote indicates, Scalia sought to use originalism to constrain not only lawmakers and presidents but also judges, starting with his Supreme Court colleagues. In his view, justices should respect the text as written, in order to honor the democratic process that ratified the original Constitution and its subsequent amendments. To Scalia, this ensured that unelected judges would not amass too much power within our democratic system. In this case, though, the majority of the court would not be constrained. They disagreed with Scalia's argument, ruling in favor of extending the right of privacy to any intimate relations between consenting adults.[36]

Despite the increasing influence of Scalia's originalism, in the end, the view has not eliminated the right to privacy. Instead, a majority of the court has rejected Scalia's brand of originalism, and has instead expanded the right to privacy to protect a woman's access to abortion, as well as gay rights.

Interestingly, after the Senate failed to confirm Bork, the justice that Reagan chose to replace him has since played a major role in expanding gay rights. That justice was Anthony Kennedy. In 1987, Edwin Meese, the attorney general who advised Reagan, admired Kennedy's libertarian principles and defense of states' rights. But Reagan's staff had doubts. They quietly circulated an internal White House memo vetting Kennedy, expressing concerns that Kennedy might decide that gay Americans had rights to privacy under the Constitution.[37] The memo claimed that Kennedy had "indicated fairly strongly that he would not uphold the validity of laws prohibiting homosexual conduct."[38] Kennedy went on to write the 2015 opinion in *Obergefell v. Hodges*, recognizing that the fundamental right of marriage applies to same-sex couples as well as opposite-sex ones. Justice Kennedy wrote eloquently in that decision, "Their hope is not to be condemned to live in loneliness, excluded from one of civilization's oldest institutions. They ask for equal dignity in the eyes of the law. The Constitution grants them that right."[39]

Questions about how to interpret the Constitution continue to divide the Supreme Court—and the American people. The battle between Biden and Bork was just the opening salvo in a clash of ideas about how we understand the requirements of the Constitution, and its broadcast on C-SPAN invited all Americans into this conversation. The confirmation hearings provided Americans—through their senators—a chance to reject an approach that was widely thought too extreme. Bork had spent much of his life among the ranks of the powerful: in the Nixon Department of Justice, at Yale Law School, and as a federal circuit court judge. But his hearing was a chance for the American people to assert their power by considering and challenging his ideas.

The role that ordinary people played illustrates how the Supreme Court nomination process is not simply one between the president and the Senate. In fact, all three branches—and the people themselves—have a responsibility to engage in serious constitutional interpretation, publicly considering and defending their views when a justice is subject to confirmation. The president should scrutinize potential nominees' views, only choosing those whose understanding of the Constitution's text and morality is sound. Senators, like Biden, should ask tough questions to make sure their "consent" to the nominee is informed, as Article II requires. Nominees, like Bork, should clearly convey their judicial philosophies. Though he was not successful in being confirmed, Bork should be admired for being forthcoming with his views, a trait all too often missing in modern hearings, where nominees say little of substance in an effort to seem uncontroversial.

The people also have an important role to play, lobbying their representatives to ask tough questions at hearings and weighing in on whether nominees share their values. Although the phrase *separation of powers* commonly describes our form of government, in instances like this, every actor in our democratic system should work together to protect the Constitution.

YOU'RE BACK at the White House, mulling over the list of possible nominees for the vacant Supreme Court seat. What qualities should you look for in a justice?

Expertise in constitutional law should be a starting point, but that alone is not enough. Bork was brilliant, diligent, and a hard worker. But he was also cocksure, insensitive, and sometimes flippant toward the office he was trying to occupy. When asked why he wanted to be a justice, his first response was that "it would be an intellectual feast"—a self-centered answer that betrayed little regard for the awesome power the court has in shaping real people's lives. He dismissed landmark precedents with the wave of his hand, and didn't seem to have the temperament of a justice. A brash intellect might make someone a famous professor or provocateur, but it is not what you should look for in a Supreme Court justice.[40]

One way to show respect for the grave impact of court decisions on the lives of ordinary Americans is by communicating clearly. A good justice strives for clarity and transparency in writing, understanding that citizens are due an explanation of the court's rulings. Here Scalia excelled. His writing remains a model of clarity. As we saw in his comment about *Lawrence*, he was blunt. But at least we knew where he stood.

Further, a great justice must also show independence from a president, even if that president is you. Looking on as the Warren court altered the face of American life, President Eisenhower once called the appointments of Chief Justice Earl Warren and Justice William Brennan, another left-leaning justice, his two biggest mistakes.[41] Yet those justices played a part in enacting basic rights that many of us take for granted, such as the Miranda Right to hear our rights read to us upon arrest or the ban on segregation in public schools in *Brown v. Board of Education of Topeka.* Justice Brennan also became the most important defender of a value-based reading of the Constitution, defending in eloquent pieces the idea that the Constitution in its various provisions respects and protects individual dignity.[42] When you pick a justice, don't look for a sycophant. Look for a person with the courage to enforce the values of the Constitution.

Also look for a team player. Like any employee, a good justice can get things done by collaborating well and building consensus among other justices. You are appointing a person, after all, not a theory. Before serving as a judge, Justice Sandra Day O'Connor was a senator in the Arizona state legislature. There, she became well known for her ability to build political coalitions to move legislation forward.[43] The same skill helped her on the bench. Look for a justice who works well with others. Such a justice will be the most influential in making real his or her vision of the Constitution; like O'Connor or Earl Warren, who had been governor of California, you might consider a politician as opposed to a judge.

O'Connor, as the first female justice to serve on the Supreme Court, helps illustrate another important factor to consider when choosing a nominee. Politicians and judges should not only defend the interests of America but should also look like America. It is important, therefore, that you consider gender, race, ethnicity, religion, and a variety of other characteristics and experiences in your judicial nominations. If this sounds extreme, consider Justice Ruth Bader Ginsburg's approach:

when people ask her how many would be enough women on the Supreme Court, she answers "nine." As she explains, "People are shocked [by that answer] . . . but there'd been nine men, and nobody's ever raised a question about that."[44] We should not go back to a time when the court is composed entirely of white men. Ensuring gender, racial, and ethnic diversity helps to alleviate a monolithic court's failure to understand the circumstances that litigants often find themselves in.

Justice Thurgood Marshall argued *Brown v. Board* before the Supreme Court and later became that court's first African American justice. Given his personal and legal background, it is undeniable that Marshall was better able to understand issues of equal protection and discrimination in ways that a white person who had never experienced Jim Crow ever could. O'Connor too spoke of being unable to land a job at a law firm—aside from as a legal secretary—a perspective that no doubt informed her decisions about the role of equal protection in guarding against gender discrimination.[45]

As you weigh your possible nominees, what should you do about the battle between originalism and value-based reading? Frankly, I think you should avoid a justice with the rigidity of Scalia's or Bork's originalism. A few years ago, when I was a visiting professor at the University of Chicago Law School, I wandered out of my office to the one next to mine. There I made an amusing discovery: Antonin Scalia's old office. Outside the door hung a plaque recognizing Scalia's time there as a professor. I remember thinking that such an acknowledgment was fittingly placed: an academic setting is where Scalia's originalism belongs.[46]

Scalia's version of originalism did have an intellectual austerity that scholars can appreciate. But it failed to account for many of our most important precedents that protect the civil liberties of Americans, like the right to privacy and the right against discrimination. Civil liberties enshrined in the Constitution come both from the text and from a reading that sees our nation's founding document as defending the values of freedom and equal protection of the laws. As president, look for justices who draw from both the Constitution's text and its values, and who can build consensus around the founding principles the court is designed to uphold.

Of course, the justice you choose might not fit neatly within old categories, and you should welcome that. Cutting-edge work about how to read the Constitution draws from originalist theories, value-based theories, and the rich area in between these two approaches. And labels matter less than substance. An ideal justice might call him- or herself a "living originalist," for instance, and still demonstrate a commitment to the Constitution's values and Supreme Court precedents, as well as to the document's text.[47]

Ultimately, if you can find a nominee with expertise in constitutional law, a clear communication style, an ability to build consensus, a willingness to maintain independence from political pressure, and a fundamental respect for the Constitution and its role as a guardian of the rights of ordinary Americans— and you make your choice with a commitment to gender, ethnic, and racial diversity—you will have chosen well.

6

The Commander-
in-Chief Power

PRINCIPLE: Congress, not the president, can declare war. Restore the original balance between your commander-in-chief power and Congress's war power.

"In no part of the Constitution is more wisdom to be found, than in the clause which confides the question of war or peace to the legislature, and not to the executive department."

—JAMES MADISON[1]

Early in your presidency, the Syrian dictator invades northern Lebanon, seeking to annex it to his country. During the presidential election, you campaigned on a foreign policy platform of "human rights for all," and you want to intervene to liberate the Lebanese from the Syrian army. You ask your military advisors to explain all of your available options to resolve the crisis—including a possible American invasion.

In this situation, you have two adversaries: the Syrian army, invading Lebanon on one side of the globe; and—you guessed it—the Framers of the Constitution. They are the ones who have limited your role as commander in chief. Under Article I, only Congress has the ability to declare war. How can you tell whether launching a military attack is within your purview as commander in chief, or if it intrudes on Congress's power to declare war?

To make matters more complicated, a member of Congress is introducing a resolution to debate going to war. Your advisors say there is no time for discussion. By the time Congress is finished talking itself to sleep, they warn, Syria will have long conquered various Lebanese outposts. But Congress wants to consider the resolution carefully, gathering input from constituents and discussing among its members whether this mission is truly worth putting American lives at risk. Should you ask for a formal declaration of war while the clock is ticking? Or should you order military action on your own?

Similar scenarios have played out many times for modern presidents. The tension between Congress and the president over war powers is one of the defining features of the presidency. Article II designates the president as "Commander in Chief of the Army and Navy of the United States."[2] This makes you the leader of the most powerful military on Earth. You are at the top of the chain of command on purpose. Among the Framers' fears was a government overseen by a military general, so they placed an elected civilian official, the president, in charge of the military.

Once Congress has declared war, you have wide discretion on how to conduct it. Though Congress can place some checks on your power, you ultimately are the most important person deciding how to allocate resources and make battle plans during war. That is precisely the reason the Framers wanted Congress to deliberate *before* a declaration is rendered: Congress is charged with declaring war, and once the war is declared, the president can focus entirely on winning it.

FROM THE perspective of the Constitution, the president's key strength of being able to react to a crisis quickly is itself also a weakness. Madison wisely predicted that the executive would be the branch "most interested in war, & most prone to it." Congress, on the other hand, could constrain those tendencies with its deliberative traditions. The Framers hoped that a president would be forced to deliberate with Congress, even while Congress deliberated with itself. That, Madison wrote, is why the Constitutional Convention "vested the question of war in the [legislature]"—the branch with the highest propensity for deliberation.[3]

Madison's concern about the rush to war continued from the Philadelphia Convention into the first presidential administration. In 1793, George Washington declared that the United States would remain neutral in a conflict between England and France. Known as the Neutrality Proclamation, this declaration was one of the first major foreign policy decisions of the United States.[4] Madison was furious about it, and Jefferson was, too. They both argued that a president's war-making powers were extremely limited—so limited, in fact, that even to make such a proclamation usurped Congress's war-making power in Article I of the Constitution. Who was Washington to say whether we would be neutral or not? Madison and Jefferson thought such a decision should have been up to Congress.

Aside from deliberation, Madison saw another important

reason for Congress's role in authorizing war: the president is more removed from democratic accountability to the American people, whose families will endure the worst of these conflicts. These arguments were revived by prominent constitutional lawyers during the Vietnam War.[5] The worry in that period was that President Nixon failed to understand the extent of the American public's opposition to the war because he was sequestered in the White House.

Alexander Hamilton clashed, as he often did, with Jefferson and Madison on the war power question. He stressed the need for broad presidential power and argued that a president needed to act with speed, wisdom, and sometimes aggression— a combination he summed up as the special "energy" of the executive, needed especially during emergencies. He wrote, "In the conduct of war, in which the energy of the Executive is the bulwark of the national security," the president must be ready to respond to threats rapidly.[6] Hamilton's words, written during a time when war was fought on horseback and sailboats, might seem even more relevant today given the faster pace of war.

Quick action, however, does not always lead to the best decisions in war. Other early interpreters of the Constitution, siding with Madison and Jefferson, thought deliberation mattered more than speed. Joseph Story, a Supreme Court justice who served from 1812 to 1845 and was one of the most prominent voices on the war powers question, argued that slow deliberation by Congress would rightly tilt the war powers against the rush to war. It would also preserve Congress's ability to set the national agenda, which might be lost if a president could simply engage the country rapidly in war. He was concerned that war "never fails to impose upon the people the most burthensome [sic] taxes, and personal sufferings."[7]

Although the Framers disagreed about many things, they did agree on a crucial point regarding constitutional war power—that it must be Congress that initiates a war, not the president. Although Madison went too far in claiming a president could not signal policy preferences about war—through making a Neutrality Proclamation, for example—he was right to fear a chief executive who claimed the sole power to commence a sustained conflict. Unfortunately, recent history has shown an alarming trend in the other direction.

The Framers were right to fear placing the war power in the hands of one person. Richard Nixon was one president who exhibited the "passion" and rash decision making the Founders feared in a commander in chief. To put this into blunt terms: an angry King George could do damage to his colonies, but imagine an angry king with his hands on the nuclear trigger and the power to literally blow up the world. In our current system, we leave that power to one person, the president. But what if this person lacks mental balance? Richard Nixon once talked flippantly about nuclear war, with some members of Congress reporting that he told them, "I can go in my office and pick up the telephone and in 25 minutes, millions of people will be dead."[8] After hearing this, Senator Alan Cranston of California was so concerned that he called Secretary of Defense James Schlesinger to tell him about "the need of keeping a berserk president from plunging us into a holocaust."[9]

Secretary Schlesinger was likely worried after hearing about this exchange, and reports of Nixon's heavy drinking could not have alleviated that concern.[10] In an earlier crisis, the Yom Kippur War had just broken out between Israel and a group of Arab states, including Egypt and Syria. British Prime Minister Edward Heath was on the phone and wanted to talk to President Nixon. Secretary of State Henry Kissinger was recorded telling Deputy National Security Advisor Brent Scowcroft in an October 11, 1973, conversation that Nixon could not come to the phone: "Can we tell them no?" asked Kissinger. "When I talked to the President he was loaded."[11]

By the time Nixon faced the threat of impeachment toward the end of his presidency, Schlesinger allegedly told the military to clear any presidential order to use nuclear weapons with either himself or Secretary Kissinger.[12] While prudent, considering Nixon's emotional state, Schlesinger's order violated the principle that the president is the commander in chief of the military. The reality is that our current system would force a secretary of defense to choose between obeying an order from the president to launch a nuclear attack and engaging in criminal civil disobedience. If presidential checks on war powers were stronger, we might never have to end up in this scary situation.

Although Nixon was often perceived as disconnected from the American people and indifferent to the suffering of war, some presidents have been deliberate and even brooding over the decision to go to war because of their personal connections to those fighting. During Vietnam, Lyndon Johnson felt the full effect of having close relatives on the battlefield when the nation was at war. One of his sons-in-law, Chuck Robb, commanded a rifle company and eventually received a bronze star for his valor in combat. Robb, who later became a US senator, sent letters and audiotapes from Vietnam on a regular basis. President Johnson would sometimes listen to these tapes and share them with cabinet and staff members.[13]

These dispatches from the front often moved Johnson and made him more critical of his decisions in Vietnam. One image, captured by White House photographer Jack Kightlinger, shows Johnson in agony, doubled over with one hand on his face as he listens to Robb's tape. In one letter, Robb, who was in his late twenties, described in gruesome detail a five-hour firefight. The story left Johnson shaken.[14] Lynda Robb, Johnson's daughter, later recalled that "I was a big pregnant reminder that it was *his* policy that was separating husbands from wives, children from parents."[15] The experience left Johnson to conclude, as he once told his vice president, "I'm not temperamentally equipped to be commander-in-chief. I'm too sentimental to give the orders."[16]

A little over a decade later, a group of congressmen decided that empathy was not enough to justify usurping the constitutionally assigned role of Congress in declaring war. In 1990, fifty-three members of the House and one senator joined a lawsuit against President George H. W. Bush's threatened war in Iraq, arguing that Bush needed congressional approval to use the military to remove Iraqi forces from Kuwait.[17]

When President George H. W. Bush wanted to commence prolonged military action in Kuwait after that country was invaded by its neighbor Iraq, Bush claimed he did not need congressional authorization. Bush set a timeline for Iraq leaving Kuwait in 1991, and he claimed that his commander-in-chief power meant he didn't need Congress to authorize him to use military force against Iraq. Later, after the lawsuit, Bush *requested* (but still did not think he needed) that Congress provide official support for a UN resolution that authorized member states to use "all necessary means" in the conflict to ensure peace.[18] Congress agreed. It passed its own resolution endorsing Bush's war.[19]

In this case, Bush eventually followed the protocol called for in the Constitution. But not all modern presidents have been as willing to take a backseat to Congress in initiating war. In 1973, toward the end of both the Nixon presidency and the war in Vietnam, Congress tried to institute a compromise between, on one end of the spectrum, a rash commander in chief, and on the other end, a slow-moving Congress. The resulting War Powers Act requires that the president alert Congress within two days whenever military forces are introduced into a new conflict.[20] It also mandates that the president end military action within sixty days if Congress has not made a formal declaration of war or officially authorized a continuation of the military operations.[21] This specifically delineated amount of time reflected growing concern in Congress that President Nixon was using a previously passed resolution about Vietnam to invade other countries like Cambodia and Laos.

By passing the War Powers Act, overriding Nixon's veto, Congress might have thought it was flexing its muscle, signaling that it would force the president to respect its ability to declare war. Now, nearly twenty years later, Bush and his lawyers argued something different: that the Act had actually delegated the power to commence war to the president. Practically every Republican senator and member of Congress was happy to let this usurpation of congressional power go unchallenged.[22] Bush's strategy was to commence war and then seek approval once the American people's patriotic fervor had been activated.

So, the case of *Dellums v. Bush* (the lawsuit the fifty-three members of the House and one senator had joined) was heard before the United States district court for the District of Columbia. Federal judge Harold H. Greene ruled that because the Gulf War had not yet begun, he could not issue a preemptive ruling. But Judge Greene wrote a crucial addition:

that the congressional representatives, including Robb, were right. Only Congress could declare war.[23] The lawyer in the case, Jules Lobel, calls the outcome a "real *Marbury v. Madison* moment,"[24] because in both *Marbury v. Madison* and *Dellums v. Bush*, the courts ruled that presidential power was limited, despite giving the president a nominal victory.[25]

Judges, however, are often reluctant to intervene to stop a war, even if it is unconstitutional. Lobel, the lawyer, also represented Congressman Tom Campbell and his colleagues in a suit against President Clinton for engaging in a sustained aerial campaign in Kosovo without congressional approval. Lobel sued on behalf of members of Congress, but this time found less success. The United States District Court for the District of Columbia refused to opine on whether Congress or the president had the power to initiate the conflict. The judge also cast doubt on the right of Campbell and his colleagues to sue in the first place, suggesting that the two branches might best work it out on their own. The bombing campaign went on.[26]

The Campbell lawsuit was a sign of things to come, and a continuation of the past. In the Vietnam War era, courts repeatedly refused to decide cases about the war's constitutionality on the merits. Although many of these suits argued that the Vietnam War was an undeclared war and thus illegal, the courts avoided answering these contentions. Often these courts relied on the "political question" doctrine, claiming that defining what constituted a war was an issue only to be resolved between the president and Congress.[27] In this sense, *Dellums v. Bush* was an aberration, in that Judge Greene acknowledged that the decision about whether the country was in a state of war was within the courts' purview to decide.

The problem with the "political question" doctrine and other refusals to intervene is that they have ceded power entirely to the executive. Without the courts as an ally, Congress has been hamstrung in stopping executive declarations of war. In the modern era, courts have continued to be hands-off when it comes to presidential war powers, leaving it to presidents and Congress to argue over where the proper authorization of war lies.

This has created real problems. The issue of presidents waging war unconstrained by courts and Congress has gotten worse in recent years. In 2011, President Obama's Office of Legal Counsel advised him that his bombing campaign in Libya, relying heavily on the use of drones, required congressional authorization under the War Powers Act after sixty days had expired. Obama ignored the advice. Instead, using arguments from the White House counsel and State Department lawyers, he determined that without ground troops deployed, he did not need authorization from Congress.[28] In doing this, Obama stepped over the remaining constraint on presidential power—his own office tasked with constitutional interpretation—further eroding the Constitution's original division of war powers. Drone strikes increased dramatically under President Trump, showing that the problem is not just confined to the Obama administration.[29]

———•———

TODAY, THE swift approach to military action by presidents is light-years away from Madison's vision of a slow, deliberate consideration of war authorized by Congress. A president in office today must be ready for attack at any time. The rise of international terrorism and the growing threat posed by rogue nuclear states like North Korea make clear the need for decisive, and possibly preemptive, military action. Some might say Madison's praise of deliberation is outdated.

I believe those defenders of our current, unchecked executive powers are wrong, and Madison was right that the Constitution requires war to be authorized by Congress. After all, the Constitution is clear that "Congress shall have power . . . to declare[30] war."[31] Madison understood that Congress, which today has 535 members, is bound to the people who serve in the military. All members of Congress will have constituents—and many will also have relatives of their own—serving in the very wars they authorize. Yes, Johnson had a deep connection with his son-in-law, and other presidents too might have personal connections to war. But it is nothing like the collective experience of members of Congress on the whole. Some members of Congress have served themselves, some have relatives in the military, and some represent parts of America where war is viewed with deep skepticism. In short, Congress is structurally more representative than any single person can be. Together, members of Congress bring a collective understanding of the dangers of war that the Founders thought would result in more cautious and better decision making.

The War Powers Act was a well-intentioned but flawed attempt to reset the balance between these two branches. Despite its Madisonian intentions to constrain the president, the War Powers Act has backfired, enabling presidents to act unilaterally, especially within the sixty days that it allows for military action without congressional approval. By the time presidents seek congressional approval, patriotic fervor is often at a high and people have already rallied behind their president and the war—pressuring Congress to support the war and further enabling executive action in a way that presidents can claim is consistent with the Act.

In my view, it is long past time for Congress to pass a new war powers bill—one that would restore the original balance between Congress's power and the president's. The legislation should state unequivocally that a president can only initiate a long-term armed conflict if Congress approves it first. It should allow a president to launch an isolated, small-scale attack unilaterally, but only when there is an imminent threat to the security of the United States. It also should allow for military commanders, when directed by the president, to engage in certain self-defensive actions in order to protect the country. This response to immediate danger in a limited amount of time is distinct from a long-term engagement in war. War should require congressional authorization and the deliberation that comes along with it.

This new law could help clarify the distinction between wars and short-term conflicts. The legislation should clarify that the president does not need to gain prior congressional approval for short-term actions, especially when they are intended to be defensive. A short-term battle that lasts only a day, the stationing of a limited number of soldiers in a country, or a single air strike should not be regarded as constitutional war of the type requiring congressional authorization. Sustained conflict, on the other hand, definitely constitutes war. Though there will be some difficulty in drawing a clear line that shows when a short-term conflict becomes a war, this is where courts can step in. It is essential for the judicial branch to opine on the president's ability to initiate long-term military action. The legislation should make clear that courts have the jurisdiction and the obligation to intervene when a president usurps Congress's power to declare war.

Nowhere is the need for such a law clearer than in the case of the use of nuclear weapons. Vice President Dick Cheney put it in the starkest terms during a 2008 interview on Fox News: "The President of the United States now for fifty years is followed at all times, twenty-four hours a day, by a military aide carrying a football that contains the nuclear codes that he would use, and be authorized to use, in the event of a nuclear attack on the United States. He could launch the kind of devastating attack the world has never seen. He doesn't have to check with anybody. He doesn't have to call Congress, he doesn't have to check with the courts."[32] Bill Perry, the secretary of defense under Bill Clinton from 1994 to 1997, confirmed how much power the president has in the nuclear arena: "The order can go directly from the president to Strategic Air Command. . . . So, in a five- or six- or seven-minute kind of decision, the secretary of defense probably never hears about it until it's too late."[33]

We know that under the War Powers Act, presidents have thought they had the sole power to launch an attack. But given how rapidly nuclear conflict can escalate, sixty days might no longer be a meaningful waiting period—in fact, we might not even have a Capitol building in which to deliberate. A nuclear launch is a de facto act of war. The danger of nuclear war lies in its speed. That's even more reason to slow down the launch process by requiring an emergency session of Congress.

On the other hand, some might say the rapidity of nuclear war and its potential to destroy the entire Earth mean that deliberation puts us at risk of catastrophic inaction. In this view, the country's immediate safety, rather than the Constitution, is the primary concern. Keeping control over nuclear weapons in the president's hands, the argument goes, is a strategic risk that can alleviate the overall risk of nuclear war. Nixon, for instance, spoke of the "madman" theory of threatening to use nukes, even if he had no intention to. He once said that "I want the North Vietnamese to believe that I've reached the point that I might do anything to stop the war."[34]

But here is the problem: nuclear war is too consequential for brash threats of attack, even if they are intended to be deterrents. The risk is too great that they might actually start the very conflict they are intended to avoid. Professor Matthew Fuhrmann argues the evidence doesn't suggest that the aggressive threat of a nuclear attack works as a deterrent to adversaries.[35] And in my view, the madman theory is too dangerous to justify overriding the Constitution to give the president such a vast power. It goes against exactly what Madison stood for.

Of course, constraining the president's power comes with risks. But that has always been the case, and some risks are unavoidable. Justice Joseph Story addressed those concerns by suggesting that the risk of waiting for congressional authorization is dwarfed by the risk of rushing to war. Story was writing in the nineteenth century, but modern scholars back up his point. Scott Sagan, a nuclear expert and Stanford University professor, details how the origins of the nuclear football itself were all about a fear of unilateral military control. Originally, a military commander had the sole ability to launch nuclear weapons. That changed during the Kennedy administration, when presidential control became the rule.[36] But the president is just one person, subject to whims and moments of possible bad judgment. We cannot rely solely on the president to make a good decision. One topic to debate when drafting a new war powers law is whether Congress should have control over nuclear weapons.

Some might object that the threat of nuclear attack is an effective deterrent only if a president can issue a fast-acting response. But with our modern technology, Congress could be convened quickly—perhaps even virtually—and could still authorize a retaliatory strike in a matter of hours. In the early 1800s, when President Jefferson faced an urgent situation of pirate attacks on American ships in Tripoli, he sought congressional approval for a defensive response.[37] If Jefferson could do that two centuries ago, we could certainly accomplish it today—and much more quickly.

In fact, technology is forcing a separate discussion about war powers, regardless of whether or when Congress decides to act. The military has made great strides in developing new weapons that may heighten the need for congressional oversight of war. Elon Musk, the CEO of Tesla, and Mustafa Suleyman of Google, recently organized a petition of 116 experts calling for a ban on the use of killer robots. They warned: "Once developed, they will permit armed conflict to be fought at a scale greater than ever, and at timescales faster than humans can comprehend." Congress will be more important than ever in the era of this new technology.[38]

Nowhere is this concern more relevant than when it comes to the president's ability to use precision drone strikes against targeted enemies. Because of the broad language of the 2001 AUMF discussed in Chapter 3, President Obama initiated drone strikes against targets in Pakistan and Somalia, despite the fact that there was never explicit congressional authorization to expand the fight against terrorism to those targets. In fact, many of the organizations targeted by his drone strikes were not a part of Al Qaeda and did not even exist at the time of the AUMF's passage.[39] This is a dangerous infringement on Congress's power to declare war and an overly broad interpretation of the authorization of force against Al Qaeda. The perpetual war on terrorism and its amorphous boundaries risk undermining the requirement that only Congress can declare war.

Citizens, too, have a role in limiting the president's war powers. Though not directly involved in the decision-making process, they can elect representatives who will demand such a law and restore the original understanding of the war powers. Checks and balances work best when Congress stands up strong. Congress is more likely to do that if constituents make their support clear. Constitutional enforcement ultimately rests on the people's willingness to demand actions by their representatives, because the Constitution is not self-enforcing. Though the details of foreign affairs might not be on the forefront of the average citizen's mind, war is something that affects all of our lives. The people's voices must ring through in all decisions relating to it.

—————

BACK IN the White House situation room, you and your advisors are working to decide what to do about Syria's invasion of Lebanon. All of your top military advisors are huddled around the room, anxiously awaiting your decision. "Just get the Office of Legal Counsel to sign off on it," chimes in one general. What should you do? In an interview with C-SPAN founder Brian Lamb, Chuck Robb—Lyndon Johnson's son-in-law who later became a senator—explained that even though his father-in-law was the president of the United States, Robb's role as a soldier was to obey the president's orders. As he put it, "mine is not to reason why, mine is but to do or die."[40] Unfortunately, when it comes to war powers, many senators now see their relationship to the president in a similarly subordinate role, as links in the chain of command and not as members of a coequal branch of government. But members of Congress bear responsibility here too, and they need to reclaim the status of equals, deliberating about whether to go to war instead of deferring to the president.

As president, the fact that you might get away with ignoring Congress's power to declare war is not a justification for doing so. The oath of office binds you to respect the limits on your power, even when the courts, Congress, and other institutions do not demand it. You have the power to restore the balance between executive power and Congress's power to declare war; it is your responsibility to use it. Bring deliberation—reasoned debate—back into the terrifying decision to go to war or to use nuclear weapons. You will have fewer travesties of war to regret. And you will show due respect for the powers of war that your oath bestowed upon you.

Your general is right that you could take military action in Syria, and you could probably get the OLC to sign off on it. But the opinion of the Office of Legal Counsel is, in my view, an insufficient reason to make a decision as consequential as going to war. In the twenty-first century, it is time for a president to demand that Congress fulfill its role in declaring war and return to the founding ideal of deciding our conflicts by deliberation. In conflicts such as Vietnam, senators such as William Fulbright later said they regretted not debating more thoroughly the decision to go to war.[41] Those decisions might have turned out differently had there been more time to deliberate. Going forward, senators should warn a future president against usurping Congress's proper role in reviewing whether or not to go to war. The Constitution requires this vetting.

Section II

"WE THE PEOPLE" AND THE BILL OF RIGHTS

7

Madison and the Creation of the Bill of Rights

PRINCIPLE: The Bill of Rights and the Fourteenth Amendment apply to the president. Internalize their principles and the constraints they put on your office.

"A Bill of Rights is what the people are entitled to against every government on earth, general or particular, and what no just government should refuse, or rest on inference."
—THOMAS JEFFERSON[1]

The Bill of Rights—the first ten amendments to the Constitution—constrains a president and articulates the values he or she should promote. We'll soon get to the details about what these rights require of you as president. But first, let's look to where these rights came from, and how they came to be incorporated into our Constitution. Yet again, we will follow our guide, James Madison, who was the chief drafter of the Bill of Rights. However, before he came to that role, Madison was actually the Bill of Rights' chief opponent.

In 1788, James Madison entered the race for Congress in Virginia's fifth congressional district. One issue dominated the campaign: whether the country needed a Bill of Rights.[2] The issue was thorny. Without a Bill of Rights, George Mason, a fellow Virginian, had refused to sign the Constitution.[3] Madison disagreed, arguing that a Bill of Rights was unnecessary, and perhaps even harmful.

Why? Madison might have felt like a master chef watching a patron pour ketchup all over his perfectly cooked steak. He considered his work crafting the Constitution so thorough that there was nothing to amend: Article I limited the powers of Congress, and Article II constrained the president. A Bill of Rights was redundant at best—and dangerous at worst. Madison worried that a specific list of rights might embolden the federal government to violate any rights that happened to be left off it. Virginians, however, not content to trust that Article I and Article II would protect their rights, demanded such a bill. Despite his original opposition to listed rights, Madison came to appreciate their importance—and he wanted to win his race. Campaigning on a commitment to introduce a Bill of Rights, Madison defeated James Monroe by 336 votes.[4,5]

Thomas Jefferson had a role to play in Madison's conversion, helping to convince Madison that it was not enough to leave the interpretation of his masterwork to popular perception. In a letter to Madison dated December 20, 1787, Jefferson urged, "a Bill of Rights is what the people are entitled to against every government on earth, general or particular, and what no just government should refuse, or rest on inference."[6] Madison came to agree. Against the threat of tyranny, he reasoned, the Bill of Rights couldn't hurt and could only help: "It is prudent to guard [against] it," Madison wrote of tyranny, "especially when the precaution can do no injury."[7]

Madison's original concern was rectified by the Ninth Amendment—perhaps the least well-known member of the ten. The Ninth Amendment made it clear that a government could not use a narrow interpretation of the Bill of Rights to infringe on the Constitution's protected liberties by clarifying that some things were protected by the document, even if not explicitly mentioned. It states: "The enumeration in the Constitution, of certain rights, shall not be construed to deny or disparage others retained by the people."[8] (Take note, originalists: the amendment spells out rather explicitly the idea that not all rights are explicit.)

Madison, though, had another fear. The Bill of Rights applied only to the federal government, not the states. In theory, then, if there were no protections in the state's constitution, a state could establish an official state religion or prosecute unpopular newspaper editors. Madison feared a federal Bill of Rights would take the focus away from the need for such protections at the state level. As a solution, Madison proposed specific language that would have applied the rights of religious freedom, press freedom, and trial by jury to the states.[9] But Madison's version of those amendments failed to win approval. Only around the start of the twentieth century would the Fourteenth Amendment, ratified decades earlier in 1868, be understood to expand the major provisions of the Bill of Rights to state governments.[10]

In a letter he wrote to Jefferson in 1788, Madison found another purpose for the Bill of Rights: creating a virtuous civic culture for the new nation. If the rights were presented as lofty aspirations, they could check untempered populism before it began. Madison wanted the rights to "acquire by degrees the character of fundamental maxims of free Government, and as they become incorporated with the national sentiment, counteract the impulses of interest and passion."[11] For a president, that means internalizing the values of the Bill of Rights and promoting its ideals.

Just as he promised, Madison introduced the Bill of Rights in Congress on June 8, 1789.[12] Together, Congress proposed the Bill of Rights on September 25, 1789, and the state legislatures ratified the ten amendments in less than twenty-seven months—a political feat never to be repeated. There was only one hiccup: Rhode Island still refused to ratify the Constitution, much less the new amendments to it. The Constitution was long ratified already, after New Hampshire became the ninth state to approve it in 1788. But Rhode Islanders were outraged that neither the Constitution nor the Bill of Rights outlawed slavery, and they thought the federal government would have too much power.[13] In protest, a group from the town of Scituate approached the state capital with guns and threatened consequences if the Constitution was ratified.[14] Only under severe threats of economic and military sanctions did Rhode Island later agree to sign in May of 1790,[15] making it the thirteenth state to do so.[16]

It wasn't long before the Bill of Rights faced its first challenge from a power-hungry president. In 1797, John Adams succeeded George Washington to become the country's second president. In contrast to Washington, who was seen as modest, President Adams was seen as haughty—often helping himself to the trappings of aristocracy that the Constitution was intended to reject.[17] He also signed a series of laws that were clear overreaches of federal power.

Madison began to wonder if President Adams was the demagogue that he had feared. But Adams was also Madison's former ally; each had helped draft a founding document—Adams the Declaration and Madison the Constitution. In 1798, Madison penned a secret letter to Jefferson, writing that Adams had strayed far from constitutional ideals as president.[18] Madison believed that among his many overreaches, Adams had not internalized the idea that the American Revolution was fought to get rid of royalty. In fact, dating back to his vice presidency, Adams believed the president should be referred to as "His highness, the President of the United States, and Protector of their Liberties."[19] (Madison, by contrast, argued successfully for calling him "Mr. President.")

But by far Adams's worst abuse—and Madison's primary cause for alarm—was the Sedition Act of 1798.[20] As we'll see in the next chapter, the Act was an attack on the press and political opponents—a classic abuse of federal power—that made it a crime to criticize or to mock the president of the United States (but left it legal to criticize the vice president, who at the time was Thomas Jefferson, a member of the opposition party). Madison could have been arrested for his political speech, as even a member of Congress could be thrown in prison. In fact, one was: Vermont congressman Matthew Lyon was imprisoned, along with other supporters of Jefferson, newspaper editors, and other prominent Democratic-Republicans. In all, approximately twenty-five people were arrested under the Act, and ten were convicted.[21]

Jefferson won the next presidential election. He promptly allowed the Sedition Act to expire and pardoned all ten convicted under it. The ordeal, however, vindicated Madison's and Jefferson's belief that the Bill of Rights should restrict the president.

———

THE BILL of Rights—and later amendments like the Fourteenth, which strengthened those original rights protections— have been underutilized for much of their history. During the nineteenth century, the Supreme Court found a ban on Chinese immigration to be constitutional, despite its basis in anti-Chinese prejudice.[22] That is partly because the Equal Protection Clause did not yet apply to the federal government, a development that would come in the 1954 case *Bolling v. Sharpe*.[23] Later, in the twentieth century, the court failed to reject the internment of Japanese Americans.[24] And it took until the twentieth century for the Bill of Rights to be invoked to stop the criminalization of political dissent.[25] Indeed, the Bill of Rights as a whole only became regularly enforced by judges in the twentieth century. Unfortunately, failures to uphold the text and values of the Bill of Rights have continued in the twenty-first century. In this section, I will try to convince you that the Bill of Rights should become a more fundamental part of pushing back against present injustices— and all future ones to come.

Why has it taken so long for the Bill of Rights to be used more strongly? It turns out that not everyone agrees with Madison: although they acknowledge the Bill of Rights enumerates the rights of *the people*, it doesn't necessarily constrain *the president*. During the George W. Bush administration, White House legal advisor John Yoo argued that the president's constitutionally granted emergency war power is "plenary,"[26] or absolute, permitting actions such as "enhanced interrogation"—a euphemism for acts of torture.[27] Yoo and other legal scholars suggest that in a time of war, the president is immune from some of the limits required by the Bill of Rights. Although Yoo is right to suggest that war necessarily does force exceptions to normal rules, a president who is completely exempt from the Bill of Rights not only defies Madison's vision but also undermines the very idea of the presidency as it is set out in the Constitution.

It's true that some of the Bill of Rights seems especially aimed at Congress, not the president—after all, the first word of the First Amendment is "Congress," and the word "president" never appears. As Stanford historian Jack Rakove argues, that is simply because the Framers assumed Congress was the branch of government most likely to violate the Bill of Rights.[28] They would not have conceived of the executive as wielding a vast bureaucracy and passing sweeping orders that resemble laws, so they thought Congress posed the greatest threat to liberty. But the Framers were still worried about a despotic president. As we've seen already, they took careful pains to avoid monarchy.

Rakove also suggests the strictness of the language is the most important aspect. The provisions of the Bill of Rights do not say Congress "ought not" do this or that. Instead, we see the more legally binding language of "shall not"—for example, "Excessive bail shall not be required" and "Congress shall make no law respecting an establishment of religion." A president who thinks that simply not being mentioned exempts him or her from the requirements of the Bill of Rights is ignoring a fundamental goal of the Constitution: to constrain all government officials, not just some. Considering how much Madison expected the Constitution to be enforced by norms, it makes sense that the Framers would have intended the Bill of Rights to apply to every citizen—including the president.[29]

Luckily, there will be people watching to make sure these ideals are upheld. If you fail to respect the limits of the Bill of Rights, then the courts, Congress, and the people can check your power. That's part of what it means to honor Washington's message in his Second Inaugural: that if he defied the limits of the Constitution, those assembled should stop him. Our modern Constitution includes the robust protections of the Bill of Rights, and your obligation is to defend the Constitution in its entirety.

The Bill of Rights should remind you that your job is bigger than just following the formal requirements of the Constitution. You should seek to promote its ideals and values, even when the other branches will not stop you. That means advancing the Bill of Rights from your bully pulpit and respecting legislation meant to strengthen it. All amendments to the Constitution, especially those in the Bill of Rights, are important for you to understand. In this section, we will focus primarily on three of the most important amendments: the First, the Eighth, and the Fourteenth. Your responsibility as president is to uphold the values of the entire Constitution, and these three amendments illustrate why that is so necessary.

8

The First Amendment and Free Speech

PRINCIPLE: The president is required to defend citizens' right of free speech. Encourage citizens to speak out, and allow criticism of public officials—including you.

"Mr. Khrushchev, operating a totalitarian system . . . has many advantages, [but also the] terrific disadvantage [of] not having the abrasive quality of the press applied to you daily."
—JOHN F. KENNEDY[1]

Midway through your first term, a series of videos is released on YouTube. In them, a narrator praises a neo-Nazi leader who advocates violent revolution to create a white republic. The videos depict you, the president, in a dunce cap cowering in the Oval Office. Your denunciations of white supremacy from the bully pulpit have made you the declared enemy of neo-Nazis throughout the country. One of the videos has been viewed ten million times. Its narrator says, "One day we all can be part of the great revolution that will make the white race supreme. Then we will all finally know the truth about our dunce of a president. In time, we will see this president executed for his crimes against the white race."

The secretary of homeland security tells you that in the name of security, free speech must have limits. The lawyers in the Office of Legal Counsel have other ideas. They tell you that the First Amendment's right to free speech must protect even the right to advocate violence. Of course, if you try to pass a law stopping such speech or order the prosecution of those who criticize you, Americans will lampoon you as an iron-fisted tyrant. But if you defend the right of this critic to speak, you might be accused of being weak on matters of national security.

———

IN THE United States, there is a long history of presidents trying to make it a crime to criticize them. As we mentioned in Chapters 2 and 7, President John Adams used the Sedition Act to silence his critics. The story behind the law is worth recounting. During the American Revolution, no ally was more instrumental to victory than the French. But by the late 1790s, the United States had signed a treaty with France's enemy, Great Britain. France was routinely attacking US merchant ships, and President Adams was making preparations for war against his country's former ally. A passionate moment of anti-French fervor had taken root in the United States. Just a few years before, the Capitol experienced one of its first major political scandals, the XYZ affair, in which French diplomats solicited bribes from American officials. Later, rumors abounded that government officials were spying for the French.

The Federalist Party controlled all three branches of government. They used the paranoia about French infiltration to pass the Alien and Sedition Acts, signed by President Adams in July 1798.[2] The laws made it a crime to criticize President Adams (although it remained legal to criticize Vice President Jefferson, who was a member of a different political party). They also revoked the rights of foreign nationals to due process. Federalists claimed this legislation was targeted at French spies. The real targets, however, were the Democratic-Republicans led by Madison and Vice President Jefferson—both of whom were criticizing the president's handling of French foreign affairs.

As we saw in the last chapter, the first person prosecuted under the Acts was not a French spy, but US congressman Matthew Lyon. Lyon was an Irish immigrant who settled in Vermont and was elected to Congress in 1797 as a Democratic-Republican. A hardscrabble Vermonter, Lyon couldn't have been more different from the scholarly Adams. Once, just ten months after taking office, Lyon spit on Roger Griswold, a congressman who had mocked him. Just weeks later, the two got into a brawl. (Lyon, ever creative, defended himself with fire tongs.) Lyon certainly did not mince words with President Adams, whom he regarded as a pompous aristocrat. Adams, as Lyon said in his public speeches and writings, was too self-absorbed to care about the public good. In his words, "Consideration of public welfare [was] swallowed up in a continual grasp for power, in an unbounded thirst for ridiculous pomp."[3]

Lyon soon found himself arrested for this statement. At his trial, Lyon pleaded not guilty and argued that the Sedition Acts were unconstitutional because they violated the newly adopted First Amendment's requirement that Congress not pass laws "abridging the freedom of speech." He also had the Speech and Debate Clause of Article I on his side; that part of the Constitution protects members of Congress from censorship. Today, Lyon's free speech claim sounds like common sense: It is the stuff of banana republics to tell members of Congress what legislation they can or cannot endorse and propose, or what they can say about a president. But at the time, Lyon's claim that his free speech had been violated fell on deaf ears. He was found guilty, fined one thousand dollars, and sentenced to a prison term of four months.[4]

The courts were filled with judges sympathetic to President Adams and the Federalist agenda. They never overturned the Alien and Sedition Acts, or even a single conviction under those Acts, based on the First Amendment. It was almost as if the newly passed Bill of Rights made no mention of free speech at all. Even Madison, the author of the Free Speech Clause, was a possible target of criminal prosecution, given his opposition to Adams.

Lyon was sent to jail, but his supporters largely paid off his $1,000 fine. While in prison, Lyon busied himself with the one task guaranteed to annoy Adams: he ran for reelection from his prison cell. He won overwhelmingly, with 3,576 votes, compared to 2,444 for his nearest competitor.[5] Nothing in the Constitution prohibits a current convict from running for the House of Representatives, and Vermonters sent a clear message to Adams and the Federalists that they stood with Lyon and the principled defense of free speech he represented.

The specter of foreign enemies, like the French panic of the 1790s, often presents a convenient excuse for limiting the political speech of opponents. The twentieth century saw the criminalization of a new kind of speech, this time under the auspices of a threat from Russia. At the turn of the twentieth century, the Indiana-born Eugene Debs was one of the most well-known American activists of his day. He was instrumental in the infamous Pullman Strike of 1894 and went on to found the Social Democratic Party, later known as the Socialist Party of America. In fact, Debs ran as the Socialist Party candidate for president five times between 1900 and 1920, campaigning on an anticapitalist, pro-worker platform that demanded policies such as collective ownership of industry and unemployment relief. Though Debs never had much of a chance to win, his candidacy was about making a statement, and he did. In 1912, Debs won 6 percent of the national popular vote.[6]

Debs's time on the national stage came in an era of tremendous upheaval. The United States, after much deliberation, entered World War I in April of 1917 and instituted a military draft. Many on the left, including anarchists and Marxists, opposed war, believing it inimical to the working class. This was a war fought among capitalists, but by worker soldiers.[7] Using heated rhetoric, they urged resistance to the draft.

In response that June, President Woodrow Wilson signed the Espionage Act, a law that outlawed political speech meant to undermine the war effort.[8] Though its stated purpose was to stop spying, the law itself was crafted amid a public frenzy of paranoia about global communism known as the first "Red Scare"—a frenzy similar to the one surrounding the 1798 Sedition Act. The Espionage Act was eventually repurposed, much like the Alien and Sedition Acts, to silence criticism of World War I. Federal prosecutors argued that criticizing the war effort amounted to aiding the enemy. In fact, an amendment to the law passed in 1918 was even called the "Sedition Act." Signed in 1918, the new Sedition Act punished "disloyal, profane, scurrilous, or abusive language about the form of government in the United States."[9]

Debs, the most prominent socialist voice in America, was a perfect target for such a law. Criticism of America's involvement in World War I was an essential part of Debs's political platform. In June 1918, at a rally in Canton, Ohio, Debs gave a speech criticizing the war from a Socialist perspective. For this, Debs was charged and tried under the Espionage Act. The jury delivered a conviction of ten years in federal prison. Before being taken away, Debs delivered a statement to the court, calling the Espionage Act a "despotic enactment in flagrant conflict with democratic principles and with the spirit of free institutions."[10] Though Debs lost his right to vote upon his arrest, he, like Lyon, ran for office from his prison cell. He won more than 914,000 votes in the 1920 presidential election.[11]

Unlike Lyon, though, Debs was no friend of the Constitution. Revolution, not democracy, was his primary project. About this he was clear: "The socialistic movement means socialistic revolution, and under it, the Constitution would be absolutely abolished, not reaffirmed," he said at one campaign speech in Berkeley, California.[12] In criticizing the president, Debs was similar to Lyon. But Debs was a different *kind* of political opponent: if his advocacy were ever successful, the result would decimate the Constitution and our system of government. The Supreme Court upheld Debs's conviction in *Debs v. United States*.[13] The court used the "clear and present danger" rule, conceived in the court's recent decision in *Schenck v. United States*.[14] That decision upheld the earlier Espionage Act and allowed the government to ban speech that posed a "clear and present danger" to the security of the United States. This meant that political speech could be limited by the court if it was deemed injurious to the government. Often, this test was used to criminalize leftist speech, even if its aim was improving the conditions of the society's poor and working class.

Most modern constitutional thinkers believe this ruling was wrong. In their view—and I count myself among them—Debs should never have been punished for his speech. The First

Amendment protects all viewpoints, even radical ones. Had Debs been elected and tried to carry out his anti-constitutional agenda, things would have been different. Holders of public office cannot act directly against the Constitution. If someone does, it is the court's role to step in. But in a modern approach to free speech, all viewpoints are protected, whether they come from a Jeffersonian Democratic-Republican like Lyon or a Socialist like Debs. To see why, we need to look at how that view emerged in the first place.

———

AROUND THE time that Debs was being hauled off to prison, a Brown University dean named Alexander Meiklejohn was sitting in his office, located in the same building I see regularly from my own window on campus. As a well-established Ivy League professor, Meiklejohn was anything but a radical, and no friend of Debs.

Nevertheless, Meiklejohn was disturbed by what happened to Debs. He went on to write prolifically in defense of free speech and expression. To explain his rationale, Meiklejohn invented a famous thought experiment. To think about what speech should be protected in our democracy, he asked his readers to imagine that they were sitting together in a town meeting.[15] In our version of this thought experiment, let's imagine that we are townspeople debating whether a bridge should be built on the north or south side of town. Suppose that the pro-north citizens have virtually no good argument: the north side is totally uninhabited, for instance. So, the town hall moderator makes a rule: in order to save everyone time, no one will hear any arguments from the pro-north side.

What would happen if we were then told to take a vote? Who would the aggrieved, victimized party be? Sure, the pro-north contingent was gagged and banned from voicing their opinion, so they face tangible harms. But the real victim, in Meiklejohn's view, would be everyone else at the meeting: when we were asked to vote at the end of the meeting, we were all denied the moral and factual information needed to make a truly free decision. Discussion and deliberation allow individuals to understand their options before making informed choices. In the case of the town meeting, the pro-north contingent was denied their right to speak. More importantly, though, everyone was denied their right to *hear*.[16]

Meiklejohn's argument was radical at the time. "Freedom of speech" was (and is) thought of as protecting minority opinions—unpopular fringe leaders, for example, like Debs. But Meiklejohn's argument showed that the greatest harm from banning speech is not to minority opinion, but to *majority* opinion—by restricting the arguments everyone gets to hear. In so doing, Meiklejohn transformed free speech from a right of personal expression into an article of democratic rule. When all viewpoints are allowed to be heard, majority votes become a better expression of informed self-rule. When it came to the opposition to war, Meiklejohn argued that speech such as that of the radical Left needed to be heard and refuted. They should not be silenced by criminal law, but challenged with reason and deliberation. Otherwise, the idea of government "by" the people would be a myth.[17]

The Espionage Act under which Debs was prosecuted was soon challenged in the Supreme Court in a case called *Abrams v. United States*. The plaintiff, Jacob Abrams, was a poor immigrant who lived in the tenements of New York City, which were then crowded with newly arrived immigrants.[18] In 1918, Abrams rented a printing shop where he and three allies printed a pamphlet criticizing President Wilson's foreign policy in a style reminiscent of Debs's criticism. The pamphlet read: "he [the president] is too much of a coward to come out openly and say: 'We capitalistic nations cannot afford to have a proletarian republic in Russia.'" It ended with a threat: "If they will use arms against the Russian people to enforce their standard of order, so will we use arms, and they shall never see the ruin of the Russian revolution."[19]

Abrams was arrested under the Sedition Act of 1918 (the amendment to the Espionage Act) and eventually convicted. He appealed his case all the way to the Supreme Court. There, in 1919, the court ruled against Abrams, using the "clear and present danger" rule conceived in *Schenck*.[20] In the court's view, Abrams's words were enough to prove that he presented this danger to national security, making his speech not protected. According to the court, "these excerpts sufficiently show that . . . the plain purpose of their propaganda was to excite, at the supreme crisis of the war, disaffection, sedition, riots, and, as they hoped, revolution."[21]

Justice Oliver Wendell Holmes wrote a famous dissent in this case, joined by fellow justice Louis Brandeis. Though Holmes had himself devised the "clear and present danger" standard in the earlier Espionage Act case, in *Abrams* Holmes modified his view. He wrote that there was a difference between holding unpatriotic or even revolutionary views, and posing an immediate danger of violent action. In his words, "it is only the present danger of immediate evil" that justifies limiting speech.[22] Holmes believed that the people's right to deliberation itself ensured that democratic constitutionalism would win out over antidemocratic viewpoints. He wrote, "The best test of truth is the power of the thought to get itself accepted in the competition of the market."[23]

Meiklejohn and Holmes lost, stuck in the minority for fifty

years. Then, in 1969, the Supreme Court heard a case called *Brandenburg v. Ohio*. The case concerned a rally that the Ku Klux Klan had planned to hold in Hamilton County, Ohio. The rally, however, was prohibited under an Ohio law that banned inflammatory speech. The court struck down the law and announced a new rule: all opinions or viewpoints would be protected under the First Amendment, unless that speech were both intended to cause "imminent lawless action" and "likely to incite or produce such action"[24]—a higher and more immediate standard than "clear and present danger."[25] Even if the political speech advocated a heinous or murderous ideology, it would be protected. Holmes and Meiklejohn's positions were vindicated: the court would not allow prosecutions of ideas alone, even dangerous ones.

Today, we can debate whether the radical Right or radical Left should be protected in public spaces such as university campuses. As the history of the court demonstrates, today's persecuted right-wing radicals might be tomorrow's persecuted leftists. Their metaphors were different, but Meiklejohn and Holmes's arguments were much the same. We should have faith in the American town meeting, and in the idea that deliberation is an achievable ideal of free speech. It is because reasoned discussion (more often than not) leads people to see the right answers that a democratic people can be allowed to criticize the democratic system itself. A sedition law, whether Adams's attack on the Democratic-Republicans or the Espionage Act's attack on anarchists, had and has no place in a self-governing society.

———•———

As PRESIDENT, you face constraints on your actions by the First Amendment and the Supreme Court. Faced with radical militants on YouTube praising a neo-Nazi leader advocating revolution, you might sympathize with Wilson's approach in the Espionage Act—crack down and lock them up. Though you don't want to abet hate speech, this kind of crackdown runs counter to the First Amendment. In other words, no matter how wrong the opinions presented to you are, you shouldn't act like the town-meeting moderator who simply shuts down opposition viewpoints.

So what can you do to reject hate speech while still protecting it? For one thing, you can use the bully pulpit to fight such views in the marketplace of ideas. Remember, your aim is not to change the minds of extremists who make incendiary videos. It is to ensure that they do not win adherents among the wider population. As president, use your bully pulpit to explain that hateful viewpoints, though constitutionally protected, should be rejected outright by the people.

Similarly, you should not crack down on hate groups by seeking to criminalize what they say. Instead, you should urge Congress to fund organizations and programs that oppose hate: the Countering Violent Extremism program in the Department of Homeland Security is one that could be enhanced to undo the influence of hate groups in the United States. Grants to programs such as Life After Hate, which works to deradicalize neo-Nazis and Klan members, have been cut or eliminated, but they are essential to keeping these groups from winning the battle of ideas.[26] You should work with Congress to fund them. We cannot return to the time when "dangerous ideas" were confused with immediate violence. Our democracy has other resources to prevent those views from winning out, without resorting to imprisoning political "opponents" like Lyon and Debs.

Constitutional law and norms have come a long way from a

time when John Adams's administration could throw his political opponents in jail. But in the modern world, security threats might seem so great that as president you want to turn back the clock and allow the prosecution of radicals. That would be a shame, and would relinquish the main advantage of the democratic system, all in the name of protecting it. John F. Kennedy explained it well when he said that even though he reacted to media criticism by "wish[ing] they didn't write it," the free speech given to the press made it an "invaluable arm of the presidency" because it showed the public what was really going on.[27]

Such criticism is what made the press beneficial to the presidency in a democracy: "Operating a totalitarian system . . . has many advantages," Kennedy joked, but also the "terrific disadvantage [of] not having the abrasive quality of the press applied to you."[28] Here Kennedy channeled Meiklejohn's support of the right to listen: even (or especially) the president needs to be able to hear criticism to do the job correctly. So do all of us, if we are to serve as the people's check on the power of the nation's highest office.

As president, you should not—and constitutionally cannot—try to prohibit or criminalize criticism of your presidency. Instead, you should take to the bully pulpit to promote liberal democracy and condemn discrimination and terrorism. More than that, you should work with Congress to seek out ways of funding the ideals and institutions of democracy so that it has the strength to stand up strongly against its opponents.

9

The First Amendment and the Freedom of Religion

PRINCIPLE: The president leads a country of people with diverse religious faiths. Speak and make policy in a way that shows your respect for the religious and secular pluralism of America.

"The example of the Colonies, now States, which rejected religious establishments altogether, proved that all Sects might be safely & advantageously put on a footing of equal & entire freedom."

—JAMES MADISON[1]

In 1953, Methodist minister Abraham Vereide organized a group of political leaders to pray together in Washington, DC. Vereide hoped to gather a fellowship devoted to Christian teaching and leadership, and in a long-shot attempt, he invited President Dwight Eisenhower to attend. Eisenhower declined. But the famous evangelist Billy Graham convinced him that the nation needed to hear from its chief executive why the country should be guided by a sense of faith.[2] Eisenhower's attendance started a tradition: every president since has attended the annual event, known as the National Prayer Breakfast.

Not everyone is so enamored of the prayer breakfast. Rob Boston, the communications director of Americans United for Separation of Church and State, criticizes the tradition. In his words, the meeting "tramples on the church-state separationist spirit that infuses the Constitution."[3]

So, does the Constitution keep you from attending the prayer breakfast? The Bill of Rights has something to say about it in its very first sentence: "Congress shall make no law respecting an establishment of religion, or prohibiting the free exercise thereof."[4] That's two requirements: the "Establishment Clause" says you can't have the government pick favorites among religions, and the "Free Exercise Clause" says you must protect everyone's right to worship however they wish. These legal restrictions, though, also evoke principles and guidelines of religious neutrality that speak to your duties as president, even if no law is violated. As a citizen, you have the right to pray as you wish. As president, you speak on behalf of the nation and should be leery of placing one religion over others as a public matter.

You can see the tension here: These two clauses affirm the value of religion in public life but also limit the role it can play. A president needs to speak for all the American people—and their many different religions. Your challenge is balancing this fundamental tension. Can you pray in a way that does not send a message of exclusion to those who do not share your religious beliefs or are not religious? Can you pray publicly at all without violating the Establishment Clause?

As you consider your answer, be mindful that when you

took the oath, you made a commitment to integrate the requirements and ethos of the Constitution into your own belief system. You must consider how all your actions can protect religion without violating the Establishment Clause. In office, you might find yourself tempted to simply ignore the Establishment Clause and proclaim America a Christian nation. You may even hold a sincere belief that America should endorse your version of Christianity, and you may want to use the bully pulpit of your office to promote it. However, you are the president now, not just a private citizen, and you must respect and incorporate the ideals of the Bill of Rights into your speech and policies.

———•———

JAMES MADISON saw the opposition to an official government religion as central to his political identity. Before the American Revolution, he vowed to oppose any law that put a particular religion above others. In 1784 and 1785, the Virginia legislature considered a bill that would use taxpayer money to fund Christian churches. Madison objected. Virginia had already banned interference in the free exercise of religion, and Madison argued that this bill, while not a direct violation of this requirement, violated its spirit. This led to one of Madison's most famous writings: the "Memorial and Remonstrance." In it, he argued that the bill funding ministers "degrades from the equal rank of Citizens all those whose opinions in Religion do not bend to those of the Legislative authority."[5] Because this bill propped up religion by funding Christian teaching, it excluded non-Christians.

Worse, thought Madison, funding ministers would entangle religious reasoning with the business of government. Although religious believers certainly deserve a place in public life, it would be inappropriate to just cite the Bible or another theological doctrine in defense of public policy when the country (and the government) is composed of many faiths. True, the bill Madison opposed bore scarce resemblance to the policy of religious intolerance practiced during the Inquisition in Europe—a policy that called for the systematic murder of nonbelievers. But as Madison put it, "distant as [the bill] may be in its present form from the Inquisition, it differs from it only in degree. The one is the first step, the other the last in the career of intolerance." [6]

Madison might seem hyperbolic, but he was capturing the Framers' views of the religious wars that had dominated European politics for centuries. Those wars were based on a theocratic desire to impose religion on believers and nonbelievers alike. By contrast, the Establishment Clause rejected even a hint of theocracy by expressly requiring that government policy not be based on particular religious beliefs.

These tradeoffs weren't always easy, even for someone as knowledgeable as Madison. In 1789, the House hired its own chaplain, a decision to which Madison did not object at the time. Later in his life, however, in 1817, Madison would question whether that hiring violated the same principles he expressed in the "Memorial and Remonstrance." He wrote, "The establishment of the chaplainship to Cong[ress] is a palpable violation of equal rights, as well as of Constitutional principles: the tenets of the chaplains elected [by the majority] shut the door of worship [against] the members whose creeds & consciences forbid a participation in that of the majority." [7] Madison here expressed regret that he did not stop the hiring of a minister. Though the Bill of Rights had not been passed at the time the chaplain was hired, Madison suggests that such a hiring would violate the principle that government not endorse one religion, later expressed in the Establishment Clause.

As president, Madison enforced the ban on establishment through the veto power. Madison saw the president, and not just the courts, as having an obligation to use the veto to protect the First Amendment. In February 1811, Congress passed a bill giving it authority over the activities of the Episcopal Church in the town of Alexandria, then part of the District of Columbia. Madison vetoed the law. According to political scientist Vincent Philip Muñoz, Madison was bothered by the way the bill would have given Congress control over the hiring and firing of ministers in the church and by the requirement that the church provide public welfare services.[8] Using the veto, Madison protected against an establishment of religion.

As much as Madison valued the notion that America had no official religion, he also believed that prayer, in a limited form, could be part of public life. On July 9, 1812, he declared a national "Day of Prayer." Washington and Adams had done the same during their terms, though Jefferson, even more cautious about the separation of church and state, never declared a "Day of Prayer" as president.[9] Did Madison, the champion of the Establishment Clause, simply contradict himself? Or, perhaps, is there a way the president can pray that includes all Americans and honors the restriction on an official government religion?

There is a way. Madison thought prayer itself could be used to opine on the meaning of the Establishment Clause. He stressed in his 1815 proclamation recommending a public day of Thanksgiving for peace that Americans would be afforded the opportunity to voluntarily pray. He also emphasized it was not a day of prayer for one denomination but for all. He used the public prayer to reiterate a commitment to the multiple traditions of the United States, stressing that a commitment to plurality of belief is the American *civic* religion. In Madison's words, "the people of every religious denomination may in their solemn assemblies unite their hearts and their voices in a freewill offering to their Heavenly Benefactor of their homage of thanksgiving and of their songs of praise."[10]

Later presidents would also emphasize the need to base government policy on more than one particular set of religious beliefs. In 1960, Senator John F. Kennedy was running to become the first Catholic president. That same year, a group of 150 Protestant ministers released a statement, writing that it was legitimate to criticize Kennedy for his religion, since his allegiance would be to the pope—not the American people. Throughout the election, anti-Catholic campaign literature proliferated in the Bible Belt.[11] In a public address, Kennedy responded to these attacks but also to the notion that America is a Christian nation. Kennedy was, he said, not a "Catholic candidate for president" but a candidate "who happens also to be a Catholic." Kennedy here tapped into the moral strictures of the Establishment Clause to keep the government secular. But he also alluded to the textual requirement of Article VI: "no religious Test shall ever be required as a Qualification to any Office or public Trust under the United States."[12] Kennedy believed that even an indirect religious test—not voting for a candidate based on his or her religious faith—"subvert[ed] Article VI of the Constitution."[13]

Kennedy made clear what he would do if he ever faced a conflict of interest. He said, "if the time should ever come—and I do not concede any conflict to be even remotely possible—when my office would require me to either violate my conscience or violate the national interest, then I would resign the office; and I hope any conscientious public servant would do the same."[14] Kennedy was defending religious freedom while giving voice to Madison's vision that it requires more than religious reasons to pass public policy. Ultimately, reasoning that can be accepted by people of all faiths must dictate government policy, lest one religion impose its will on the population as a whole.

RELIGION CAN publicly be invoked to reaffirm the Establishment Clause, as Madison and Jefferson demonstrated. Many of our great civic movements, like those for the abolition of slavery and the promotion of civil rights, have invoked the call of a higher power. Lately, however, religion has inserted itself into our politics in a way that might have troubled Madison and some other Framers.

The Establishment Clause and the Free Exercise Clause make the relationship between the president and religion complicated. On one hand, a president must reject theocracy or rule by a particular church. As Justice Sandra Day O'Connor wrote, "The Establishment Clause prohibits government from making adherence to a religion relevant in any way to a person's standing in the political community."[15] On the other hand, it gives the president a role in publicly praising the many religions welcomed in the United States.

When I was still a student, I was once invited to a dinner with a prominent federal judge who had been discussed as a potential Supreme Court nominee. At dinner, the judge began to complain about Christmas pageants being limited in public schools to make children of all faiths not feel excluded. The judge told me the Jewish kids loved participating. It was unfair to them, as well as to Christian students, the judge said, that the pageants were being discontinued. That observation had led the judge to believe that many of the limits on government speech posed by the Establishment Clause were wrong. I smiled and enjoyed my steak.

As the judge made this case, I thought about how I grew up Jewish, and how a Christmas pageant at my school would not have included or represented kids like me. I thought that prayer had a place in America, even in a school, but only if it could be made clear that it was part of an overall message that we are all Americans, regardless of our religion or whether we believe in God at all. In my view, religion has a place in public life, but not at the exclusion of those who do not practice the dominant religion.

There is significant pressure on the president to use the bully pulpit as a religious pulpit, but we should be wary of presidential invocations of religion. Endorsing a particular religion in the capacity as a spokesperson for all Americans can too easily exclude some Americans. Avoiding the establishment of a religion doesn't just mean that the government can't coerce people. It means that the government cannot exclude people in any form on the basis of religion. The message of government should be that America is not defined by identifying with one particular religious denomination.

Public schools could simply celebrate winter holidays with no reference to religion—but that would be a mistake. It's crucial we don't overcorrect against the establishment of religion, such that we avoid celebration of religion in the public sphere entirely. Part of the ideal of the Free Exercise Clause is that we welcome, recognize, and value religion. Instead of pushing religion out of the public sphere, we should embrace it and appreciate a plurality of religious and secular views—whether on the public school stage or in broader public life. This is not hard to do. All it takes is a pageant that includes multiple religions, not just one. Add some Hanukkah and Kwanzaa songs, and at other times of the year, recognize religious traditions like Ramadan. Read a poem in the secular humanist tradition. The key is to make the message of the pageant consistent with the Constitution's vision of religious pluralism. As Justice Sandra Day O'Connor wrote, the Establishment Clause prohibits government from making adherence to a religion relevant in any way to a person's standing in the political community.[16]

Beyond school stages, the threats to the Establishment Clause become more serious. In 1954, Congress passed the Johnson Amendment, a law that bars 501(c)(3) nonprofit organizations—including churches—from supporting or opposing candidates for public office. The Johnson Amendment made clear the federal government's position that religion should not mix with politics. It has been a foundation of modern policy for sixty years.[17]

In recent years, though, religious leaders have not hesitated to express political views from the pulpit. President Trump's executive order on "Promoting Free Speech and Religious Liberty" from May 2017 warns the IRS not to engage in "discrimination" against churches when it comes to their nonprofit status.[18] Given no evidence of such behavior by the agency, it is possible the IRS will interpret the order as intending for the agency not to enforce the ban on religious groups engaging in electioneering.

If churches engage in electioneering, then taxpayer dollars are potentially funding the kind of entanglement between church and state that violates the spirit of the Establishment Clause. Churches that do not accept the benefits of tax deductibility are free to campaign, but those that are subsidized by the government should respect the ban on political campaigning that all other 501(c)(3) nonprofits have to abide by.

As PRESIDENT, you should follow Madison's example. When he vetoed laws that would have infringed upon religious freedom in the District of Columbia, Madison was going beyond what courts would have demanded of him to protect the principle of antiestablishment. In this tradition, you can fight efforts to repeal the Johnson Amendment and sign an executive order reaffirming your commitment to see it enforced. Even if no court rules that the Johnson Amendment is constitutionally required, preserving it supports the values embedded in the religion clauses. The notion of churches subsidized by the government is strikingly similar to the funding for religious ministers in Virginia, funding that Madison had opposed. But repealing the Johnson Amendment would be even worse. By using tax dollars to subsidize ministers seeking to influence our elections, we inch toward a government where religion gains even more influence over politics.

Your leadership on the question of the establishment of religion has as much to do with the way you speak as it does with how you defend laws. How should you talk about religion? We have already seen some examples from President Madison. Let us now consider some examples from pastors themselves on how to talk about religion as it relates to politics and public life.

The Minnesota state legislature has long had a tradition of inviting a religious leader to offer a prayer at their session. That is how Rev. Bradlee Dean ended up standing before Minnesota legislators on the morning of May 20, 2011. Dressed in a tracksuit with long, flowing hair, Dean offered his vision of religion in America. A few minutes into his sermon, he remarked that he was supposed to offer a nondenominational prayer—words that would unite Minnesotans of all faiths—but then he flagrantly disobeyed. Dean launched into an exposition of his political beliefs, claiming that Jesus Christ was the head of "the denomination" of the United States. He added a shot at President Obama as well, criticizing him for failing to acknowledge Jesus as the chief symbol of the country.[19]

To some religious Americans, Dean was expressing his vision of America. Undoubtedly, many agreed with him. But make no mistake: Dean does not understand the history we just reviewed. America is not a congregation, its people are not parishioners, and the president is not a pastor. The notion that Christ is the guiding light of the country would certainly have surprised Madison, who warned that even funding churches was inching toward the Inquisition.[20] To some religiously unaffiliated Americans, Dean was a strong example of the dangers of religion in public life. But as we've seen, trying to banish religion from public discourse also violates the spirit of the First Amendment. So, what example should you follow?

If you want to find a pastor you should seek to emulate as president, look to the Reverend Dr. Martin Luther King Jr. Perhaps no public speaker has better invoked religion to call us to our founding ideals and better angels. King often spoke of the "mountaintop," using biblical imagery like this to help Americans imagine themselves as a people headed toward shared ideals together. During the Montgomery protests against segregation, King invoked the Book of Amos: "We are determined here in Montgomery to work and fight until justice runs down like water, and righteousness like a mighty stream." In his "I Have a Dream" speech, King famously called on all religious faiths to embrace this mission: "black men and white men, Jews and Gentiles, Protestants and Catholics" must come together in the fight for freedom.[21]

King gives the best argument for supporting prayer in public life, as long as that prayer has an inclusive message. That inclusivity is why the government-sponsored memorial to him on the National Mall is a celebration of the ideal of the Establishment Clause, not a violation of it. Bradlee Dean's message, on the other hand, is one of animus, claiming that one cannot lead the country if one does not accept Jesus Christ—a clear violation of our requirement that government is not based on an exclusive conception of religion. In honoring King—not Dean—with a national holiday, the government endorses his vision of how the state can speak while respecting religious and secular views alike and avoiding the endorsement of any one religious viewpoint.

King should be a model for how you talk about religion as president. King used religious language in his speeches, but he was always careful to incorporate secular values as well. This made it clear, in both form and content, that the American ideals he invoked could be shared by religious and nonreligious people alike. So, you do have the freedom to speak with religious idioms. In fact, this language may help you convey your message powerfully. But you must always be careful to explain how that message applies to all Americans—including those who are secular or whose religious beliefs are different from your own.

———•——

WHY DOES any of this talk about prayer matter? Isn't it just talk, not policy? Some might dismiss discussion of prayer as mere symbolic politics.

It is not. Madison cared about the Establishment Clause

because it informs our constitutional culture and every debate we'll ever have. The way we speak in public elucidates the values we will use to make law. When we debate what the state should say and how, we are really talking about how it should reason about the most important issues of the day.

In 2014, the Supreme Court affirmed in *Town of Greece v. Galloway* the right of government to offer public prayers so long as they are voluntary. The opinion takes a page from Madison, suggesting that government-sponsored proselytizing or prayers that degrade some religions or ethnicities have no place under our Establishment Clause, even though that clause does allow some government-sponsored prayer.[22] The question is not *whether* to invoke religion as president, but *how* to do so. What is most important here is to avoid exclusive appeals to religion, not just when you speak but also when you sign executive orders or decide on whether a bill should be the law of the land.

Thinking back to that dinner as a student all those years ago, I often imagine what I should have said to the federal judge. I should have reminded the judge of Madison's commitment to the nation: all government speech—and public prayer—must be inclusive of people of all faiths because of America's commitment to avoid theocracy, or the rule of one religion over others. As Madison would have put it, a school-sponsored Christmas pageant, while doubtless an innocent endeavor, still shares a kernel of the reasoning that led to the European wars of religion.[23]

We can also look as an example to George Washington's 1790 letter to the small Touro Synagogue, which still sits on a side street in Newport, Rhode Island.[24] In his letter, Washington wrote of the difference between tolerating minority religions and honoring their equal place at the table: "it is now no more that toleration is spoken of as if it were the indulgence of one class of people, that another enjoyed the free exercise of their inherent natural rights."[25] The idea of America is that minority religions don't have to sit quietly and watch the pageant of bigger religions take place on a larger stage. Rather, we need to craft our plays, our government's speech, and our policy with an ear to including all Americans, regardless of their faith.

So, attend the prayer breakfast. But use your prayer to stress the meaning of the Establishment Clause and the Free Exercise Clause. We are a nation that refuses to establish one religion as true or official. Our Constitution celebrates people of any faith, and none at all. Instead of calling America a Christian nation or a nation defined by any one religion, you should strive to strike a balance between acknowledging the cultural and historical importance of religion to America, while being careful not to exclude any of your fellow citizens. As president, you need not pray, but if you do so, try to pray for all of America—not just those who share your religious beliefs or supported your campaign. Our constitutional commitments welcome a place for a plurality of religious beliefs to be recognized as equals at the dinner table, even in the presence of a federal judge.

10

The Eighth Amendment and the Ban on Torture

PRINCIPLE: Kings tortured their subjects to dominate them; presidents are required to respect their citizens and others in their custody with dignity. Reject all forms of torture and deliberate infliction of pain by the state.

"The United States is not like the terrorists. We have no grief for them, but what we are is a nation that upholds values and standards of behavior and treatment of all people, no matter how evil or bad they are."
—JOHN MCCAIN[1]

Five minutes after your inauguration, a military aide appears with a forty-five-pound briefcase: the nuclear football. In your first week, you tour some of the most important and secret locations in American intelligence: the CIA, the NSA, the FBI, the Pentagon, the White House Situation Room, the emergency bunker. All of this is a reminder, your advisors tell you, of one of your most important jobs: overseeing the national security apparatus that is fighting America's ongoing "war on terrorism"—against enemies like ISIS and Al Qaeda—and more importantly, keeping the country safe.

One day, the CIA director makes a personal visit to the White House to deliver your morning briefing. He informs you that a member of ISIS was captured on the battlefield in Syria, and was transferred last night to Guantanamo Bay—the American military outpost and prison that the United States operates on the island of Cuba. The CIA suspects that the ISIS captive may have information about an imminent attack planned to take place on American soil.

Then your CIA director does something startling: he asks you to sign a letter granting the agency express permission to use "enhanced interrogation." This is a euphemism for harsh questioning techniques that include waterboarding, a process by which a detainee fastened to a board has water poured over his face. It simulates, with nauseating precision, the exact sensation of drowning to death. This technique has been classified as torture by many institutions, and according to some,[2] it violates the Geneva Conventions, to which the United States is a party.[3] But your advisor warns you that there's simply no time to ask for permission to use these techniques every time they are necessary. "We need to be ready," he says. If the CIA wastes precious minutes "asking the suspect nicely," as he puts it, the attack may happen before we get the information to stop it.

Such dramatic scenarios are usually the stuff of movies. As president, though, you may well confront one in real life. However, your lawyers tell you there's a problem: the Eighth Amendment bans "cruel and unusual punishment," such as drawing and quartering or torture, as punishment for a crime.[4] But one of your counsels raises a counterargument: the Eighth Amendment has never been found by the Supreme Court to prohibit torture for information gathering before conviction (though it has ruled that post-conviction torture is prohibited). So, would the Eighth Amendment apply to the CIA's suggestion of waterboarding and prevent you from taking such action to extract information from a detainee? And even if the Eighth Amendment does not ban "enhanced interrogation," are there other provisions in the Constitution that do so, like the writ of habeas corpus or the Fifth Amendment's Due Process Clause?

————

IN 2002, this was precisely the question faced by senior White House officials in the Bush administration. As we saw in Chapter 3, John Yoo and Jay Bybee wrote President Bush a series of legal memos that defended the use of "enhanced interrogation" and supported an expansion of presidential power in situations where the country's security was at stake.[5] Yoo and Bybee were not alone in saying the Constitution did not ban torture. On the television show *60 Minutes*, Justice Scalia argued that the Eighth Amendment's ban on cruel and unusual punishment did not establish an absolute limit on torture. Scalia's reasoning was that the Eighth Amendment refers to "cruel and unusual *punishment*." Even if torturing to extract information is cruel, he argued, it is not literally "punishment," so the Eighth Amendment does not limit a president who wishes to use torture to obtain information.[6]

Scalia's argument is clever, but modern victims of enhanced interrogation would certainly understand that waterboarding is indeed a punishment—for failing to comply with the demands of their interrogators. A quick detour into British history also shows that Scalia's argument ignores critical context behind the Framers' language in the Eighth Amendment. As an originalist, Scalia made his legal arguments by referring to the precise meaning of the words used by the Framers. His argument, then, would suggest that those who passed the Eighth Amendment made a strict distinction between formal punishment after conviction and the kind of torture used to extract information. However, the words "cruel and unusual punishment" are taken directly from the British Bill of Rights, passed by the British in 1689 to put an end to the arbitrary and cruel abuses—especially torture—committed by kings and queens against their subjects.[7] These abuses did not fit neatly into the pattern of punishment meted out to convicted criminals. In some cases, tortured subjects were simply political opponents who had dared to speak out against the king and were judged guilty by the king's kangaroo court. In others, subjects were simply imprisoned and tortured without any formal charge.

King Charles I, for example, engaged in the kind of brutality so agonizing and bloody that it would be too intense for a horror movie. Throughout the 1600s, Charles made use of the "Star Chamber," a special court where judges loyal to the king dealt harshly with anyone who spoke out against him. Although the Star Chamber did not have the power to impose the death penalty, the judges handed down sentences of cruel, strange, and "unusual" punishment to demonstrate the king's disdain and to display his power to would-be adversaries.[8]

One of the "guilty" was William Prynne, a political opponent of King Charles. In 1637, he was dragged to the "Star Chamber" (for the second time, in fact), where he was convicted on a charge of sedition. Here is the description of what happened to him from writer John Rushworth, a contemporary of Prynne's: "Mr. Prynne's cheeks were seared with an iron made exceeding hot; which done, the executioner cut off one of his ears and a piece of his cheek with it."[9]

Parliament responded to King Charles's abuses by passing legislation aimed at limiting kingly power. The Habeas

Corpus Act of 1640 demanded legal explanations for all those imprisoned, asserting that anyone imprisoned could apply for a writ of habeas corpus—a protection against unjustified imprisonment. The Act also abolished the Star Chamber.[10] By instituting some procedural safeguards for those accused of crimes, the idea behind the Act was that kingly torture would be limited. This Habeas Act was an important precursor to our Constitution's provision in Article I that "the privilege of the Writ of Habeas Corpus shall not be suspended, unless when in Cases of Rebellion or Invasion the public Safety may require it."[11] It is also a precursor, though less explicitly, to the limit on cruel and unusual punishment in the Eighth Amendment.

But the situation in seventeenth-century England didn't get better; it got worse. A later king, James II, inflicted on a group of Protestant political opponents some of the most severe punishments ever recorded, in a series of trials known as the "bloody assizes." The crackdown began with the beheading of an elderly woman, Alice Lisle, whose crime was to have offered shelter to rebels after their defeat by James.[12]

After James was deposed, Parliament resolved to put an end to excessive punishment for good. In 1689, they passed a new Bill of Rights. In its preamble, which explains the reason for the newly imposed limits, it speaks of "cruel" and "illegal" punishments by the British king, seemingly a reference to the assizes and the earlier torture of people like William Prynne. The British Bill of Rights specified its limit on such actions by the king, requiring "that excessive bail ought not to be required, nor excessive fines imposed, nor cruel and unusual punishments inflicted."[13] The word "unusual" has often puzzled historians and judges, but it likely was influenced by the strange kind of punishments meted out at the Star Chamber. It turns out that the British, just like their American counterparts one hundred years later, had similar worries about a despotic executive.

Madison knew all too well the horror of Charles I. We can imagine him reeling in disgust as he read Rushworth's multivolume history of England—a book that sat in Jefferson's home library in Monticello and that both often turned to as a source.[14] Jefferson authored the Declaration of Independence to include a list of the king's abuses, just as the British Bill of Rights did. Madison also used the British Bill of Rights for inspiration in his railing against kingly abuse. Our Bill of Rights replicates, essentially word for word, the British language prohibiting "cruel and unusual" punishment. Scalia's suggestion that it would not apply to presidentially sanctioned torture during interrogation would be news to the Framers.

By 2005, the Bush administration was running a horror show that, though less extreme, still evoked the total control that Charles I's tactics imposed on his subjects. Under Bush, detainees were subject not only to intense pain, but to a kind of pain deployed methodically in order to extract information. More often than not, these "interrogation" methods yielded nothing at all. In 2014, a Senate Intelligence Committee report revealed the CIA's incredibly harsh interrogation tactics—methods that included waterboarding, near-drowning, nonstop interrogation, and forced rectal feeding, that had been used during the Bush administration.[15] The report concluded that no intelligence about impending terrorist attacks was obtained by these interrogation methods.[16] Furthermore, the report showed that at nearly every opportunity, the CIA lied and misled other government officials and the public about the torture program—including masking its most basic premise, which was that the program was run by experts. It was actually run by James Mitchell and Bruce Jessen, two Air Force psychologists without any experience in the subtle art of information extraction.[17]

The report also showed something else: that Khalid Sheikh Mohammed, one of the masterminds of the 9/11 attacks, was being held abroad at a CIA-operated base. There, Mohammed—whom the FBI had identified by using proven, noncoercive interrogation methods on another terrorist, Abu Zubaydah—was subject to brutal treatment by the CIA.[18] The agency repeatedly waterboarded Mohammed, pouring water over him a total of 183 times in a single month. The CIA also forced him into standing sleep deprivation, and performed dangerous rectal hydration procedures. A CIA official even concluded that waterboarding "has proven ineffective."[19] Yet the use of torturous techniques went on.[20]

When he came into office, President Obama stopped using euphemisms, instead explaining what happened in the bluntest of terms: "We tortured some folks." This was an acknowledgment of wrongdoing by one administration, distancing itself from the previous one.

Long before Obama took office, Congress had passed the Detainee Treatment Act of 2005, which banned torture. Specifically, the law required the Department of Defense to abide by the *Army Field Manual*, which places strict limits on the kinds of interrogation techniques that can be authorized.[21] That manual outlaws waterboarding and other extraction techniques that fall under "enhanced interrogation." Later, in 2009, President Obama issued an executive order requiring the CIA and other intelligence agencies to also abide by the manual.[22] Further, the 2005 law also mandated that no person in US custody could be subjected to "cruel, inhuman, or degrading treatment or punishment," bringing the United

States into compliance with international law.[23] Passing the Detainee Treatment Act also vindicated the original meaning of the Cruel and Unusual Clause, specifying that no government official, including the president, was exempt from limits on how detainees must be treated.

In passing the Detainee Treatment Act of 2005, Congress was likely responding to public pressure: Americans had recently seen images of Iraqi prisoners tortured at Abu Ghraib prison during the Iraq war. Senator John McCain of Arizona, a member of Bush's own party, had himself been tortured while a prisoner in Vietnam. On the day that the anti-torture bill passed, McCain said, "What we are is a nation that upholds values and standards of behavior and treatment of all people, no matter how evil or bad they are."[24] He understood that torture, no matter who it was directed against, was contrary to the values held by the United States and embedded in our Constitution.

The significance of Congress's 2005 Detainee Treatment Act was not lost on anyone. Beforehand, the president's lawyers argued that the lack of prior legislation banning torture meant it was a legal gray area, a crucial part of the argument that allowed the president's lawyers to authorize it. Somewhat like Truman in *Youngstown*, federal officials thought their war powers authorized them to do whatever they could to stop a potential terrorist attack. But the passage of the 2005 act directly undercut this argument. As the *Youngstown* ruling showed, presidential power is at its lowest when the president acts against congressional legislation.[25] Congress's intention was to bolster the constitutional ban on torture, wherever it may occur and by whatever public official attempts to carry it out: The law they sent to the president's desk reflected that. As we saw in Chapter 3, Bush signed the bill, but he wiggled out of the dilemma by using a signing statement. The statement seemed to suggest that his administration's tactics did not count as torture, rendering Congress's law suddenly toothless.

Chapter 3 taught us that if Bush wanted to oppose the bill, he should have vetoed it. Using a signing statement in this way blurred the distinction between executing the law and making it. But for our purposes here, the problem was that the signing statement seemed to signal that enhanced interrogation would continue. Understood in the way described above, this revealed a commitment to violate the Eighth Amendment.

WAS THERE a need for legislation to stop presidents from torturing to extract information? Or does the Eighth Amendment already prohibit such action? Given the amendment's text and history, Scalia's argument—that the Cruel and Unusual Clause does not prohibit torture—is wrong. The Bill of Rights was designed to prevent such abuses by a president with monarchical ambitions. Here, "punishment" is a broad category. The fact that the king's punishments were both "cruel" and "illegal" shows that, contrary to Scalia's claim, the Framers were not concerned only with formal or legal punishment. They were concerned with kingly actions that expressed opposition to the rule of law. Thus, the restrictive legislation passed by Congress simply reiterated a constitutional limit on presidential power that should already have been understood.

The prohibition against torture comes from the Constitution's values as well as its text.[26] Cruel actions deliberately inflict pain on people, disregarding their basic dignity. The values of the Constitution, however, affirm the dignity of all people: disrespecting a person's dignity is thus disrespecting the meaning of the Constitution. Since Justice Jackson's prosecutions at Nuremberg, 163 countries have become party to a treaty outlawing intentional torture.[27] The principles in this Convention Against Torture echo our own Eighth Amendment. To disregard these requirements would be to violate core principles of constitutional government, ones that we have helped spread throughout the world.

There is a problem, though: the Supreme Court has never applied the Eighth Amendment to limit torture endorsed by a president, let alone torture against foreign nationals. Nevertheless, the Supreme Court has set the stage for such a ruling. The Bush administration tried to argue that its policies toward suspected terrorists at Guantanamo Bay were beyond the reach of the courts, citing a case about a military tribunal during World War II in which habeas corpus protections were not guaranteed.[28] However, in a rebuke, the Supreme Court denied these claims in a case called *Boumediene v. Bush*.[29] The court held that there was a right to suspend the writ of habeas corpus, which protects against prisoners being detained without cause, but that Congress must provide an "adequate substitute." The court quoted Hamilton's *Federalist* 84 at length:

> The practice of arbitrary imprisonments, have been, in all ages, the favorite and most formidable instruments of tyranny. The observations of the judicious Blackstone . . . are well worthy of recital: "To bereave a man of life . . . or by violence to confiscate his estate, without accusation or trial, would be so gross and notorious an act of despotism as must at once convey the alarm of tyranny throughout the whole nation; but confinement of the person, by secretly hurrying him to jail, where his sufferings are unknown or forgotten, is a less public, a less striking, and therefore a *more dangerous engine* of arbitrary government.[30]

The writ of habeas corpus protects the most basic rights of citizens and noncitizens from arbitrary power exercised by any level of government. The court never addressed explicitly the issue of torture. But its rebuke of the right of the president to ignore habeas corpus should go hand in hand with a rejection of the right of the government to torture. Of course, it is possible that the writ could be granted while torture was upheld. In the law, one is an issue of legal process, and the other an issue of physical action upon a prisoner; put another way, one is a procedural right, the other a substantive one. But a president who respects the meaning of habeas corpus and the ban on cruel and unusual punishment would see their commonality too. Both are meant to stop the abuse of a "subject" intended to reinforce the absolute power of government. A crucial component of liberty under the Constitution is the right to avoid domination by the government. There could be no clearer expression of such domination than presidentially endorsed torture.

You might also look beyond the Eighth Amendment and habeas corpus to the Fifth and Fourteenth Amendments. From the standpoint of American case law, these offer additional protections against torture. The Supreme Court has not yet ruled that torture *before* a conviction is an unconstitutional "cruel and unusual punishment." However, the court has rejected such torture under the doctrine of Due Process. As president, you should find a way to affirm the values of the Eighth Amendment together with the Fifth and Fourteenth Amendments' Due Process Clauses: each applies to the humane treatment of all people.

In *Rochin v. California*, the court examined whether the Due Process Clause protected an American whose stomach was pumped against his will as the police attempted to uncover evidence in a drug case. The court made clear that the issue was about more than just the process of legal investigation; it involved a moral concern about the integrity of persons subject to state control. The opinion referred to the treatment of the detainee as "conduct that shocks the conscience" and is "too close to the rack and the screw to permit of constitutional differentiation."[31] Although the court is making an argument about due process here, its reasoning bolsters what we have said about the Eighth Amendment: the Constitution prohibits arbitrary treatment and torture, regardless of whether there has been a conviction.

But what about torture of noncitizens? It is true that the Eighth Amendment's limits do not apply on the battlefield. Inevitably soldiers will commit acts upon each other that would be prohibited outside of war. Still, the Eighth Amendment should apply in any circumstance in which the United States has control over detainees. When torture is used abroad, it undermines the kind of character a president is supposed to exhibit. A president's duty to enforce the ideals of the Constitution go beyond its strict legal limits. In all official interactions, a president should express the ideal that torture is wrong and refuse to allow it.

Aside from the battlefield, we must not let presidents exert total control over other human beings with the aim of subjugating them. Human freedom, protected by the Constitution, demands as much. No government official, no matter how high, should have the ability to dominate another person's body completely. The rule of law requires respect for all persons—citizens and noncitizens alike. It is incompatible with the inherent dehumanization inflicted by physical torture, regardless of how pressing the reason for it might be.

———

As PRESIDENT, you will certainly want to do whatever you can to avoid a terrorist attack on US soil. You might even be tempted to take extreme measures like authorizing CIA agents to engage in torture to extract information. But this would be a violation of US law passed by Congress and an affront to the very meaning of the Cruel and Unusual Clause. As president, you should refrain from agreeing to enhanced interrogation and condemn those who suggest it. On the one hand, the Supreme Court has not ruled enhanced interrogation unconstitutional. On the other hand, the Detainee Treatment Act of 2005 prohibits it. As president, though you may not have clear guidance from the Court, the oath requires you to respect the text and values of the Constitution and ban torture under your watch.

In so doing, you should avoid the shortcomings of presidents. Speaking in general about how the Bush administration dealt with terrorism, Cofer Black, a head of the CIA's Counterterrorist Center, said, "After 9/11, the gloves come off."[32] The phrase "the gloves come off," now associated with the Bush administration, is an affront to the core idea of Article II: the Constitution places "gloves" on a president in all areas, and for good reason. Donald Trump seemed to disregard these gloves when he suggested as a candidate that the United States should return to these torturous tactics—and worse. He stated that waterboarding is "not tough enough," and that the United States should "take out" the families of suspected terrorists.[33] These ideas "shock the conscience," as *Rochin* put it, and are also in violation of the Eighth Amendment.

By proclaiming that torture violates multiple provisions of our Constitution, the principles we adopted in the eighteenth century from the British Bill of Rights, and modern international norms, you can help reestablish the United States as a moral leader against torture. Your bully pulpit can reach beyond American soil, and with an issue as important to human dignity and freedom as torture, you have a responsibility to use it.

11

The Fourteenth and Fifth Amendments and the Guarantee of Equal Protection of the Laws

PRINCIPLE: The president is bound to the guarantee of equal protection of the law to all. Never make policy based on racial or ethnic prejudice—including against noncitizens.

"We conclude that, in the field of public education, the doctrine of 'separate but equal' has no place. Separate educational facilities are inherently unequal."
—Chief Justice Earl Warren[1]

During your presidency, tensions with Russia reach a fever pitch. Kremlin-backed hackers have broken into a White House server and stolen reams of classified information. The head of your Department of Homeland Security, a holdover from a previous administration, denounces all Russians living in the United States as "spies" and "criminals." She even proposes to deport all Russian green card holders.

The response from your Office of Legal Counsel is swift and clear: such a policy would violate the equal protection of the law, a provision written into the Constitution in the Fourteenth Amendment and later applied to the federal government under the Fifth Amendment. But Homeland Security has lawyers, too. They cite obscure nineteenth-century precedents upholding the president's power to discriminate based on nationality. Who is right? To answer that question, we'll need to delve deeply into the Equal Protection Clause of the Fourteenth Amendment and the history that brought it about.

———•———

IN THE Bill of Rights and the Constitution, statements about protecting liberty stand alongside provisions protecting slavery, including a mandate that the slave trade remain legal until at least 1808.[2] Many states, too, failed to live up to the credo of liberty, and the Bill of Rights—limiting only the federal government—did nothing to stop states from legalizing the enslavement of human beings. Worse, in the infamous *Dred Scott v. Sandford* decision in 1857, the Supreme Court refused to grant legal standing to Dred Scott, an enslaved person who had been brought into a free territory. Scott had sued for his freedom, arguing that he was entitled to it because he had been brought into Illinois and the Wisconsin Territories, where slavery was prohibited. The court, in perhaps its worst opinion of all time, held that Scott was property and not even entitled to be seen or recognized in court.[3]

Specifically, the court argued that due process was an entitlement of property owners. In this case, that meant slaveholders, but not enslaved persons.[4] The Civil War was largely fought over the question of slavery and the need to rectify the

Dred Scott decision. When the war ended, Congress passed what are known as the Reconstruction Amendments in an attempt to rectify this original sin against equality. The Thirteenth Amendment banned slavery, and the Fifteenth Amendment ratified the right to vote regardless of skin color.[5]

But the amendment that has by far had the most lasting impact on American life is the Fourteenth Amendment, ratified in 1868 after a dramatic struggle that helped lead to the impeachment (and near removal) of a president.

The Fourteenth Amendment can seem complex. It is often referenced in American political life, but is little understood. The amendment has five sections and does three main things. First, it applies the fundamental protections of the Bill of Rights to state government actions. (This happened gradually, and long after the amendment passed.) Second, it grants citizenship to all persons born in the United States, overturning *Dred Scott*, which had ruled that African Americans born in the United States were not entitled to citizenship. Third, and most importantly, it guarantees equal protection under the law.[6]

Until the passage of the Fourteenth Amendment, state governments were free to discriminate against people on the basis of race or religion. The Equal Protection Clause legally changed all that by guaranteeing that no person, regardless of race, religion, or ethnicity—later expanded to include gender—could be discriminated against by the government. Here, crucially, the Equal Protection Clause is rightly understood to apply to everyone—not just citizens. We know this because the text speaks about not denying equal protection of law to "any person," not "any citizen."[7]

This amendment was a major accomplishment, but passing an amendment does not always lead to change overnight. Big changes often occur slowly, and an amendment or law merely plants the seeds of an idea that can require years to take hold. In this case, it took decades: states long ignored the meaning of the Fourteenth Amendment, allowing blatant ethnic discrimination at the US border and implementing what are now known as Jim Crow laws codifying segregation. The Supreme Court could have intervened in this despicable arrangement. Instead, it refused to combat racial prejudice, both in immigration law and domestic segregation.

In the 1880s, the United States was in the feverish throes of anti-Chinese sentiment. A wave of Chinese immigrants had arrived in the growing West Coast states, and like the Irish, Germans, and many other nationalities at different periods of American history, the Chinese were the hated immigrant group of the moment. Often, they came seeking opportunity and a better life, working at dirt-poor wages and in unsafe conditions. Anti-Chinese sentiment got so bad that in 1885, a mob in Tacoma, Washington, was granted authority by the local government to forcibly remove members of the Chinese community and razed their buildings.[8] This anti-Chinese local policy had no rational basis—the Chinese were neither a security threat nor a significant economic threat; Chinese immigrants to the United States represented less than 1 percent of the American population at the time. This was racial discrimination, not sound policy.

The anti-Chinese sentiment hit home at the time for Chae Chan Ping, an immigrant who left his family in China to settle in California. He had built a life for himself there, working and contributing to the economy for twelve years. But he was not yet a naturalized citizen. In 1887, Ping decided to head back to China to visit. These trips were common, and according to the law, immigrants who wanted to visit home merely needed a certificate from a customs official. Ping secured such a certificate in San Francisco, and with the promise of later reentry, he returned to his home in China.

Things turned out differently than Ping had planned. In September of 1888, he boarded a steamship called the *Belgic*, leaving China to return to the same San Francisco port from which he had left a year earlier.[9] When he arrived on October 8, 1888, he was barred from entering the country, despite his reentry certificate. While he was gone, the nation had succumbed to anti-Chinese fervor: in 1888, Congress passed and President Grover Cleveland signed the Scott Act[10]—a law that expanded the earlier Chinese Exclusion Act to prohibit Chinese laborers who were abroad from returning to the United States.[11]

When Ping arrived and was denied reentry, he faced a choice: return home, or try to sue for entry into the country. He chose the latter. As his legal case unfolded, he was held on the ship for close to seven agonizing months. Finally, in 1889, the Supreme Court heard his case.

The case pitted Chae Chan Ping against Congress and the president of the United States. Ping argued that he was being held illegally and that his certificate gave him the right to reenter. President Cleveland, through his solicitor general, claimed that under the Constitution, Congress and the president have plenary—or absolute—power to legislate immigration policy. Because they had this power, they were authorized to exclude Ping.

The court ruled against Ping, holding that the president, acting with the approval of Congress, had the power to determine who can enter the country and who cannot. The president's power, the court reasoned, may be limited domestically by Article II, but in international affairs, Congress can authorize the president to do whatever he or she sees as best for the country. According to this ruling, due process and equal protection were irrelevant in immigration matters.[12] Unchecked executive power, it seemed, had won out over the Fourteenth Amendment's protections, at least for noncitizens like Ping wishing to enter the country.

Just seven years after Ping's case, the court again declined to enforce the Equal Protection Clause, this time domestically in a case called *Plessy v. Ferguson*. In 1890, the state of Louisiana passed a law mandating that railway companies have segregated coaches for blacks and whites.[13] In 1892, Homer Adolph Plessy, a man of mixed race, refused to leave a section of the railway car that was reserved for whites. The case reached the Supreme Court, which ruled that the law requiring segregated railway cars was constitutionally permissible as long as the accommodations were separate but equal.

This decision in *Plessy v. Ferguson* began a new era in which government-mandated segregation was tolerated as constitutional. Discriminatory Jim Crow laws proliferated, undermining the promise of equal protection throughout much of the American South.[14] Though *Plessy* did not deal specifically with presidential or other federal government action, the Jim Crow laws it permitted should serve as a stark reminder of our country's history of discrimination. A president committed to upholding the values of the Constitution should, both then and today, speak out against such blatant violations of the value of equality—and disallow them when possible.

Unfortunately, the court continued its failure to apply real equal protection well into the twentieth century, in more ways than just allowing the evils of segregation. After the attack on Pearl Harbor in December of 1941, the United States did what today seems like an unthinkable act: it limited the movement of

Japanese American citizens to discrete "military zones," sometimes even forcibly relocating them to internment camps.[15]

In 1942, President Franklin Roosevelt signed Executive Order 9066, authorizing the secretary of war to carry out an involuntary internment of innocent Japanese Americans. Children and families with no connection to our wartime enemies were placed in internment camps. The rationale for the order was security. Today, however, there is wide agreement among historians—bolstered by the revelations of a contemporaneous report from the Office of Naval Intelligence that had been deliberately hidden by a member of Roosevelt's administration—that the mass internment served no security purpose.[16] And even if the internment order had improved security, it was still tainted by racial prejudice. Significantly fewer German Americans, for instance, were rounded up and interned, despite the fact that the United States was also at war with Germany.

During World War II, a Japanese American citizen named Fred Korematsu was living in San Leandro, California, a suburban community close to the Oakland airport. In September 1942, Korematsu was convicted of violating a "civilian exclusion order." His family had been ordered to report to a nearby racetrack where they would await transfer to the internment camp. Fred Korematsu refused to go. He sued to overturn his conviction, and the lawsuit reached the Supreme Court.[17]

In that decision in *Korematsu v. United States*, the court, ruling in a six-to-three-vote majority, admitted that the policy discriminated based on ethnicity, but claimed the executive order was justified due to security concerns.[18] Though "all legal restrictions which curtail the civil rights of a single racial group are immediately suspect" under the Equal Protection Clause, "that is not to say that all such restrictions are unconstitutional."[19] Just as in *Chae Chan Ping*, in *Korematsu* the court deferred to a president's discriminatory policy in the interest of security. Even the great civil libertarian and future chief justice Earl Warren was complicit in the policy.[20] During World War II and before he joined the court, Warren had served as attorney general and governor of California. In those positions, he helped Roosevelt carry out the internment on the West Coast.[21]

Not everyone on the court was so ready to grant this power to the president, though. Writing in a powerful dissent, Justice Robert Jackson—whom we have already seen was deeply concerned about authoritarian overreach in the executive—argued that the United States had succumbed to racial animus. "The Court for all time has validated the principle of racial discrimination in criminal procedure and of transplanting American citizens. The principle then lies about like a loaded weapon, ready for the hand of any authority that can bring forward a plausible claim of an urgent need."[22]

Although the Equal Protection Clause speaks of lofty ideals and high ambition, it was often betrayed throughout its early history—a good reminder, as we discussed early on, of the difference between a document that citizens meaningfully enforce, and one that is a mere "parchment [barrier]."[23] The Chinese Exclusion Act undermined the clause at the border, and *Plessy v. Ferguson* undermined it at home. It would be more than fifty years before the ideal of nondiscrimination finally began to wipe away the stain of segregation. Still today, the Equal Protection Clause is interpreted weakly when it comes to the rights of those beyond our borders. It is time for that to change.

THE MID-TWENTIETH century saw a reversal of *Plessy*, and with it, a new hope that the Equal Protection Clause would eradicate governmental prejudice. Domestically, the court overturned and rebuked the "separate but equal" logic of *Plessy*.[24] But in regard to immigration, though the court has made strides to undermine the logic of *Chae Chan Ping*, the case has not yet been formally overturned and some still argue it should not be. However, the court's principles, history, and precedent, as well as the text of the Constitution, all suggest that the time has come to do so.

In my view, the Court should explicitly deny the president plenary or absolute powers in matters of immigration. Applying the Equal Protection Clause, the court should also demand that presidents not engage in racial or ethnic discrimination at the border, just as they cannot at home. We can see the need to overturn *Chae Chan Ping* by looking closely at the court's logic in overturning *Plessy*.

In 1954, Justice Earl Warren, who had earlier aided in Japanese internment as California's attorney general and as its governor, wrote the opinion in the court's most important repudiation of racial discrimination: *Brown v. Board of Education of Topeka*. In Topeka, Kansas, a third-grader named Linda Brown became the lead plaintiff in a lawsuit against the Topeka Board of Education, which was excluding them from the local white elementary school. Brown was joined in the lawsuit by a group of nineteen fellow students of color. Topeka, like many other southern towns, maintained one set of schools for black children and another for whites.

Under the "separate but equal" logic of *Plessy*, Brown's lawyers could have made a more limited argument, one that said the black schools were inferior to the white schools in the district. Instead, they made a bolder argument, asserting that segregation itself was inherently unequal because it sent a message of inferiority to black students. Lead lawyer Thurgood

Marshall presented evidence that black schoolchildren, when asked if they preferred white or black dolls, chose white dolls overwhelmingly—indicating that views of racial inferiority were inculcated even at a young age. The system was not one of "separation"—it was akin to a racial hierarchy, with whites on top. Ever the savvy politician, Warren cobbled together a coalition to issue a ruling in *Brown v. Board*, one that went far beyond Linda Brown's specific case, instead issuing a full repudiation of *Plessy v. Ferguson*. In Warren's ruling, the court famously ruled that in public education, separate was inherently unequal.[25] That decision was unanimous.

Did this ban on segregation apply to noncitizens? Later, the court clarified that the equal protection of the law was afforded to all those in the country, independent of citizenship. In *Plyler v. Doe*, the court made clear that the rights of noncitizen children were also protected by the Equal Protection Clause, which refers to "any person," not just to citizens. In that case, the court protected school funds for the children of undocumented parents.[26]

In domestic law, the Equal Protection Clause since *Brown* and *Plyler* has advanced so far that it now limits what a president and Congress can do if their actions are clearly prejudiced. And importantly, in *Bolling v. Sharpe*, decided on the same day as *Brown*, the Supreme Court made it clear that the ban on racial discrimination placed on the states also applied to the federal government. It ruled that there was an equal protection dimension to the Fifth Amendment's Due Process Clause that courts were obliged to protect. Even though the *words* "equal protection" are not found in the Fifth Amendment's text, the court correctly determined that the *value* of equal protection became embedded within the amendment in the post–Civil War Constitution.

One of the most important developments in the court's

recent equal protection jurisprudence has to do with the doctrine of "animus." In 2013, the court heard the case *United States v. Windsor.*[27] Edith Windsor was a widow who had tried to claim the estate of her deceased wife, but was forbidden due to a 1996 law called the Defense of Marriage Act (DOMA) that prevented gay spouses from making claims for a federal estate tax exemption.[28]

The Supreme Court found that Windsor had been discriminated against: federal policy based in prejudice, in this case against same-sex couples, violates the Equal Protection Clause. Justice Kennedy argued that DOMA's name revealed its prejudice, as there was no reason marriage needed to be "defended" from gay couples. In his interpretation, the clause required that government policy must be based in a rational purpose; the government could not just make arbitrary policy. Prejudice, by definition, is not rational. Thus the law, based on irrational bigotry toward gay couples—or "animus," as the court called it—is unconstitutional.[29]

On the other hand, in the international realm, the Equal Protection Clause is still too weak. Fred Korematsu had his sentence overturned in 1983 by a federal district court judge in northern California, and in 1988, President Reagan signed a law[30] that granted reparations to the victims of Japanese internment and formally apologized on behalf of the United States.[31] Despite these moves in the right direction, the Supreme Court has never overturned the legal precedent that allowed internment to happen.

In 2017, the court was given an opportunity to formally overturn *Korematsu*, but it chose not to, at least not immediately. During the 2016 presidential campaign, candidate Donald Trump had promised to ban all Muslims traveling to the United States—precisely the kind of religious test prohibited by the Constitution. A few days after taking office, Trump made good on the promise, signing an executive order banning immigration and travel from seven Muslim-majority countries and suspending the previous administration's refugee program for ninety days.[32] His lawyers likely informed him that an explicit Muslim ban would violate the First Amendment's Free Exercise Clause and the Fourteenth Amendment's Equal Protection Clause. They redrafted the ban to avoid criticism that it targeted Muslims, but the president, in an interview with the Christian Broadcasting Network,[33] had previously explained that the ban favored exceptions for Christian refugees at the expense of Muslim ones.[34]

Due in part to Trump's own statements about the travel ban, several federal district courts and two appellate courts have ruled against the various iterations of the ban. The Fourth Circuit Court of Appeals, for example, held that the travel ban constituted a violation of the Establishment Clause, which, like the Equal Protection Clause, outlaws policies based in animus.[35] But in December of 2017, the Supreme Court ruled that the third version of the ban could take effect while legal challenges went through federal appeals courts.[36] In January of 2018, the Court announced that it would hear challenges to this version of the administration's travel ban. As of this writing, the case has not been decided.

The next chance the Supreme Court has to overturn *Korematsu* and *Chae Chan Ping*, it should strongly repudiate the holdings in those two cases. The court should clearly say that animus based on race, religion, ethnicity, gender, or sexual orientation has no place in US policy at home or abroad. It should also clarify that national security is never an excuse for animus-based policy. Such a statement would make clear that *Korematsu* and *Chae Chan Ping* were wrongly decided and undermined the values of the Constitution. No president should see them as good law today. Any policy—whether the travel ban or otherwise—that follows in the tradition of animus present in these cases is unconstitutional and should be seen that way. As the concurrence of the Fourth Circuit Court of Appeals' ruling in the travel ban case asserted:

> Invidious discrimination that is shrouded in layers of legality is no less an insult to our Constitution than naked invidious discrimination. We have matured from the lessons learned by past experiences documented . . . in *Dred Scott* and *Korematsu*. But we again encounter the affront of invidious discrimination.[37]

This concurrence by Judge James A. Wynn confirms the idea that prejudice by a president has no place in our constitutional culture. This principle is the basis of our modern equal protection case law, even if the opposite view prevailed in the nineteenth century.

Some might argue that a president's power must remain strong internationally given the unprecedented threat of international terrorism; they would see *Chae Chan Ping* as a good decision, one that allows the president to do what it takes to fight terrorism. But both domestically and internationally, discriminatory acts by the US government that are intended to combat terrorism often do no such thing, and instead undermine American values or sow deepening negative feelings about our country around the world. One lesson of *Korematsu* is that trying to act tough in the name of security instead often amounts to weak and impulsive presidential action. It is long past time for the Supreme Court to recognize this, and to repudiate its decisions in *Korematsu* and *Chae Chan Ping*.

We need to allow our notion of the president's foreign policy power to be limited by the Equal Protection Clause. No purposeless and prejudicial policy—domestic or foreign—should stand constitutional muster.

PRESIDENT REAGAN's apology regarding *Korematsu* was an important acknowledgment of the mistaken policy of Japanese internment. Yet the real tribute that Fred Korematsu deserves should be in ensuring that a president never relies on prejudice to make government policy. You should listen carefully to the words of John Tateishi, who grew up in an internment camp: "There is a saying in the Japanese culture, 'kodomo no tame ni,' which means, 'for the sake of the children.' And for us . . . it's the legacy we're handing down to them and to the nation to say that, 'You can make this mistake, but you also have to correct it—and by correcting it, hopefully not repeat it again.' "[38]

With these powerful words in mind, heed your Office of Legal Counsel's advice over that of Homeland Security. The advisor who told you to deport all Russians is proposing a policy that will do little to protect American national security, and may even harm it: she is advising you to violate the Constitution. No president should repeat the evils that the Supreme Court failed to overturn in *Plessy*, *Chae Chan Ping*, and *Korematsu*—and you should make sure you're no exception. Instead of deporting all Russians in the United States, take to your bully pulpit to affirm to the country that a person's race, gender, religion, ethnicity, and national origin should not stand in the way of their equal protection under American law.

Section III

CHECKS ON THE PRESIDENT

12

How to Stop a President

PRINCIPLE: A president who disregards the oath can be stopped in a variety of ways. The ultimate power to stop you lies with the people, acting through the other branches and the states.

> *"The people are the only legitimate fountain of power, and it is from them that the constitutional charter, under which the several branches of government hold their power, is derived."*
>
> —JAMES MADISON[1]

W e've learned about the constitutional duties of the president and how a good president can carry them out. We've also seen how the Constitution can limit the impact of a bad president. But the Constitution has a dangerous loophole: What happens if a president simply refuses to comply with the limits placed on him or her by the Constitution?

In tackling this question, we will transition in this section from thinking about the limits on a president to what we should do when a president oversteps them. As president, you need to understand the modes of recourse that citizens can take if you stray from the oath. As Madison argued in the *Federalist Papers*, people are not angels,[2] and constitutional violations will happen—even by presidents with the best of intentions (like you, perhaps). No matter what, you'll likely face normal political resistance as you pursue your agenda. That is just democracy in action. But if you show deep disregard for the oath of office, you should be met by more profound opposition.

To see why this matters, consider the following scenarios: a president assaults a protestor at a rally; a president lobbies for and signs a Twenty-First Century Sedition Act, making it a crime to criticize the chief executive; a president disregards the Emoluments Clauses, selling the office of the presidency for personal profit. In each of these cases, the president plainly disregards the Constitution. What should we do?

Such a president must be stopped. Thankfully, the Constitution offers tools to make this possible. The checks on a president do not just work on their own, however. They rely on an active citizenry and on legislative and judicial branches that are committed to upholding the Constitution. In this chapter, by introducing how the judiciary, the states, and the legislative branch can check the president, we again find ourselves learning from our guide, James Madison. Not only did he design these checks and balances, but he also demonstrated the best ways to leverage them in his political life after the Constitution was ratified.

———•———

MADISON PLACED the first hints of these tools in a little-known speech that George Washington never delivered. In the months before he would be sworn in as the first president, Washington labored over his draft of the first inaugural address, originally seventy-three pages long. Struggling, Washington turned for help to James Madison, the person whom he regarded as the foremost expert on the Constitution.

Madison agreed to help, and Washington mailed him a draft of the speech, marked "confidential." Madison thought the draft was an "extraordinary production," and later worked with Washington to trim the speech, focusing more on civic duty and broad goals for government than specific legislative proposals.[3]

In these early drafts, Washington's address contained some clues about why the people have the power to oppose a president who disregards constitutional norms. In his words, "This Constitution is really in its formation a government of the people; that is to say, a government in which all power is derived from, and at stated periods reverts to them."[4] One draft of the address hints at an answer as to *how* the people might—within the constitutional system—reclaim their power from a president who violates the oath. It notes: "the balances, arising from the distribution of the Legislative—Executive—& Judicial powers, are the best that have been instituted."[5] We should take from this the idea that the other two branches should intercede when the president goes too far. On my view, these balances are the "best" because they provide real mechanisms to stop a president who feels unconstrained by informal norms. Ideally, a president will internalize the ethos of the Constitution, but if he or she does not, the people must use the other branches to intervene.

Washington never elaborated on the details of how to stop a president. But four years later, in his second inaugural address, he made clear that "constitutional punishment" and the "upbraidings of all who are now witnesses of the present solemn ceremony" were necessary to resist a president who disregards the oath.[6] The drafts of Washington's first inaugural address might have served as a guide for the people on how to stop a president by using the levers of the other branches, showing us how to make good on his later idea of "constitutional punishment." Though the first president did not deliver those words about the people's power in his first inaugural, they can still serve as an inspiration for how the people can stop an errant president.

———

THE FIRST check on presidential power is also the most tenuous: the judiciary. Today, when the Supreme Court makes a ruling, the president obeys it. This is a remarkable achievement. After all, no branch is more powerless to force the president to comply with its rulings. Whereas the executive might rely on the police power and the legislature on its power of the purse, the judiciary has nothing but norms to make the other branches comply with its orders.

The Framers designed the judicial branch with the hope that presidents who violated the law would, indeed, be stopped by the courts. In *Federalist* 78, published in 1788, Alexander Hamilton described this check on the president: if the Constitution were the supreme law of the land, and judges were charged with enforcing the law, then by definition judges would also need to enforce the Constitution—even if it were the president who had violated it.[7]

What would happen if a president simply refused to follow a court order? Today, such an act would be seen as a gross violation of the oath of office. But in 1800, it lay distinctly in the realm of possibility, because constitutional norms about compliance with judicial orders were not yet well established. So, how could the judiciary resist a president who disdains judicial authority itself? It turns out that judges can get creative in how they enforce the Constitution on presidents, even when presidents themselves are unwilling to adhere to court rulings.

Nowhere was the creativity on better display than in the Supreme Court case that essentially invented judicial oversight: *Marbury v. Madison*, which we first discussed in Chapter 5.[8] Today, we accept that judges can overturn unconstitutional laws. In the first few years of the nation's history, however, this was not obvious at all. Although it had been discussed in *Federalist* 78 and an earlier Supreme Court case, judicial review wasn't yet firmly established in practice.[9] It would have to be invented—in this case, forged in a clash between the president and the chief justice of the Supreme Court.

It began on the last night of John Adams's presidency in 1801. That evening, the Federalist Adams sent out a series of envelopes containing judicial appointments—the famous "midnight appointments." This was a mad dash to squeeze a few more Federalist judges onto the bench before Jefferson, from the rival Democratic-Republican party, could take office the following morning. Several envelopes, however, were mistakenly never delivered—including one addressed to a loyal Maryland Federalist named William Marbury.[10]

When Jefferson took office, he refused to deliver the letters— an attempt to prevent more of Adams's Federalist judges from joining the judiciary. But from Marbury's perspective, he couldn't be denied his appointment just because an envelope wasn't delivered. So, Marbury (along with three other men whose judicial appointments went undelivered) sued Jefferson's administration. Since James Madison was now Jefferson's new secretary of state, the case became known as *Marbury v. Madison*.[11]

Secretary Madison thought the Constitution supported judicial review—the ability of the courts to overturn unconstitutional laws.[12] But President Jefferson, while not explicitly rejecting judicial review, strongly opposed the idea of judicial supremacy—that judges have a monopoly on interpreting the law—writing that "to consider the judges as the ultimate arbiters of all constitutional questions . . . would place us under the despotism of an Oligarchy."[13] Instead, he thought that at least in some circumstances, each branch should interpret for itself the meaning of the Constitution, with the judiciary occasionally deferring to the president's judgment on some matters.[14] Jefferson also didn't trust Chief Justice John Marshall, a well-known Federalist and ally of John Adams. Jefferson did not believe that a Federalist-sympathizing court should have special say over whether he was a faithful executor of the Constitution he had sworn to uphold.[15]

Twelve years earlier, in 1789, Congress had passed a law called the Judiciary Act, which established America's federal court system.[16] According to Marbury's lawyers, the law gave the newly created Supreme Court the power to act as a trial court, one that could issue a writ of mandamus to compel government action.[17] So, they argued, the court should issue a writ requiring that Madison deliver the commission and make good on Marbury's appointment. In other words, if Madison and the Jefferson administration would not deliver the commissions voluntarily, the Supreme Court was entitled to force their hand to make the appointment.

The stakes were considerable. If Marshall issued the order to honor the appointment, Jefferson could simply ignore it. This would have shown the young country the true weakness of the judicial branch. Marshall had to find some way to outsmart Jefferson, establishing judicial authority while getting Jefferson to go along with it.

In his famous ruling, that is exactly what Marshall did. The court ruled that Marbury was not entitled to his appointment—handing a victory to Jefferson. But the court did so by striking down part of the Judiciary Act of 1789, arguing that nothing in Article III of the Constitution gave the Supreme Court the power to act as a trial-level court that could compel a judicial appointment. (The court left open the possibility that it could compel an appointment at the appeal stage.) Marshall found a way to rule "for" Jefferson on the immediate question, while asserting the judiciary's power of judicial review by striking down an aspect of a law that it deemed unconstitutional. In so doing, Marshall put Jefferson, who could hardly quibble with his legal victory, in a clever checkmate.[18]

Although Justice Marshall decided not to challenge Jefferson directly, over time we have come to understand the Supreme Court's central role in interpreting the Constitution to, if need be, stop a president. Every president has a duty to respect judicial orders; no president has the right to disregard them. As president, it is essential that you respect the power of judicial review, even when you disagree with a court's opinion.

Today, other judicial checks on presidential power are more controversial. In the next chapter, we will explore the difficult question of whether the president can be tried for a crime or sued by a private citizen. That possibility all began with Marshall's vital defense of judicial power in 1803.

———

THE SECOND check on presidential power is legislatures, both at the federal and state level. In Chapter 14 we discuss how state officials should step in to protect rights, showing the central role that Madison played to establish how this check could be used. Here again, Madison played a central role. As we have already seen, when Congress passed the Alien and Sedition Acts in 1798—making it a crime to criticize the president and revoking foreign nationals' rights to due process—Madison objected vehemently to the laws' passage. When President Adams signed them anyway, Madison was left to consider other options for resistance.[19] We return to the Acts here to show one powerful way to oppose a president who disregards the Constitution.

Madison knew the Alien and Sedition Acts were unconstitutional. But the options he had to resist them seemed limited. He could not go to the courts, because they were stacked with justices loyal to Adams. He could not turn to Congress, because the same Federalists who passed the law and supported Adams would not suddenly decide to impeach the president.

Stymied by these limits, Madison devised an altogether different strategy, and returned to Virginia to carry it out. The Tenth Amendment states: "The powers not delegated to the United States by the Constitution, nor prohibited by it to the States, are reserved to the States respectively, or to the people."[20] Madison saw that this affirmed the people's ability to use the states to claim their individual rights. So, since he had been a member of the state legislature, he decided to deploy his connections there to resist Adams's attempt at unconstitutional federal censorship. Later in this section, we will detail how Madison accomplished this by drafting a resolution that would be passed by the Virginia legislature proclaiming the acts unconstitutional.[21] In this instance, the power of state government was essential to stop a president who disregarded the oath.

Though Madison and Jefferson had to look to state legislatures to stop Adams, Congress can also use its own powers to resist a president. Congress has the responsibility to pass good laws, closely scrutinize nominees, and hold investigative hearings. Members of Congress also swear an oath to the Constitution, so no matter what is happening in the executive branch, they have an obligation to uphold their constitutional duties.[22] When a president commits "high crimes" against the Constitution, this obligation might even take the form of impeachment. In Chapter 15, we examine the role of Congress in impeaching a president.

———•———

ALL OF these checks require an active citizenry to be truly effective. Few citizens will ever occupy as many branches of government as Madison did, and none have had as much influence on the structure of the Constitution. But Madison's words and actions—and the principles that Washington detailed in the second draft of his first inaugural address—emphasize the critical role that citizens can play in defending the Constitution, even if they never hold government office. There are at least four major ways the people can stop a president who disregards the Constitution. Whether you're reading this guide as a president or as a citizen, you should keep these principles in mind in your votes and in your actions.

First, citizens can hold a president accountable through elections. Citizens with a thorough understanding of the Constitution are less likely to mistake a demagogue for a legitimate seeker of the presidency—one who intends to "protect and defend" the Constitution.

Second, Americans can use the judiciary by bringing or supporting cases filed by citizens who have been harmed by a president's reckless actions. Of course, presidents have always argued for immunity from such suits, but Madison's argument in the *Federalist Papers* counteracts those claims. A president—in clear contrast to a king—is not above the law.

Third, citizens can pressure their local and state officials to resist presidential attempts to encroach on their rights. As the court has interpreted it, the Tenth Amendment grants state officials the ability to resist unconstitutional federal laws that violate individual rights.

Fourth, citizens can demand that Congress use the power of impeachment to remove a president who violates the Constitution. Impeachment, of course, is the most explosive and popularly known check on the president. While it has not often been used, impeachment is the most direct way to stop a president who disregards the oath.

None of these four methods is possible without the fundamental weapon that underlies each of them: public understanding of the Constitution. Jefferson put it in terms of a metaphor that we would do well to remember. He feared that if we left constitutional interpretation to courts alone, the document would become like "wax in the hands of the judiciary, which they may twist, and shape into any form they please."[23] Jefferson's metaphor extends beyond the courts: no one branch has the exclusive power to interpret the document. It is up to us, the citizens, to interpret the Constitution, and to demand that when a president tries to undermine it, the other branches spring into action.

As president, you may think that a discussion of how to thwart your actions or even remove you is disloyal. We are, after all, talking about principles and techniques that might apply to you if you fail to live up to the oath of office. But President Washington's words on resistance in his undelivered first inaugural address and official second inaugural show that perceived personal disloyalty to a president can actually be the highest form of loyalty to the office. To take the oath of office seriously, you should challenge the people and the other branches to stop you if you fail to "preserve, protect and defend" the Constitution of the United States.[24]

In the next three chapters, we will look at real stories from American history that demonstrate how citizens have managed to defend the Constitution from presidents who would abuse it. We will also explore current and possible future abuses, examining what citizens can do to counter them.

13

The Judicial Check on a President

PRINCIPLE: The president is not above the law. You can be criminally indicted in the name of the people.

"No man is above the law, and no man is below it."
—Theodore Roosevelt[1]

Imagine a rather gruesome scenario: the president is meeting with legislators in the Oval Office about his proposed health care bill. Suddenly, the discussion becomes heated. The president screams in the face of the Senate Minority Leader, a member of a different party. Then, with ten witnesses present, the president punches the minority leader three times, continuing to do so while he lies on the ground.

In any normal circumstance, this person would be charged with assault. If you think this sounds too far-fetched, consider that something similar happened in Canada, an event infamously remembered as the "Shawinigan handshake." In 1996, Canadian prime minister Jean Chrétien, who hailed from the town of

Shawinigan, was speaking at an event in Quebec when the crowd began to heckle him, protesting recent changes to the country's unemployment laws. The hecklers disrupted the prime minister's speech, chanting, "Chrétien to the unemployment line!" in French. As he pushed his way out of the event, the infuriated Chrétien lost his cool, grabbing one protestor by the throat and shoving him aside, where police wrestled him to the ground.[2]

What should happen in a circumstance like this? In Canada, the prime minister is subject to the law and Chrétian was charged with assault. (The charges were rejected by the minister of justice of Quebec.)[3] But in the United States, some legal scholars have argued that the president is immune from criminal indictment—being formally accused of or charged with a serious crime—while serving in office. Lawyers for both Presidents Nixon and Clinton made precisely this argument, suggesting that a presidential indictment would cripple the executive branch. As president, you might be confronted with a similar situation. Are these lawyers right?

DURING THE Watergate scandal, Nixon's Office of Legal Counsel argued that the president enjoyed certain executive privileges that allowed him to resist indictment by courts, at least while he was in office.[4] In that scandal, President Nixon was suspected of ordering the break-in at the Democratic headquarters at the Watergate Hotel and subsequently covering up the incident with hush money. A number of his aides were eventually charged with hiring "plumbers" to tap phones illegally in order to gather information that could give Nixon a strategic political advantage over his rivals. Nixon's aides were also later convicted of breaking into the office of the leaker

Daniel Ellsberg's psychiatrist to find information that might undermine Ellsberg's credibility.[5]

In 1974, Watergate special prosecutor Archibald Cox made a dramatic announcement: he had gotten a court to subpoena Nixon's private tapes that recorded conversations in the Oval Office.[6] These tapes possibly revealed the president discussing a conspiracy and cover-up of Watergate. But Nixon refused to surrender the tapes. His lawyers argued that the Supreme Court could not demand them, because to do so would violate executive privilege and the need to protect the confidentiality required for the president to receive candid and objective advice.

In the Supreme Court case *United States v. Nixon*, the court had to determine how much latitude the Constitution gave to the president. In a dramatic 8–0 ruling, the court drastically curtailed the notion of executive privilege, asserting that "the impediment that an absolute, unqualified privilege would place in the way of the primary constitutional duty of the Judicial Branch . . . would plainly conflict with the function of the courts under Art. III."[7] On the question of confidentiality, the court solved this problem by ruling that the lower district court could review the tapes privately and determine which parts needed to be kept secret and which parts could be released to the public. With a simple practical adjustment, the court was able to refute Nixon's claim that the functioning of the executive branch required legal immunity for the president. In their decision, the court referenced *Marbury* and a simple but fundamental principle of American democracy: the president is not above the law.[8]

It was now established that Nixon could not block the subpoena against him. But that just raised an entirely new question: If the subpoena revealed wrongdoing, what would happen next? Could Nixon, a sitting president, be indicted and brought to trial?

Not surprisingly, Nixon's lawyers argued vehemently that the president was immune from indictment. How did they argue this, just days after the Supreme Court had clearly stated that the president was not above the law? The lawyers claimed that the logic of *United States v. Nixon* did not extend to *indictments*. Because the occupant of the Oval Office is synonymous with the branch as a whole, an indictment or criminal prosecution would be the equivalent of waging war on the executive branch. It would "interfere with the President's unique official duties, most of which cannot be performed by anyone else."9

In other words, Nixon argued that even if a subpoena did not imperil the branch, a criminal trial would. After all, a criminal defendant is required to attend trial, and the president may not be exempt from that requirement. The president is a busy person. His work running the free world doesn't allow him a lot of free time to sit in a courtroom. A criminal indictment would be unlawful, essentially, because of a scheduling conflict and the distractions that an indictment would entail.

In the end, this interesting question was never resolved. As we know from history, Nixon did not face a criminal court: he resigned to avoid impeachment and then received a pardon from President Gerald Ford. Nixon's aides had even considered having Nixon try to pardon himself, but lawyers from his Office of Legal Counsel talked him out of it.10 Article II grants the president "Power to grant Reprieves and Pardons for Offences against the United States, except in Cases of Impeachment."11 According to the memo from Nixon's OLC lawyers, this broad power does not extend to a president's right to be a "judge in his own case."

Even after the specifics of Nixon's ordeal were over, his

case continued to raise fascinating questions about the limits of executive privilege. In the American justice system, a person exonerated or pardoned for a criminal offense may still be sued in civil court, where private legal disputes between persons are settled. Years after he left office, Nixon found himself facing several civil lawsuits. One suit was filed by former US Air Force analyst A. Ernest Fitzgerald, who alleged that Nixon retaliated against him after the aide publicly broke ranks with Nixon during congressional testimony.[12]

Now the question had become whether the president could be brought to court on civil charges *after* leaving office. Nixon's lawyers made their old argument in a new way: allowing lawsuits against the president would cripple the executive branch, even if the president were out of office. After all, the president faces countless life-or-death decisions with only seconds to respond. In such crucial moments, do we really want the president's attention elsewhere, pondering whether or not he or she will be sued in retirement for actions taken in office?

The Supreme Court, in a 5–4 decision, ruled in the controversial case *Nixon v. Fitzgerald* that a president was immune from civil suits for his official acts while in office. (It's important to note that *Fitzgerald* specified an "outer perimeter" to that protection from civil suits. As women who have accused Donald Trump of sexual misconduct sue for defamation, claiming that he lied about the encounters, the court may have to determine where the "outer perimeter" sits.) However, the court said nothing about what should happen when the president commits criminal acts while in office.[13] In the 1990s, President Clinton was under investigation by an independent counsel named Kenneth Starr. As we discussed in Chapter 4, the inquiry eventually revealed that Clinton had misled investigators over his sexual relationship with White House intern Monica Lewinsky.[14]

Suddenly, the Nixon question roared back to life: Could Starr ask a grand jury to criminally indict the president? Like Nixon, President Clinton asked his Office of Legal Counsel for advice. They assured Clinton he could not be criminally indicted, agreeing with the defense that Nixon's lawyers had prepared before his resignation and citing the ruling in favor of Nixon in the *Fitzgerald* case. They argued that a president had absolute immunity from criminal indictments during office, because such an indictment would cripple the functioning of the entire executive branch.[15]

Clinton was never indicted, but the issue of whether a president could be subject to a civil suit while in office (for actions taken before becoming president) soon found itself before the Supreme Court. In the case *Clinton v. Jones*, a former government employee named Paula Jones sued Bill Clinton for sexual harassment and retaliation that had allegedly taken place when he was governor of Arkansas. When he was ordered to testify in his own defense, Clinton claimed he had a logistical conflict that would interfere with his testimony: being president. He asked the court to reschedule to a more convenient time—namely, after his term as president had ended. Clinton became the living embodiment of Nixon's once-theoretical argument: a grand jury could not indict and a prosecutor could not even depose the president without debilitating the executive branch.

Unfortunately for Clinton, the court in *Clinton v. Jones* disagreed. There was nothing about a deposition that would require a president to abandon all of his duties. They could schedule it in a way that would not harm national interests. Ultimately, careful calendaring resolved a supposedly insurmountable constitutional problem. The court rejected arguments that a president was too busy to be sued for acts committed before he or she took office.[16]

LET'S NOW return to our hypothetical, where our poor Senate minority leader is wheezing on the floor, as aides frantically pry the president off of him. Can a president who assaults someone in the Oval Office be prosecuted for such a crime, either while in office or after? The Supreme Court has never definitively answered the question. On the one hand, *Nixon v. Fitzgerald* suggests that, unlike the prime minister of Canada, the US president might be immune from such a lawsuit. Yet two other cases, *United States v. Nixon* and *Clinton v. Jones*, suggest the opposite.

The truth is, we do not know how courts would rule in such a case. However, there are a few arguments that a court might consider if such a case does reach its docket. These arguments suggest that a president is in fact liable to prosecution.

The first argument has to do with the spirit of the Constitution. All criminal cases initiated by the federal government are, because of the government's democratic nature, brought on behalf of "the people." Immunizing a president from a criminal suit would literally place the chief executive beyond the boundaries of the law and outside the control of the people. That hardly seems like what the Framers would have wanted. Kings were immune from lawsuits precisely because they were regarded as above the people. In the United States, it is the people—not their elected officials—who are sovereign. If we are governed by laws, and not individuals, then no president should be immune from a criminal indictment.

Furthermore, the notion that an indictment would debilitate the executive branch is false. It is true that a trial would be demanding on the president's time—but scheduling is a solvable problem. The White House Office of Presidential Advance (formerly known as the White House Department of Scheduling and Advance) is one of the least well-known yet most impressive teams in the building. Usually made up of a few dozen staff members, it has pulled off incredible feats. In one case, the staffers were required—with only minutes to spare, and with a snowstorm approaching—to find a secret location for President Obama and Secretary of State Clinton to meet with the Chinese premier. The nuclear briefcase, Secret Service, advance team, and traveling advisors all had to be in the same place within minutes. The travel office pulled off this logistical feat with ease. Compared to that, finding an afternoon for the president to appear in a courtroom should not be too hard to pull off.[17] Not surprisingly, when Bill Clinton was ordered to show up for that deposition, he was miraculously able to fit it into his schedule.

And there are other creative solutions for working around the burdens of scheduling. A president might be indicted, but the trial itself can be delayed until he or she is no longer in office. This would not be longer than a four- or eight-year period (depending on whether a president is reelected), leaving the possibility of legal recourse open. If it were necessary, a court might excuse a president from being present at his or her own trial but still allow the trial to take place.

Yet there is a deeper, more existential question: The Framers surely wanted the president to be held accountable, but was a criminal indictment their preferred solution for presidential misdeeds? They already gave us a powerful tool for removal whose basis was not in the criminal law. This tool is impeachment, and it is a political punishment that does not require any proof of breaking the law.

Impeachment, as we will see, is meant to be reserved for actions by a president that undermine the oath of office. For instance, disregarding a judicial order or refusing to implement and protect fundamental constitutional rights are actions that I believe to be distinct from violations of the criminal law. An incident like the "Shawinigan handshake" might not rise to the level of a constitutional offense, even if it is an illegal act. It is important, therefore, that a president can be criminally indicted to ensure that assaults and other crimes do not go unpunished simply because the perpetrator occupies the nation's highest office.

If, as president, you find yourself committing a crime while in office, perhaps you should not be there in the first place. If it does happen, however, you can likely find a lawyer to try to argue that you are immune from prosecution. But, as your constitutional advisor, my role is to tell you what the law requires. As I see it, you can be indicted. Despite how powerful your office may seem, you are not above the law.

14

Federalism

PRINCIPLE: Local officials can resist the unconstitutional policies of an errant president. Federalism will rightly limit your power.

> *"The States . . . have the right, and are in duty bound . . .*
> *[to arrest] the progress of the evil, and [to maintain]*
> *within their respective limits, the authorities, rights and*
> *liberties appertaining to them."*
>
> —JAMES MADISON[1]

One October day in 1798, two American statesmen met in Virginia to plot a resistance movement against President Adams. It was a risky undertaking, since both men were current or former public employees high up in the federal government. But they had both watched in horror while the Alien and Sedition Acts—which criminalized criticism of the president and revoked the rights of foreign nationals to due process—sped through Congress and were signed by Adams. Each felt compelled to action. For weeks, the two plotted their next steps in a series of private letters. They complained that the sitting president was a royalist who never distanced himself from the system of monarchy, hinting that he saw himself as the chief royal. At last, they agreed on a plan: while a resistance movement from within the federal government would be impossible, they might have a chance of resisting Adams from farther away. And so, Thomas Jefferson and James Madison set out to work against the president of the United States.[2]

Today, resistance is a popular watchword, and rightfully so. When the president fails to uphold and protect the Constitution, citizens and other public officials must themselves act as guardians of the document. Federalism—the concept enshrined in the Tenth Amendment that states retain powers independent of the federal government—can be a critical tool in the arsenal of resistance. There could hardly be a better place to look for precedent for such constitutional action than at what Jefferson and Madison did: the sitting vice president and a prominent former congressman convened their own plan to challenge a sitting president who was acting unconstitutionally. In so doing, they not only showed us how resistance is patriotic, but they also showed us how to do it.

Specifically, their plot revolved around the Tenth Amendment. It is the provision in the Constitution clarifying that "The powers not delegated to the United States by the Constitution, nor prohibited by it to the States, are reserved to the States respectively, or to the people."[3] Jefferson and Madison believed that any federal law, such as the Alien and Sedition Acts, that undermined the people's basic constitutional rights should not be imposed on the states. Thus, they would try to appeal to state governments to demonstrate that the Alien and Sedition Acts were unconstitutional.

At Jefferson's home in Monticello, both he and Madison reasoned that in order to stop the new laws, state legislatures should declare them unconstitutional and should find legal ways to protect the rights of those prosecuted under them. Jefferson, going beyond Madison, even believed that the states should "nullify" unconstitutional federal laws by refusing to enforce them. For the next month, the two men worked feverishly, writing letters to state leaders and hosting delegates from state legislatures, trying to drum up support for the idea.

Finally, they gathered up interest in the idea among leaders of two key states: Virginia, then the largest and most politically influential state in the union, and Kentucky. In the capitals of those two states, each legislature passed a similar resolution. In what became known as the Kentucky[4] and Virginia resolutions, passed in November and December 1798, respectively, the two states declared that the Alien and Sedition Acts were unconstitutional, citing the First Amendment's freedom of the press and the Tenth Amendment's limitation on federal power.[5] The Virginia resolution calls on other states to join it in "maintaining the Authorities, Rights, and Liberties, referred to the States respectively, or to the people," although it does not specify how it will maintain them.[6] A draft of Kentucky's resolution, written by Jefferson, goes further, declaring a "nullification" of the laws.[7]

The Virginia and Kentucky resolutions were effective in halting a tyrannical law that blatantly violated the First Amendment guarantee of freedom of speech and press. Although they did not end the Alien and Sedition Acts overnight, they sent a powerful signal to citizens of the young country that a vocal minority would not accept unconstitutional federal action. Aided by the opposition to the acts that the resolutions spurred, Jefferson defeated Adams in the presidential election of 1800, and the Sedition Act was allowed to expire in 1801.

The resolutions, however, later backfired in a serious way that Madison never intended. In the 1820s and the 1830s, as the country moved closer to civil war, secessionists and advocates for slavery began to draw on the Kentucky and Virginia resolutions as a rationale for seceding from the union. One of them was Senator John C. Calhoun of South Carolina, who expressed the belief that "the right of judging . . . is an essential attribute of sovereignty, of which the States cannot be divested without losing their sovereignty itself."[8] To address his concern about sovereignty—the authority of states to govern themselves—Calhoun focused in on one word in Jefferson's draft of the Kentucky resolution: nullification. Jefferson had written that since the Alien and Sedition Acts were unconstitutional, they were "therefore not law, but utterly void and of no force."[9] Calhoun used the concept of nullification to argue that states could essentially veto federal law. Moreover, Calhoun was arguing that the states remained sovereign under the Constitution, and that they could invalidate any federal law they viewed as unconstitutional. South Carolina used that idea when it sought to invalidate a federal tariff or tax on imports.[10]

Now an elder statesman, Madison was horrified to learn that Calhoun had drawn on his and Jefferson's ideas to support secession from the union.[11] Jefferson used the term *nullify* in his draft of the Kentucky resolution, in explaining what the state sought to do to the censorship law.[12] But Madison had avoided such language in the Virginia resolution. It's important for us to see why he was right to do so. While the Kentucky resolution went so far as to claim that federal law could be declared "void" and "nullified" (and thus invalidated), Madison's Virginia resolution only claimed that the states should use their influence to persuade Congress to change such unconstitutional laws. (If that did not succeed, Madison implied the states should work together to pass a constitutional amendment.) He also opened the door to legal ways that states might protect those prosecuted under the acts. This was a nuanced yet crucial difference that reflects the legitimacy of federal supremacy, using what Madison called means "strictly within the limits of the Constitution."[13]

Near the end of his life, Madison explicitly disavowed Calhoun's view of the Constitution: "It follows from no view of the subject, that a nullification of a law of the U.S. can as is now contended, belong rightfully to a single State. . . . A plainer contradiction in terms, or a more fatal inlet of anarchy cannot be imagined."[14] In my view, Madison's resistance to Adams had been about the right of the states to resist unconstitutional laws by speaking out and encouraging Congress to change them. It was never an attack like Calhoun's on the power of the federal government itself. Calhoun thought that a single state had the right to resist or nullify federal law. By contrast, Madison rejected nullification, and thought resistance to federal law was only justified on the grounds of protecting individual rights. It is the tradition of Madison's Virginia resolution—limited and legal resistance to unconstitutional federal action—rather than the Kentucky resolution's and Calhoun's tradition of nullification, that I believe should guide government officials seeking to resist an errant president.

Not surprisingly, Madison's plea against nullification was conveniently ignored by defenders of slavery and by segregationists (and also by many later history books, which still teach the Virginia and Kentucky resolutions as the Confederacy's basis for secession). In the twentieth century, the nullification strategy was revived in the effort to resist the racial integration of public schools. It was especially popular among those who tried to impeach Chief Justice Earl Warren. These defenders of "states' rights" invoked Calhoun's nullification doctrine, and thus indirectly Jefferson's draft of the Kentucky Resolution, to argue against the Fourteenth Amendment and, later, the attempts by the federal government to enforce it.[15]

THAT HISTORY has damaged our sense of how important and necessary the Virginia resolution really is—and what a useful precedent it can set for resistance to unconstitutional acts that threaten civil liberties. Imagine if Earl Warren, governor of California in the 1940s and 1950s, had followed Madison's example by publicly declaring that building internment camps in his state was unconstitutional and should be resisted. What if he had tried to convince California's congressional delegation to pass a federal law prohibiting internment on the basis of ethnicity or national origin? Such actions could have mobilized public opposition to internment and put pressure on President Roosevelt and Congress to respect the civil rights of Japanese Americans.

In our own time, the moment has arrived to follow the example of the Virginia resolution in defense of civil liberties and the Fourteenth Amendment. Since at least the 1990s, the number of undocumented immigrants in the United States has grown.[16] Throughout Democratic and Republican administrations alike, the federal government has largely treated this issue the same way: devoting the resources of federal agencies, like Immigration and Customs Enforcement, to deporting only undocumented residents who are violent criminals or who pose a threat to their community. The law-abiding and children have generally been spared. The reason for this decision was not based in weakness or mercy, but evidence.

Exhaustive economic research has shown, over and over, that immigrants are a net benefit to American society and do not "take" American jobs.[17] Instead, they create more businesses and take more entrepreneurial risks.[18]

The same research has shown, again repeatedly, that documented or undocumented immigrants are more law-abiding on average than the citizen population. When the federal government has tried deporting otherwise law-abiding undocumented immigrants, some cities have seen criminal activity increase, increasing the burden on local police.[19] This is because undocumented residents stop reporting crimes to the police; if there's a risk of being deported, why trust your neighborhood police officer?

There is one more reason for the previous bipartisan consensus about the appropriate government response to undocumented immigrants. The bedrock of our society and civics is the sanctity of the American family. Many undocumented adults—coaching little league, contributing to the local economy, even sometimes serving in law enforcement—themselves have children who are American citizens. To deport these individuals would mean tearing their families apart.

Miguel Marquez understood intimately how important these policies were to keeping families together. Marquez's parents had emigrated from Mexico, and neither had received much formal education, but he went on to earn degrees from Berkeley and Harvard. His gratitude for programs like Head Start convinced him to pursue public service. In 2012, Marquez became a judge, also becoming the first Latino to sit on California's Sixth District Court of Appeals.[20]

After four years, though, Marquez decided to take a role that would give him the ability to be proactive in public service, rather than waiting for cases to come to him. He resigned a high-level judgeship to go back to working in Santa Clara government as the chief operating officer. This job put him in a position to solve pressing problems in his county—including threats to the rights of undocumented people living there.

The chance to make change came quickly. In the first year of the Trump administration, the federal government changed its immigration policy to engage in what experts describe as mass deportation.[21] One major change was reinstating the Secure Communities program, which began under President Bush in 2008 and continued under the Obama administration until he discontinued it in 2014.[22] Now that the program has been revived, Immigration and Customs Enforcement (ICE) asks local police departments to hold suspected undocumented individuals in custody for longer periods of time if they are even suspected of being undocumented, so that ICE agents can show up in time to detain them. President Trump also signed executive order 13768, which threatened to revoke any federal funds shared with "sanctuary cities"—cities, towns, and counties where local law enforcement doesn't cooperate with ICE's deportation plans.[23]

Now granted more leeway in deportations, ICE is having a real impact on ordinary families, looking for reasons to deport otherwise law-abiding residents. One ICE tactic is to wait for undocumented adults at courthouses, as people stop in for routine summons like traffic tickets.[24] There are cases of ICE agents stalking people at motels and churches, and even a case of agents stalking undocumented parents who had brought their infant to the hospital.[25] They have also intervened against state and local traditions that lend support to the undocumented.

Marquez knew full well that Santa Clara County, where he still lives, has a large Latino population and a long history of not cooperating with ICE requests,[26] and so was at risk of being targeted.[27] As a result, he worked with his community to help Santa Clara refuse to cooperate with ICE deportations. Marquez's plan was in the tradition of Jefferson and Madison—local resistance to federal overreach.

But was it legal? Yes.

Under the Tenth Amendment, policing is mostly a local matter, and local governments need not always take orders from the federal government. In a Supreme Court case in 1997 called *Printz v. United States*, the court ruled that, generally speaking, the federal government could not force local officials to do the government's bidding.[28] Nothing in *Printz* took away from the requirement that states need to respect the Fourteenth Amendment—including its guarantee of equal protection—and other minimum federal standards protecting individuals. In other words, the ruling did not at all endorse the nullification doctrine expressed in the Kentucky resolution. *Printz*, however, did give state officials the tools to resist being commanded or "commandeered" by the federal government, and it enabled the kind of constitutional resistance Madison endorsed.

Such commands by the federal government include drastic funding threats like the one Trump made, which, in a case called *South Dakota v. Dole*, the court identified as a form of coercion. In *Dole*, the court ruled that the federal government could incentivize local governments by rewarding them with grants—and could even pressure them with the threat of withdrawing some money. However, the threat of revoking all or nearly all federal funds as punishment for not obeying was unlawful.[29]

In February 2017, Marquez helped lead Santa Clara County in bringing a lawsuit against the federal government in San Francisco's federal district court. They relied largely on the Tenth Amendment and "states' rights" jurisprudence pioneered by conservative judges in cases like *Printz* and *Dole*. Marquez, like Madison before him, sought to use local power to protect individual rights. Marquez and his colleagues believed they could use it to protect the civil rights of those suspected of being undocumented in cities that sought to shield them from federal overreach. In court, lawyers for the federal government argued the law was not coercive and states had to comply. But Marquez argued that Trump's orders constituted coercion: because Trump threatened to revoke all funds, and not some grants, he believed it was a clear violation of the court's holding in *Dole*.

In April, Judge William Orrick issued his ruling: Marquez and his colleagues won. Orrick ruled that the executive order violated the requirements of federalism as made clear in the *Printz* and *Dole* cases.[30] The federal government could not threaten to revoke the funds of "sanctuary cities." As of this writing, the case is subject to review. But whatever future courts say, Marquez made his stand and vindicated the original tradition of Jefferson and Madison: resisting federal tyranny by appealing to state and local power.

———

MARQUEZ'S STORY is a powerful example of the wisdom of Madison's Alien and Sedition strategy of resisting an unconstitutional policy by invoking the Tenth Amendment. It's also a good example of how "states' rights" is not just a shorthand for bad or bigoted policy, but can be used to defend civil liberties.

Marquez's strategy is a controversial way to resist, though, because the method doesn't guarantee anything about the morality of the cause. Seemingly similar in principle to the Kentucky and Virginia resolutions, the "Southern Manifesto," signed by nineteen senators and eighty-two representatives in

1956, declared that the *Brown v. Board* decision desegregating public schools violated the Constitution. The Manifesto also pledged resistance, writing, "we commend the motives of those states which have declared the intention to resist forced integration by any lawful means."[31] That sounds a lot like Marquez's strategy. Can we distinguish Marquez from the southern segregationists?

Yes. It is important to see that Marquez is not opposing a role for the federal government in rights protection. Rather, he argued that when the federal government itself violates rights like due process and equal protection of the law, state resistance is called for. This is more in line with Madison's version of legal resistance than it is with Jefferson and Calhoun's idea of nullification. We can distinguish the two by remembering how Madison hoped his resistance would lead the federal government to change its policies and begin to respect the rights of the people, such as the right to free speech. Madison acknowledged that the federal government had legitimate power, but that it was exercising that power unconstitutionally. In contrast, Calhoun and later the signers of the Southern Manifesto were rejecting the whole idea of strong federal power to enforce civil rights—they weren't just opposing one specific policy. Marquez's strategy is squarely in the tradition of Madison, not that of defenders of segregation and slavery.

Marquez's example shows that federalism can be used to defend civil rights instead of oppose them. The Tenth Amendment—just one sentence long—talks about the rights "reserved to the states" as well as to "the people."[32] The idea in the text is that the state governments should be used to defend individual rights. Further, states cannot be compelled to violate constitutional rights. For example, under the Secure Communities program, states are being asked to violate the due process rights of undocumented people. Resisting this kind of program upholds constitutional rights; resisting civil rights protections, however, undermines them.

As president, you might be frustrated by the constitutional right of the states and local governments to resist your policies. But you are not the only public official who takes an oath to uphold the Constitution: if you fail in that duty, those officials have obligations to resist you. George Washington told us in his second inaugural that a president must respect rather than despise officials who challenge a president whose actions violate the oath. Indeed, Washington, a Virginian like Madison, might have been proud of the creative "upbraidings" delivered by officials like Marquez.[33]

15

The Congressional Check and Impeachment

PRINCIPLE: The president can be impeached for, and convicted of, "Treason, Bribery, or other high Crimes and Misdemeanors." You should be removed if you violate your oath—even if you commit no criminal act.

"The subjects of its jurisdiction [of impeachment] are those offenses which proceed from the misconduct of public men, or, in other words, from the abuse or violation of some public trust."

—ALEXANDER HAMILTON[1]

I have spent the bulk of this book talking about what the oath of office, Article II of the Constitution, and the Bill of Rights oblige you to do as president. We have seen ways to stop a president who refuses to abide by the oath of office. But there is a severe and rarely used check on a president who continually disregards the oath and imperils the nation: impeachment by the House of Representatives, and then conviction and removal from office by the Senate.[2]

As president, you should be guided by President Washington's second inaugural, in which he demanded "constitutional punishment" if he disregarded the oath.[3] The most powerful punishment for a president who recklessly disregards the oath is neither indictment nor resistance from state or local governments, although those are important ways of stopping an errant president. It is removal from office by Congress, through the impeachment procedure outlined in Article I of the Constitution, that gives Congress sole discretion about when and whether to remove a president.[4] That procedure runs like this: first, the House of Representatives has to take a majority vote to impeach the president. Then, the president is tried before the Senate, which has to take a two-thirds vote in order to remove the president.

Because the decision is solely in the hands of Congress, it is not surprising that presidents might worry about abusing the procedure for partisan purposes. One president who felt that way was John F. Kennedy, who in 1957—four years before he took the oath of office—won a Pulitzer Prize for a book called *Profiles in Courage*.[5] (Later, his aide, Ted Sorensen, would admit he had ghost-written it.) One chapter profiles Senator Edmund Ross of Kansas, a Republican who voted not to convict President Andrew Johnson after Johnson was impeached for accusations of illegally firing his secretary of war.[6] In Kennedy's view, the impeachment proceedings were merely a partisan affair. To him, Ross, who broke with his party, was a nonpartisan hero.

Kennedy was both right and wrong. He was right that the Senate focused on a frivolous reason for impeaching Johnson. In fact, the Tenure of Office Act that Johnson was accused of violating is today seen as unconstitutional itself, meaning that Johnson was impeached for conduct that was likely within his authority as president.[7] But Kennedy was wrong to think that there was no good reason for Johnson's impeachment and that those who opposed Johnson's removal should be lauded. Rightly understood, impeachment is a decision about a failure to live up to the oath. Distinct from a legal process, it is the primary example of what Washington called "constitutional punishment" in his second inaugural address.

"Impeachment" is described in Article II as a punishment for "Treason, Bribery, or other high Crimes and Misdemeanors."[8] Can a president be impeached for a "high crime," even if he or she commits no statutory crime? Can the people use impeachment to remove a president who disregards the oath?

———

THERE HAVE been two impeachments of presidents in American history.[9] Interestingly, both procedures imagined the "high crimes" as severe legal violations. The legal advisors to Congress in both the nineteenth-century case of President Johnson and the twentieth-century case of President Clinton focused on legal materials and violations of statutes. Both groups assumed the process should be couched in legal terms, not political ones.

One complication to those approaches, however, is that there is no category of "high crime" in the criminal law.[10] The phrase was commonly used as a basis for impeaching advisors to British kings. The king, of course, could not be impeached, but advisors could be removed by Parliament through impeachment for a variety of so-called "high crimes." For instance, one advisor was removed for giving out a military commission to a friend. Another was impeached for giving bad advice.[11] These were not violations of the law, but Parliament believed they merited impeachment because they fundamentally violated the duties of the king's ministers.

When the Framers wrote a process of impeachment for "high crimes" into the Constitution, they clearly meant to allow for removal for acts distinct from criminal violations. Removing a president is consistent with our constitutional process, even if it is only to be used in dire circumstances. The "high crimes" referred to by the Constitution would be committed against "the people" by the head of state, the president, acknowledging that the president is not above the law. Alexander Hamilton wrote in the *Federalist Papers*:

> The subjects of its [impeachment's] jurisdiction are those offenses which proceed from the misconduct of public men, or, in other words, from the abuse or violation of some public trust. They are of a nature which may with peculiar propriety be denominated political, as they relate chiefly to injuries done immediately to the society itself.[12]

In other words, the scope of impeachable offenses exceeds mere crimes: it encompasses violations of the duty to the people and a lack of respect for the Constitution.[13]

The process for impeachment outlined in Article I is not a legal process. The president is subject to "indictment" (the bringing of charges) by the House of Representatives, and faces a "trial" in the Senate.[14] Those words mimic the criminal justice process, but they are distinct from the proceedings in a court of law. There is not an independent prosecutor charged with law enforcement in this process. There is not a jury of average citizens. Elected officials will ultimately vote on impeachment and removal.

Andrew Johnson's impeachment in 1868 was the first presidential impeachment in American history. The impeachment proceedings supposedly centered on his violation of the law when he fired his secretary of war.[15] But what was really on trial was Johnson's political agenda. The Radical Republicans—a group of pro–civil rights legislators in Congress[16]—thought he was not acting fast enough to grant former slaves rights after they were freed. In 1865 and 1866, states and towns in the South passed a series of "black codes" to essentially keep African Americans in bondage after slavery was abolished. African Americans were denied rights to employment, property, and voting. In 1866, Congress passed a Civil Rights Act that would end these discriminatory laws. Johnson vetoed it, claiming the bill went beyond the scope of government power and discriminated against whites in favor of black Americans, among a host of other reasons.[17]

Congress overturned Johnson's veto. Then, to make perfectly clear how wrong Johnson was, Congress passed the Fourteenth Amendment just two months later, sending it out to ratification by the states, forever altering the structure and meaning of the United States Constitution.[18] The guarantee of equal protection of the law and due process would apply to all persons throughout the United States, limiting how any locality, including the southern states, could treat former slaves or any person. Johnson opposed this amendment too, deliberately refusing to enforce the Reconstruction laws, especially the one requiring southern states to allow African Americans to vote, which would give the amendment a better chance at being ratified.[19]

Johnson found himself at the helm of the republic with a Congress that had repeatedly fought him and won. Congress was committed to a civil rights agenda that Johnson rejected. It had a vision of America enshrined in the Fourteenth Amendment and civil rights for all, while Johnson clung to an older vision of the pre–Civil War South, where African Americans were second-class citizens, if even considered citizens at all.

When Johnson met with leading abolitionist Frederick Douglass in February of 1866, the two men's different visions of America came to a head. Douglass challenged the president to support Reconstruction and the end of discrimination in voting. Johnson retorted that African Americans who could not find equal treatment in the South should migrate and go elsewhere. He accused Douglass of not recognizing that Johnson was an ally, not an opponent.[20]

Douglass attempted to reason with Johnson, stressing that the president was not doing enough to protect the civil rights of African Americans. The legal end of slavery would mean nothing if Johnson did not ensure that African Americans had rights to vote and to work free from discrimination. Douglass described how the master-slave relationship in the United States had to be transformed through the vote and federal protections: If "his master then decides for him where he shall go, where he shall work, how much he shall work—in fact, he is divested of all political power. He is absolutely in the hands of those men."[21]

The meeting did not end well. Both men left pledging to take their case to the American people. "The president sends us to the people, and we go to the people," Douglass concluded. Johnson did not back down: "Yes, sir, I have great faith in the people. I believe they will do what is right." Johnson's blatant racism surfaced shortly after Douglass left, as Johnson reportedly told his aide: "Douglass; he's just like any other n***** and he would sooner cut a white man's throat than not."[22]

That battle of words was followed up with a barnstorming tour by Johnson, traversing the Northeast and Midwest from August to September of 1866 to pledge his support for white supremacy. He took his case to the people, declaring that "there are many white people in this country that need emancipation. . . . Let white men stand erect and free." [23] He went on to attack the supporters of African American suffrage. Johnson's speeches drew strong backlash, and eventually helped the Radical Republicans capture a veto-proof majority in Congress in the 1866 elections. By 1868, the House of Representatives had enough votes for impeachment. The Radical Republicans thought, for good reason, that the president was sympathetic to the former order of white supremacy. They also feared Johnson would not implement the new constitutional guarantee of rights to all people within the United States.

But in drafting the articles of impeachment, the congressmen made a crucial error. Rather than putting their grievances up front, the Republicans focused on a technical and legal issue that they believed constituted the "high crime" necessary for impeachment. In this case, the alleged high crime was Johnson's maneuvering to fire a cabinet official, which they alleged violated the Tenure of Office Act, a bill that limited the president's ability to fire certain officeholders without consent of the Senate.[24] Out of all the grievances against Johnson, this was near the bottom. But the Republicans decided that they needed to make their impeachment and trial look legal and politically neutral. This was a mistake: the firing was arguably legal (since the act declaring it illegal was likely unconstitutional itself). But even if the firing were illegal, violating it would at best be a minor crime. Everyone observing the proceedings knew this charge was a ruse.

In 1866, Douglass denounced Johnson in an article published in the *Atlantic Monthly* magazine, one of the most influential periodicals of its time. This article was the guide to the impeachment that Congress should have used. He called Johnson's refusal to support civil rights "treacherous."[25] Calling the president's actions "treacherous" was not a legal accusation, of course, but it was a political accusation that fit with the language of the Constitution's impeachment provision. That standard, as I suggested, is the right one, even if it is not the same as one that would be required in a courtroom.

An impeachment using Douglass's criterion of "treachery" would have focused on Johnson's failure to "take care" that the civil rights of African Americans were protected.[26] That would have been more honest and transparent, since it would have refocused the impeachment process around an actual "high crime," rather than resorting to a legal sham. As I see it, Johnson's failure to enforce the Thirteenth Amendment and implement the civil rights agenda of Congress ultimately led to long and disastrous neglect for freed blacks in the post–Civil War South—giving Congress sufficient grounds for impeachment. Had Johnson refused to implement a less significant piece of legislation, such drastic Congressional action might not have been warranted. But he blocked the execution of the core laws of the post–Civil War Constitution. Faced with such a blatant violation of presidential duty, Congress was obligated to impeach him for that high crime, not for the arguably legal firing of a cabinet official.

There has only been one other impeachment and trial of a president in American history. One hundred thirty years after Johnson's impeachment, Bill Clinton was impeached for lying about sexual relations with White House intern Monica Lewinsky. In the course of an investigation about financial impropriety involving a land deal and a sexual harassment lawsuit by Paula Jones, it was discovered that Clinton had an affair with an intern. When asked about it under oath, he denied having a sexual relationship with Lewinsky.[27]

The articles of impeachment brought against Clinton accused him of perjury—lying under oath—and obstruction of justice. Did these actions constitute a "high crime"? Although the House impeached him, the Senate ultimately did not remove Clinton, partly under the belief that Clinton's perjury didn't constitute a violation of the Constitution. On the count of perjury, fifty-five senators (including ten Republicans) voted not guilty. On the count of obstruction of justice, the vote was a fifty-to-fifty split. Neither vote rose to the two-thirds majority required for removal.[28] The Senate, it seems, determined that Clinton's perjury and obstruction of justice did not rise to the level of "high crimes." After the vote, Senator Susan Collins, for example, said that she did not want to "exonerate"[29] Clinton on the facts, but that his actions did not constitute impeachable offenses.

However, the question of whether obstruction of justice is an impeachable offense is not easily answered. In fact, one of the articles of impeachment against Nixon noted his obstruction of justice in covering up Watergate. Although the Constitution's text does not mention obstruction of justice, obstruction undermines the ideal of the rule of law central to the distinction between a president and a monarch—a distinction the Framers took great lengths to emphasize in the Constitution. Further, a president who conspires to commit crimes violates the values of the oath of office by placing him- or herself at odds with equal treatment under the law. So take note, future presidents: Clinton and Nixon avoided punishment when they were accused of obstruction of justice. But if you do the same, the outcome might be different.

Though the perjury and obstruction charges against Clinton did not succeed, there is another argument for why Clinton should, in fact, have been impeached and removed. It was made by Ann Coulter, the right-wing provocateur. In a book published in 2002,[30] she showed that in British history, a "high crime" was political, not legal. She urged the Senate to make the case that Clinton violated the "public trust," in Hamilton's sense. She argued that Clinton's "high crime" was sexual relations in the Oval Office.[31]

Coulter was right about the history, but she was wrong in explaining how it translates into our Constitution. While sexual immorality might have in fact been a crime in monarchical England, the Founders were referring to offenses against our Constitution. The burden should have been on the Senate to show that a political crime occurred, as an offense to the democratic rights of the people, not to public decency. No accusation was made that Clinton offended the Bill of Rights or any other part of the Constitution.

———

IMPEACHMENT IS a political process, but that does not mean it should be deployed on a president who is merely unpopular, even dreadfully so. In parliamentary systems, Parliament may vote "no confidence" if it feels that the prime minister is not performing well.[32] Our system, however, is different. The legislative and executive branches are separate and equal, and allowing Congress to recall the president any time they do not approve of him or her would subsume the executive under the legislature. Presidents elected from a party different from the one in control in Congress would face the process of impeachment immediately upon their election, undermining the equality of the branches the Framers so carefully built into the Constitution.

Requiring Congress to demonstrate that the president has committed major constitutional violations is not the same as a no-confidence vote in Parliament. It would require demonstration of major offenses against the people that go beyond those like the alleged crimes of Bill Clinton. Ultimately, since Congress is a representative body, it is up to the people to determine what makes up such a constitutional offense, and to demand that this power not be used for petty partisan politics. The question is not whether a particular act is a crime; it is whether it is a "high crime." Undermining the integrity of our electoral process, abusing the trust of your governmental office to personally profit, or deliberately issuing executive orders that flout the Constitution's requirements, for example, certainly would constitute such "high crimes."

One important counterargument: a "political" impeachment, one brought in the absence of a literal crime, might violate basic norms of the rule of law. The Constitution, for instance, bans laws that single out individuals or punish people retroactively.[33] According to Charles Black, a law professor who wrote a seminal guide to impeachment in the 1970s, those requirements should apply to the impeachment process as well.[34]

I disagree. Those protections are in place for criminal violations, not for firing the nation's most powerful public official. Unlike for criminal punishments, there is no jail time that comes with impeachment; Article I limits the punishment of impeachment to removal from office and disqualification from holding public office in the future.[35] In contrast, an impeachment by the House and conviction by the Senate is a recognition by the people's representatives that the president violated the duty to uphold the oath and the people's trust.

In sum, even if impeachment mimics a legal process, it is not one. It is entirely left to the Congress—a political body—

to proceed with it. We must recognize that this political body is not bound by a legal or criminal standard. Instead, the role of impeachment is to ensure that the oath is upheld. Pretending otherwise only confuses criminal law with the fundamental duty of the president to uphold the Constitution.

LET US get specific about what a high crime might be. Washington was legendary for his honesty, but the truth is, he was far from perfect. In 1758, Washington ran for office in the Virginia House of Burgesses. To win the delegates' favor, he purchased for them 160 gallons of rum, wine, beer, and cider. Even though acts like these were common at the time, Virginia quickly realized it was a problem, and soon passed a law banning such practices, understanding that such gifts could become a handy way to buy off votes. Winning elections should be a contest of ideas, not of who has the most spirits—or wealth.[36]

Washington later took this lesson with him: the Framers could not have been clearer about the problems of corruption and moneyed interests. At the root of this concern was the fear of a new aristocracy. Aristocracy was fundamentally offensive to the idea of an American society based on freedom and mobility. Jefferson, for example, hoped to "crush in its birth the aristocracy of our monied corporations which dare already to challenge our government to a trial of strength, and to bid defiance to the laws of their country."[37] Madison cautioned that a government "resting on the minority is an aristocracy, not a Republic."[38] All this may seem ironic, in view of the political reality of the era—a racially hierarchical world in which effectively only propertied white males could partake in government. But despite the Framers' elitism, they still point to important political principles that can be of use in a more inclusive polity.

As with everything the Framers worried about, these concerns stemmed from the experience of Britain. Under monarchies, kings and their courts isolated themselves from the public. They pursued the financial interests of the aristocracy at the expense of the people. Corruption had long been the hallmark of royalty, with leaders often acting for personal financial benefit. They used foreign policy to enrich themselves and their families.[39]

To avoid these issues, the Framers placed two main provisions in the Constitution to guard against corruption—including, and especially, corruption by a sitting president. The first provision, found in Article I, was a ban on royal titles—such as conferring a lordship or a knightship on a loyal constituent, a practice kings and queens long used.[40] The second provision in the Constitution banned the receipt of "emoluments"—a term meaning benefits or payments. Article I banned emoluments from foreign governments, and Article II from domestic ones.[41]

Both provisions included the president, as it was the office most susceptible to resembling monarchy. The Emoluments Clauses in particular highlighted the Framers' greater concern: a president, given the power of the office, might be more interested in selling favors than serving the public good. Even if a president was loyal to the country and its people, the Framers understood that power corrupts, and money is the driver of that corruption. The Emoluments Clauses were the clearest example we have that the Framers wanted a government free from the influence of money or gifts.

The mythos of Washington as someone who could not tell a lie about chopping down a cherry tree is meant to portray him as a leader beyond fault. But the Washington who used apple cider to influence votes suggests a truer picture: the Framers weren't angels—and that's the point. They had a keen understanding of human nature, worrying that a self-dealing government would be out of touch with its people and risk its own destruction. The reality is far more complicated. Corruption, broadly construed, has been protected by the Constitution in various ways throughout the American tradition. If a president wanted a vote in Congress to go a certain way, he or she could entice members with lucrative positions or patronage in government in exchange for their vote.

When a president's corruption goes so far as to violate one of the Emoluments Clauses, there is good reason to see it as a "high crime." In Washington's first inaugural address, he claimed that he would take no salary or other "emolument." As commanding general in the Revolutionary War, he agreed that a salary would tarnish his pure patriotic motivation. He claimed the same as president, trying to refuse his salary. But Congress, carrying out the Constitution's provision for a presidential salary, made sure that he received one.[42] Perhaps he wanted to stay clear of the kind of corruption he had engaged in when running for office in Virginia. In fact, his challenge to give him "constitutional punishment" suggests he never forgot the earlier apple cider error, and wanted it never to be repeated by a future president.[43] It also suggests that the constitutional process of impeachment—apart from the question of whether judicial intervention is needed—is the appropriate recourse for addressing violations of the Emoluments Clauses.

In the spirit of Washington, every modern president except for Donald Trump has divested their assets or put them in a blind trust. This guards against the risk that they might benefit (directly or indirectly) from foreign or domestic government actions they play a role in while serving as president.[44] Famously, President Carter even sold his peanut farm to avoid any possible financial conflicts of interest.[45] Even apart from the question of whether failing to divest assets is a legal crime, Washington's address makes it clear that it violates the anticorruption ethos that permeates the Constitution, and thus could be an impeachable offense. The Framers worried about a president who would act like a king, and that is why the Foreign Emoluments Clause is placed in the midst of the prohibition on royal titles. The trappings of monarchy, not just its institutionalization, are outlawed because a president's motivation is supposed to be about the common good.

Finally, what about unconstitutional actions a president takes or unconstitutional laws a president signs? If *Korematsu* was the wrong decision, should President Roosevelt have been impeached for his role in the internment? What, then, of every Supreme Court ruling that has gone against a president, such as Justice Jackson's rebuke to President Truman in *Youngstown*? Of course, many presidents have enacted or supported policies that were later ruled unconstitutional. But there is a difference between specific policies that might violate the Constitution and a continual disregard or disrespect for the oath of office. Presidents are not elected with a mandate to act however they wish. As we've seen, the oath requires respect for the limits of what a president can do and the obligations that come with the power that is granted to him or her. A president who continually defies those demands—whether by engaging in torture, taking repeated action based on prejudice, or fundamentally violating the Constitution in the ways we've seen in this guide—should not just be stopped in court. Such a president should be removed by Congress through impeachment proceedings. If you, as president, show contempt for the oath or the Constitution, merely reciting or reading them without internalizing their demands, you too should be removed from office.

In 1974, President Richard Nixon faced a looming impeachment from the House of Representatives for his role in the Watergate scandal, which ultimately led to his resignation. The House Judiciary Committee considered and ultimately approved three articles of impeachment against Nixon, with seven Republicans and all twenty-one Democrats voting for at least one of the articles. Representative Robert McClory from Illinois was one of those Republicans. He voted yes on two of the articles of impeachment, and implored the Committee to vote for constitutional reasons, not partisan ones. As he put it, "if we are to establish our proceedings as a guide for future presidents, we should speak in terms of the Constitution and specifically in terms of the President's oath and his obligation under the Constitution. . . . It will aid future presidents to know this Congress and this House Judiciary Committee will hold them to an oath of office and an obligation to 'take care' to see that the laws are 'faithfully executed.'"[46] McClory is right: it is imperative that future presidents know there will be consequences if they disregard the oath and the limits on the office it requires.

In America, we have presidents, not kings. As president, your oath of office makes it incumbent on you to know the difference and not abuse the office by violating constitutional principles or securing personal financial gain. The public has entrusted you to uphold your office responsibly. Use this trust well, or you might soon find yourself out of a job.

Conclusion

S o, after reading this guide, are you ready to be president? The answer will depend on how well you've internalized the principles we've discussed.

As president, you must serve as one of the interpreters of the Constitution. You must decide where the limits of your office lie and what you are allowed and expected to do. You should be guided by the primary constitutional values we have stressed: the rule of law, which constrains even the most powerful members of our society; liberties, such as those of speech, religion, and privacy; and equal protection under law. Your first task must be to internalize your basic responsibilities: make policy without bigotry or religious bias, respect free speech, accept limits on your power to enforce the law, and strike a balance between your role as commander in chief and Congress's right to declare war. If you fail to do so, the other branches might take action. If need be, the courts can stop you from advancing unconstitutional policies. If you really fail to heed my warnings, Congress can impeach you.

But you shouldn't wait until that crisis moment to reflect on your office. You need to start now. Think about what you would want to accomplish as president and how to do it within the constraints of the Constitution. Think about how you can best promote the values of the document: by respecting dissenters, embracing your own religion while also embracing religious pluralism, or advancing dignity by rejecting torture. You should also recognize the failures of past presidents to live up to these ideals, whether by promoting slavery, sanctioning Jim Crow laws, or advocating for Chinese exclusion. Keep in mind the awful consequences of previous presidents' violations. History is a harsh judge.

You can avoid these pitfalls by carefully considering constitutional text, principles, and cases. You should use your bully pulpit to encourage the nation to read the Constitution and to internalize its lessons. This will advance both your citizens' understanding of and your own compliance with the document. Of course, understanding the Constitution alone does not ensure that you will be a great president. However, it is a necessary start to ensure that, at the very least, you do not undermine the oath of office, and that ideally, you go beyond what is required, continually promoting the best ideals of our founding document.

Rituals often become dull and lose their meaning. There is a risk that without a deep understanding of the oath of office, it will become a vacant utterance performed once every four years. So, when you are ready to raise your right hand and say the words "I do solemnly swear," you should understand these words deeply and be ready to put them into action as you serve in the highest office in the land.[1]

And what if you don't become president? Even if the highest government "office" you will ever seek is that of a citizen, it is imperative to begin thinking about these issues. As a citizen, you have a role to play in promoting the constitutional ideals of America. You can use your own bully pulpit, even if it's a bit smaller than the president's, to promote the Constitution's values wherever you are. Around the dinner table, think about how you can talk to your family about the importance of defending free speech, even for those people who criticize a president. In your religious community, think about how you can embrace your beliefs but preach the importance of respecting other religions. As a parent, think about how you can encourage your child's school to teach the history of the United States honestly and in a way that encourages students to support constitutional values like equal protection.

Of course, our task isn't complete if few Americans embrace the values of the Constitution. We also need to convince others to embrace those values in order to keep them alive in our polity. Experts in messaging often look for the one perfect word to capture an idea. In our case, that word is *respect*. The idea of respect encapsulates much of what's been said throughout this book, and much of what has guided our country through tumultuous times. Today, as we always have, we need a polity and a future president who respect the rule of law and the fundamental rights of the American people. And we all need to respect the Constitution and our fellow citizens—even when we disagree. The Constitution is one of the most important documents in history; it's not a product to be "sold" to the people. So think of convincing others not as a sales pitch, but as a principled call to action. The more Americans recognize the value of the Constitution, the better off all of us—citizens and presidents alike—can be.

With James Madison's help, I have tried to guide you by looking to the victories and pitfalls of past presidents. Certainly, Madison crafted an outline of principles for you to use thanks to his role in crafting the Constitution, writing the

Federalist Papers, and being a president himself. But ultimately, the Constitution's fate does not rest on words on parchment. It does not rest on the beliefs of Framers like Madison. It does not even rest only on today's public officials. It rests on you, whether you are a future president or citizen.

It is your job—as it is all of ours—to preserve, protect, and defend the values of the Constitution.

Acknowledgments

I have studied and taught politics and constitutional law professionally for nearly all of my adult life, but I was unprepared for anything like the 2016 presidential campaign. Suddenly proposals to violate the Constitution that had been the stuff of far-fetched classroom hypotheticals became just another part of the agenda for a presidential candidate who would soon win the election. In response to this, that summer I began writing this book in the form of articles for *Politico*, *Time.com*, and the *New York Times*. Along the way, I was encouraged by my parents and stepparents, Susan Brettschneider, Robert Klopfer, Eric Brettschneider, Jeanne Rostaing, my sister, Kim Brettschneider, my mother-in-law, Virginia Weisz, my father-in-law, John Weisz, and my brother-in-law, Patrick Heppell. I also began regularly discussing constitutional issues related to the presidency on the *Dan Yorke Show* and radio program, John Fugelsang's *Tell Me Everything*, *Rising Up with Sonali*, the *David Feldman Show*, and various news and television programs for BBC. Callers to those shows and the hosts made it clear that a book clarifying the role and limits of the president was essential.

But while those articles and discussions were inspired by

the 2016 moment, I have endeavored in this book to think seriously about the constitutional limits on the office of president at any point in time. Thus the book emphasizes both future and past presidents, looking for the timeless principles of the presidency.

I wrote the book with the encouragement of and in discussion with my wife, Allison Brettschneider, who also commented on multiple drafts and made many valuable suggestions. The book is dedicated to our daughter, Sophie Brettschneider. I've been inspired by Sophie's concern for, interest in, and talent for discussing politics. Our many conversations about this book on our walks to her elementary school in the morning have been similarly uplifting. Despite her young age, she, like others of her generation, knows that politics is not a spectator sport. It has real consequences for everyone's lives.

I want to thank the numerous people who have read drafts at various stages, helped with research, and aided in putting together the final version. Quynh Do, my editor at W. W. Norton, has been a terrific guide on all aspects of the book from proposal to final draft, as has my agent, Rafe Sagalyn. Quynh also deserves much credit for the clever idea of writing this book for "future presidents," and she drew inspiration from Richard A. Muller's *Physics for Future Presidents*. Ben Wofford read multiple drafts and worked with me to edit the book in a way that would make it accessible and engaging to a wider audience of readers than political scientists or constitutional lawyers. I am indebted to him for his keen ear, amazing editing, and overall guidance on how to write for a broad audience. Aidan Calvelli brought this book home, serving as a tireless, invaluable, and brilliant editor and research assistant from early drafts to the final product. Hans Britsch worked tirelessly on research and edits and had enormous impact, especially in regard to Chapter 13, for which he introduced me to his uncle, Miguel Marquez, a focus of that chapter. I also want to thank Basundhara Mukherjee, Gwen Everett, Isabel Gensler, and Shrey Sharma for their assistance, including fact-checking the manuscript and providing important comments. I am particularly grateful to Zach Helfand and Minh Ly for their thorough fact-checking. Minh also contributed important insights into democratic theory and the political thought of James Madison.

Among the many friends and colleagues who gave comments and talked with me about this project at various stages, I am particularly indebted to the following: Nancy Rosenblum, David Estlund, James Morone, Steven Calabresi, Sabeel Rahman, Jules Lobel, Jeffrey Tulis, Herschel Nachlis, Julie Rose, Elizabeth Beaumont, Frank Spain, Tobin Marcus, Nelson Tebbe, Dennis Rasmussen, Erika Kiss, Jan-Werner Müller, Joshua Braver, Jason Zimba, Jed Sugarman, Ethan Leib, Peter Andreas, Paul Gowder, Alex Gourevitch, David Feldman, Elizabeth Cohen, Gordon Silverstein, David McNamee, Andrew Kent, Benjamin Hoekstra, Skylar Albertson, and Alex McGrath. I benefited greatly from teaching the book to my senior and graduate seminars at Brown in Fall 2017, and in particular want to thank my students K. R. White, Nick Geiser, Jeanine Mojum, Hans Britsch, Aidan Calvelli, and Sasha Lobel.

Notes

Introduction: The Oath

1. NCC Staff, "Is Andrew Johnson the Worst President in American History?" National Constitution Center, 29 December 2016, https://constitutioncenter.org/blog/is-andrew-johnson-the-worst-president-in-american-history-2.
2. Albert Castel, *The Presidency of Andrew Johnson* (Lawrence: University Press of Kansas, 1979).
3. David H. Donald, *Lincoln* (New York: Simon & Schuster, 1996).
4. George Kateb, *Lincoln's Political Thought* (Cambridge: Harvard University Press, 2015).
5. U.S. Const. art. II, § 1. Article II, Section I gives the president the option to either "swear" or "affirm" the oath of office.
6. U.S. Const. art. II.
7. Jed Shugerman and Ethan J. Leib, "This overlooked part of the Constitution could stop Trump from abusing his pardon power," *Washington Post* 14 March 2018, https://www.washingtonpost.com/opinions/this-overlooked-part-of-the-constitution-could-stop-trump-from-abusing-his-pardon-power/2018/03/14/265b045a-26dd-11e8-874b-d517e912f125_story.html?utm_term=.6feec5bbd624.
8. Edward M. Riley, "Philadelphia: The Nation's Capital, 1790–1800," *Pennsylvania History: A Journal of Mid-Atlantic Studies* 20, no. 4 (1953): 378.
9. George Washington, "Second Inaugural Address of George Washington," The Avalon Project, 1973, http://avalon.law.yale.edu/18th_century/wash2.asp.

10. James Madison, "The Federalist Papers: No. 48," The Avalon Project, 2008, http://avalon.law.yale.edu/18th_century/fed48.asp.
11. "Flushing Meadows Corona Park," NYC Parks, n.d., https://www.nycgovparks.org/parks/flushing-meadows-corona-park/history.
12. Richard Neustadt, *Presidential Power: The Politics of Leadership* (Hoboken, NJ: John Wiley and Sons, 1960), 10.
13. Neustadt, *Presidential Power.*
14. Neustadt, *Presidential Power and the Modern Presidents: The Politics of Leadership from Roosevelt to Reagan* (New York: Free Press, 1990), xvi.
15. Neustadt, *Presidential Power and the Modern Presidents*, xvii.
16. Clinton Rossiter, ed., *The Federalist Papers* (New York: New American Library, 1961).
17. Madison, "The Federalist Papers: No. 46," The Avalon Project, 2008, http://avalon.law.yale.edu/18th_century/fed46.asp.
18. Andrew Glass, "James Madison Signals His Aim To Seek A Bill of Rights, May 4, 1989," *Politico*, 4 May 2016, https://www.politico.com/story/2016/05/madison-signals-his-aim-to-seek-a-bill-of-rights-may-4-1789-222709.
19. "Removal Power of the President, [19 May] 1789," National Archives, 26 November 2017, http://founders.archives.gov/documents/Madison/01-12-02-0109.
20. Ben Brantley, "Review: 'Hamilton,' Young Rebels Changing History and Theater," *New York Times*, 6 August 2015, https://www.nytimes.com/2015/08/07/theater/review-hamilton-young-rebels-changing-history-and-theater.html?_r=0.
21. Alexander Hamilton, "The Federalist Papers: No. 70, 18 March 1788," The Avalon Project, 2008, http://avalon.law.yale.edu/18th_century/fed70.asp.
22. Jan Werner-Müller, *What is Populism?* (Philadelphia: University of Pennsylvania Press, 2016).
23. Abraham Lincoln, "First Inaugural Address of Abraham Lincoln," The Avalon Project, http://avalon.law.yale.edu/19th_century/lincoln1.asp.
24. John Adams, *A Defence of the Constitutions of Government of the United States of America* (Boston: Edmund Freeman, 1787).
25. Madison, "The Federalist Papers: No. 51," The Avalon Project, 2008, http://avalon.law.yale.edu/18th_century/fed51.asp.

26. Niccolo Machiavelli, *The Prince*, Project Gutenberg, 2006, https://www.gutenberg.org/files/1232/1232-h/1232-h.htm.
27. Corey Brettschneider, *Democratic Rights: The Substance of Self-Government* (Princeton, NJ: Princeton University Press, 2007). Ronald Dworkin, *Freedom's Law* (Cambridge: Harvard University Press, 1997), Introduction.

1: Article II and the Limited Presidency

1. Merle Miller, *Plain Speaking: An Oral Biography of Harry S. Truman* (New York: Berkley Publishing, 1974), 288.
2. U.S. Const. art. VII.
3. Brent Tarter, "George Mason and The Conservation of History," *The Virginia Magazine of History and Biography* 99, no. 3 (1991): 292.
4. George Washington and Executive Power," Center for Civic Education, 2015. http://www.civiced.org/resources/curriculum/washington.
5. Benjamin Brown, "Hot, Hot, Hot: The Summer of 1787," National Constitution Center, 2012, https://constitutioncenter.org/blog/hot-hot-hot-the-summer-of-1787.
6. "Presiding Over the Convention: The Indispensable Man," Mount Vernon, 2017, http://www.mountvernon.org/george-washington/constitutional-convention/convention-president/.
7. John R. Vile, *The Constitutional Convention of 1787: A Comprehensive Encyclopedia of America's Founding* (Santa Barbara, CA: ABC CLIO, 2005), 216.
8. "Massachusetts Declaration of Rights, 1780," Teaching American History, 2017, http://teachingamericanhistory.org/library/document/massachusetts-declaration-of-rights/.
9. Alexander Hamilton, "The Federalist Papers: No. 1," The Avalon Project, 2008, http://avalon.law.yale.edu/18th_century/fed01.asp.
10. "From George Washington to Edward Carrington, 1 May 1796," The National Archives, 2017, https://founders.archives.gov/documents/Washington/99-01-02-00479.
11. "The First Public Printing from the Pennsylvania Packet," Historical Society of Pennsylvania, n.d., https://hsp.org/history-online/

exhibits/constitution-on-display/the-first-public-printing-from-the-pennsylvania-packet.

12. Pauline Maier, *Ratification: The People Debate the Constitution, 1787–1788* (New York: Simon & Schuster, 2011), 148.

13. Hamilton, "The Federalist Papers, No. 69," The Avalon Project, 2008, http://avalon.law.yale.edu/18th_century/fed69.asp.

14. Thomas Jefferson, et al., Declaration of Independence, 4 July 1776.

15. Charles A. Beard, *History of the United States* (Pantianos Classics, 2016 [1921]), 39.

16. James Madison, "The Federalist Papers: No. 10," The Avalon Project, 2008, http://avalon.law.yale.edu/18th_century/fed10.asp.

17. "Chasing Congress Away," History, Art & Archives: The House of Representatives, 2015, http://history.house.gov/Blog/Detail/15032422770.

18. U.S. Const. art. I.

19. Hamilton and Madison, "The Federalist Papers: No. 62," The Avalon Project, 2008, http://avalon.law.yale.edu/18th_century/fed62.asp.

20. Gordon Lloyd, "The Constitutional Convention: Debates in the Federal Convention of 1787 by James Madison: Friday, June 1," TeachingAmericanHistory.org, 2017, http://teachingamericanhistory.org/convention/debates/0601-2/.

21. Lloyd, "The Constitutional Convention."

22. Lloyd, "The Constitutional Convention."

23. U.S. Const. art. II.

24. U.S. Const. art. II, § 1.

25. U.S. Const. art. II, § 1.

26. Hamilton or Madison, "The Federalist Papers: No. 57," The Avalon Project, 2008, http://avalon.law.yale.edu/18th_century/fed57.asp.

27. *The Papers of James Madison*, ed. William T. Hutchinson et al. (Chicago: University of Chicago Press, 1962), http://press-pubs.uchicago.edu/founders/documents/v1ch13s36.html.

28. George Washington to Lafayette, 25 July 1785, The National Archives, 2017, https://founders.archives.gov/documents/Washington/04-03-02-0143.

29. Evan Andrews, "How Many U.S. Presidents Owned Slaves?"

History.com, 19 July 2017, https://www.history.com/news/ask
-history/how-many-u-s-presidents-owned-slaves.

30. George Washington, "George Washington's 1799 Will," George
Washington's Mount Vernon, 2017, http://www.mountvernon
.org/the-estate-gardens/the-tombs/george-washingtons-1799-
will/.

31. "The Meaning of July Fourth for the Negro," PBS, n.d., https://
www.pbs.org/wgbh/aia/part4/4h2927t.html.

32. "The Meaning of July Fourth for the Negro."

33. Some scholars do think that the use of *he* in Article II was
meant to be gender-inclusive. See Steven Nelson, "Are Women
Allowed to Be President?," *US News*, 30 October 2015, https://
www.usnews.com/news/articles/2015/10/30/are-women-allowed-
to-be-president.

34. From a speech delivered by Elizabeth Cady Stanton at a meeting of the International Council of Women in Washington, DC,
March 25–April 1, 1888.

35. There is a debate on what "natural-born" means as it applies to
the presidency. For more, see, Thomas H. Lee, "Natural Born
Citizen," *American University Law Review* 67 No. 327 (2017),
Fordham Law Legal Studies Research Paper No. 3100411,
https://papers.ssrn.com/sol3/papers.cfm?abstract_id=3100411.

36. Some experts argue it is fewer. See David Law and Mila Versteeg,
"The Declining Influence of The United States Constitution,"
NYU Law Review (2012), http://www.nyulawreview.org/sites/
default/files/pdf/NYULawReview-87-3-Law-Versteeg_0.pdf.

37. John Greenwald, "The World: A Gift to All Nations," *Time*, 6
July 1987, http://content.time.com/time/magazine/article/0,9171
,964901,00.html.

38. Boris Munoz, "The Media and the Citizen in Venezuela," *New
Yorker*, 2013, https://www.newyorker.com/business/currency/the-
media-and-the-citizen-in-venezuela.

39. *Extra-Legal Power and Legitimacy: Perspectives on Prerogative*, ed.
Clement Fatovic and Benjamin A. Kleinerman (Oxford: Oxford
University Press, 2013).

40. Martin Flaherty, "The Most Dangerous Branch Abroad,"
Harvard Journal of Law and Public Policy 30, no. 1 (2006),
http://www.law.harvard.edu/students/orgs/jlpp/Vol30_No1_
Flahertyonline.pdf.

41. Michael W. McConnell, "The Logical Structure of Article Two," 2016, http://www.law.northwestern.edu/research-faculty/colloqui um/constitutionallaw/documents/2016_Fall_McConnell_Art.pdf.

42. On the point that most of the prerogatives of the Crown were given to Congress in the Constitution, see Forrest McDonald, *Novus Ordo Seclorum: The Intellectual Origins of the Constitution* (Lawrence: University Press of Kansas, 1985), 247–48. For a detailed and good discussion, see Robert J. Reinstein, "The Limits of Executive Power," *American University Law Review* 59, no. 259 (2009), 271–307.

43. Hamilton, "The Federalist Papers: No. 74, 25 March 1788," The Avalon Project, 2008, http://avalon.law.yale.edu/18th_century/ fed74.asp.

44. Joseph M. Bessette and Gary J. Schmitt, "The Powers and Duties of the President: Recovering the Logic and Meaning of Article II," in *The Constitutional Presidency*, ed. Joseph M. Bessette and Jeffrey K. Tulis (Baltimore: Johns Hopkins University Press, 2009).

45. U.S. Const. art. II, § 3.

2: *The Bully Pulpit*

1. William Safire, "On Language: Right Stuff in the Bully Pulpit," *New York Times*, 27 February 1983, http://www.nytimes .com/1983/02/27/magazine/on-language-right-stuff-in-the-bully-pulpit.html?pagewanted=all.

2. U.S. Const. art. II, § 3.

3. Gerhard Peters, "State of the Union Address and Message," The American Presidency Project, 2017, http://www .presidency.ucsb.edu/sou.php.

4. "Bully Pulpit," *Merriam-Webster Dictionary*, 1 December 2017, https://www.merriam-webster.com/dictionary/bully%20pulpit.

5. Corey Brettschneider, *When the State Speaks, What Should It Say?* (Princeton, NJ: Princeton University Press, 2016).

6. Jeffrey K. Tulis, *The Rhetorical Presidency* (Princeton, NJ: Princeton University Press, 1987).

7. Richard E. Farley, "The Fascinating History of the White House Press Room," *Town and Country*, 17 January 2017, http://

www.townandcountrymag.com/society/politics/news/a9263/
history-white-house-press-room-pool/.

8. Doris Kearns Goodwin, *The Bully Pulpit: Theodore Roosevelt, William Howard Taft, and the Golden Age of Journalism* (New York: Simon & Schuster, 2013).

9. Theodore Roosevelt, "Special Message to the Senate and House of Representatives," 4 June 1906, http://www.presidency.ucsb.edu/ws/?pid=69670.

10. "The Pure Food and Drug Act," History, Art & Archives, 23 June 1906, http://history.house.gov/HistoricalHighlight/Detail/1503239 3280.

11. Richard Neustadt, *Presidential Power and the Modern Presidents: The Politics of Leadership from Roosevelt to Reagan* (New York: Free Press, 1990).

12. Tulis, *The Rhetorical Presidency.*

13. Alexander Hamilton, "The Federalist Papers: No. 1," The Avalon Project, 2008, http://avalon.law.yale.edu/18th_century/fed01.asp.

14. Joanne Freeman, "The Election of 1800: A Study of the Logic of Political Change," *The Yale Law Journal* 108, no. 8 (1999 [1986]), JSTOR, http://www.jstor.org/stable/pdf/797378.pdf.

15. Renée Critcher Lyons, "United by Voice and Vision: Thomas Jefferson's First Inauguration, March 4, 1801," The National Children's Book and Literacy Alliance, 2016, http://ourwhitehouse.org/united-by-voice-and-vision-thomas-jeffersons-first-inauguration-march-4-1801/.

16. Thomas Jefferson, "First Inaugural Address: 4 March 1801," The Avalon Project, 2008, http://avalon.law.yale.edu/19th_century/jefinau1.asp.

17. Andres Burstein, *Jefferson's Secrets* (New York: Basic Books, 2005), 195.

18. Tulis, *The Rhetorical Presidency.*

19. Woodrow Wilson, *The New Freedom* (New York: Doubleday, 1913), Project Gutenberg, https://www.gutenberg.org/files/14811/14811-h/14811-h.htm.

20. Wilson, *The New Freedom.*

21. Christine A. Lunardini and Thomas J. Knock, "Woodrow Wilson and Women's Suffrage: A New Look," *Political Science Quarterly* 95, no. 4 (Winter 1980–1981): 655–71, JSTOR, www.jstor.org/stable/2150609.

22. U.S. Const. amend. XIV.

23. Plessy v. Ferguson, 163 U.S. 537, 548 (1896).

24. Plessy v. Ferguson, 163 U.S. 537, 552–564 (1896) (J. Harlan, dissenting).

25. Dick Lehr, "The Racist Legacy of Woodrow Wilson," *The Atlantic*, 27 November 2015, https://www.theatlantic.com/politics/archive/2015/11/wilson-legacy-racism/417549/.

26. "Remembering William Monroe Trotter: The First and Only Black Man to Be Thrown out of the Oval Office," *The Journal of Blacks in Higher Education*, no. 46 (2004): 50–51, JSTOR, http://www.jstor.org/stable/4133672.

27. Eric S. Yellin, *Racism in the Nation's Service: Government Workers and the Color Line in Woodrow Wilson's America* (Chapel Hill: UNC Press, 2013), 164.

28. A. Scott Berg, *Wilson* (New York: Berkley Publishing, 2014).

29. For this discussion of Wilson, I owe much gratitude to Erika Kiss, director of the University Center for Human Values Film Forum at Princeton University.

30. Thomas Nast, "The Union as it was / The Lost Cause, worse than slavery," *Harper's Weekly* 18, no. 930 (1874), 878, http://www.history.org/history/teaching/enewsletter/volume10/feb12/primsource.cfm.

31. The quote from Wilson's book, which the film adapted, actually reads: "The white men of the South were aroused by the mere instinct of self-preservation. . . . Every country-side wished to have its own Ku Klux, founded in secrecy and mystery like the mother 'Den' at Pulaski, until at last there had sprung into existence a great Ku Klux Klan, an 'Invisible Empire of the South,' bound together in loose organization to protect the southern country from some of the ugliest hazards of a time of revolution." From Woodrow Wilson, *A History of the American People* (New York: Best Books, 1918), https://ia800202.us.archive.org/5/items/historyofamerica05wils/historyofamerica05wils.pdf.

32. Berg, *Wilson*.

33. "Inside the 1915 Protest to Ban *Birth of a Nation*," *The Atlantic*, 2 February 2017, https://www.theatlantic.com/video/index/515352/birth-of-a-movement-william-trotter/.

34. "Tonight at 8:00pm," 11 June 1963, JFK Library, 2017, https://www.jfklibrary.org/Civil-Rights-Microsite/Shared-Content/

Chapters/Address-to-the-American-People/The-Address/
Tune-in-Tonight.aspx.
35. Heart of Atlanta Motel Inc. v. United States, 379 U.S. 241 (1964).
36. Katzenbach v. McClung, 379 U.S. 294 (1964).
37. John F. Kennedy, "Radio and Television Report to the American People on Civil Rights, June 11, 1963," JFK Library, 2017, https://www.jfklibrary.org/Research/Research-Aids/JFK-Speeches/Civil-Rights-Radio-and-Television-Report_19630611.aspx.
38. David Greenberg, "Dog-Whistling Dixie," *Slate*, 20 November 2007, http://www.slate.com/articles/news_and_politics/history_lesson/2007/11/dogwhistling_dixie.html.
39. Roger Simon, "The GOP and Willie Horton: Together Again," *Politico*, 19 May 2015, https://www.politico.com/story/2015/05/jeb-bush-willie-horton-118061.
40. Rick Perlstein, "Exclusive: Lee Atwater's Infamous 1981 Interview on the Southern Strategy," *The Nation*, 13 November 2012, https://www.thenation.com/article/exclusive-lee-atwaters-infamous-1981-interview-southern-strategy/.
41. David Corn, "Reagan and the Media: A Love Story," *The Nation*, 10 June 2004, https://www.thenation.com/article/reagan-and-media-love-story/.
42. "John F. Kennedy and the Press," JFK Library, 2017, https://www.jfklibrary.org/JFK/JFK-in-History/John-F-Kennedy-and-the-Press.aspx.
43. Michael Barbaro, "Pithy, Mean and Powerful: How Donald Trump Mastered Twitter for 2016," *New York Times*, 5 October 2015, https://www.nytimes.com/2015/10/06/us/politics/donald-trump-twitter-use-campaign-2016.html.
44. Kathryn Watson, "Trump on Charlottesville: 'I Think There's Blame on Both Sides,'" CBS News, 15 August 2017, https://www.cbsnews.com/news/trump-on-charlottesville-i-think-theres-blame-on-both-sides/.
45. "Text: President Bush Addresses the Nation," *Washington Post*, 20 September 2001, http://www.washingtonpost.com/wp-srv/nation/specials/attacked/transcripts/bushaddress_092001.html.
46. John Hudson, "The U.S. Has Bought $70,000 in TV Ads in Pakistan Denouncing Anti-Islam Film," *The Atlantic*, 20 September 2012, https://www.theatlantic.com/international/archive/2012/09/pakistan-obama-administration-dropping-70000-ads-denouncing-anti-islam-film/323413/.

3: The Power to Execute the Laws

1. Youngstown v. Sawyer, 343 U.S. 579, 655 (1952).

2. For civilian employment in the executive branch, see United States Office of Personnel Management, *Sizing Up the Executive Branch Fiscal Year 2016* (Washington, DC: United States Office of Personnel Management, June 2017)," PPA-02900-06-17, https://www.opm.gov/policy-data-oversight/data-analysis-documentation/federal-employment-reports/reports-publications/sizing-up-the-executive-branch-2016.pdf. For military employment, see Defense Manpower Data Center, "Military and Civilian Personnel by Service/Agency by State/Country (September 2017)," https://www.dmdc.osd.mil/appj/dwp/dwp_reports.jsp.

3. Harry S. Truman, Executive Order 9981—Establishing the President's Committee on Equality of Treatment and Opportunity in the Armed Services, 26 July 1948, online by Gerhard Peters and John T. Woolley, The American Presidency Project, http://www.presidency.ucsb.edu/ws/?pid=60737.

4. Franklin D. Roosevelt, Executive Order 9066—Authorizing the Secretary of War to Prescribe Military Areas, 19 February 1942, online by Gerhard Peters and John T. Woolley, The American Presidency Project, 2018, http://www.presidency.ucsb.edu/ws/?pid=61698.

5. "Executive Orders—Washington to Trump," The American Presidency Project, 2018, http://www.presidency.ucsb.edu/data/orders.php.

6. Cleve R. Wootson Jr., "What Trump Could Learn From George Washington's First Executive Order," *Washington Post*, 10 February 2017, https://www.washingtonpost.com/news/the-fix/wp/2017/02/10/what-trump-could-learn-from-george-washingtons-first-executive-order/?utm_term=.daea00498271.

7. The average number of executive orders from Kennedy through Obama was 191.85 per term. See "Executive Orders: Washington–Trump," The American Presidency Project, 2018, http://www.presidency.ucsb.edu/data/orders.php.

8. "Fact Sheet: New Executive Actions to Reduce Gun Violence and Make Our Communities Safer," The White House Office of the Press Secretary, 4 January 2016, https://obamawhitehouse.archives.gov/the-press-office/2016/01/04/

fact-sheet-new-executive-actions-reduce-gun-violence-and-make-our.

9. The *Saturday Night Live* sketch appeared on 22 November 2014 on NBC. For a recording of the sketch from the *SNL* YouTube page, see https://www.youtube.com/watch?v=JUDSeb2zHQo. For news coverage, see Zachary A. Goldfarb, "SNL skit suggests Obama's immigration executive action is unconstitutional," *Washington Post*, 23 November 2014, https://www.washingtonpost.com/news/wonk/wp/2014/11/23/snl-skit-suggests-obamas-immigration-executive-action-is-unconstitutional/?utm_term=.370da3fd0295.

10. Lyndon B. Johnson, Executive Order 11375—Amending Executive Order No. 11246, Relating to Equal Employment Opportunity, 13 October 1967, online by Gerhard Peters and John T. Woolley, The American Presidency Project, http://www.presidency.ucsb.edu/ws/?pid=60553.

11. Harry S. Truman, Executive Order 9981—Establishing the President's Committee on Equality of Treatment and Opportunity in the Armed Services, 26 July 1948, online by Gerhard Peters and John T. Woolley, The American Presidency Project, http://www.presidency.ucsb.edu/ws/?pid=60737.

12. U.S. Const. art. II, § 3.

13. Maeva Marcus, *Truman and the Steel Seizure Case: The Limits of Presidential Power* (Durham: Duke University Press, 1994), 74.

14. Harry S. Truman, Executive Order 10340—Directing the Secretary of Commerce to Take Possession of and Operate the Plants and Facilities of Certain Steel Companies, 8 April 1952, online by Gerhard Peters and John T. Woolley, The American Presidency Project, http://www.presidency.ucsb.edu/ws/?pid=78454.

15. Youngstown Sheet & Tube Co. v. Sawyer, 343 U.S. 579, 582 (1952).

16. Youngstown v. Sawyer, 343 U.S. 579, 667–710 (1952) (C. J. Vinson, dissenting).

17. Youngstown v. Sawyer, 343 U.S. 579, 655 (1952) (J. Jackson, concurring).

18. Youngstown v. Sawyer, 343 U.S. 579, 637 (1952) (J. Jackson, concurring).

19. Youngstown v. Sawyer, 343 U.S. 579, 655 (1952).

20. Youngstown v. Sawyer, 343 U.S. 579, 637 (1952) (J. Jackson, concurring).

21. Youngstown v. Sawyer, 343 U.S. 579, 647 (1952).
22. Benjamin Carter Hett, *Burning the Reichstag* (Oxford: Oxford University Press, 2014).
23. Germany (Territory under Allied occupation, 1945—US Zone) Military Tribunals, *Trials of war criminals before the Nuremberg Military Tribunals under Control Council law no. 10*, vol. 3 (Washington, DC: US Government Printing Office, 1951), 262, https://www.loc.gov/rr/frd/Military_Law/pdf/NT_war-criminals_Vol-III.pdf.
24. The International Military Tribunal Nuremberg, *Trial of the Major War Criminals before the International Military Tribunal Nuremberg*, vol. 9, 14 November 1945–1 October 1946 (Nuremberg, Germany: Secretariat of the International Military Tribunal, 1947), 433, https://www.loc.gov/rr/frd/Military_Law/pdf/NT_Vol-IX.pdf.
25. Office of the United States Chief Counsel for Prosecution of Axis Criminality, *Nazi Conspiracy & Aggression* Volume I, Chapter XII, Washington: United States Government Printing Office, 1946, pp. 980–82.
26. U.S. Const. art. I, § 9.
27. Jackson references the collapse of Weimar in his concurrence: "Germany, after the First World War, framed the Weimar Constitution, designed to secure her liberties in the Western tradition. However, the President of the Republic, without concurrence of the Reichstag, was empowered temporarily to suspend any or all individual rights if public safety and order were seriously disturbed or endangered. This proved a temptation to every government, whatever its shade of opinion, and, in 13 years, suspension of rights was invoked on more than 250 occasions. Finally, Hitler persuaded President Von Hindenberg to suspend all such rights, and they were never restored." Youngstown v. Sawyer, 343 U.S. 579, 651 (1952) (J. Jackson, concurring).
28. Neil Lewis, "A Guide to the Memos on Torture," *New York Times International*, 2005, http://www.nytimes.com/ref/international/24MEMO-GUIDE.html.
29. Jay Bybee, "Memorandum for Alberto R. Gonzales, Counsel to the President," U.S. Department of Justice Office of the Assistant Attorney General, 1 August 2002, https://nsarchive2.gwu.edu//NSAEBB/NSAEBB127/02.08.01.pdf.
30. Adam Liptak, "The Reach of War: Penal Law; Legal Scholars

Criticize Torture Memos," *New York Times*, 25 June 2004, http://www.nytimes.com/2004/06/25/world/the-reach-of-war-penal-law-legal-scholars-criticize-memos-on-torture.html.

31. "Detainee Treatment Act of 2005," Title X of Division A of the Defense Appropriations Act of Fiscal Year 2006 (Public Law 109-148 of December 30, 2007, Title X; 119 STAT. 2739). For the text, see Office of the Director of National Intelligence, *Legal Reference Book*, https://www.dni.gov/index.php/ic-legal-reference-book/detainee-treatment-act-of-2005.

32. Eric Schmitt, "President Backs McCain Measure on Inmate Abuse," *New York Times*, 16 December 2005, http://www.nytimes.com/2005/12/16/politics/president-backs-mccain-measure-on-inmate-abuse.html.

33. Charlie Savage, "Bush Could Bypass New Torture Ban," *Boston Globe*, 4 January 2006, http://archive.boston.com/news/nation/articles/2006/01/04/bush_could_bypass_new_torture_ban/.

34. Mike Rappaport, "President Obama's Decision to Sign and Not Enforce," Liberty Law Site, 27 April 2014, http://www.libertylawsite.org/2014/04/27/president-obamas-decision-to-sign-and-not-enforce/.

35. J. W. Hampton, Jr. & Co. v. United States, 276 U.S. 394, 409 (1928).

36. As long as Congress offers an "intelligible" guiding principle for the executive branch to base its rules on. See Scalia in Whitman v. American Trucking Association, Inc., 531 U.S. 457, 474 (2001).

37. Public Law 107-40, codified at 115 Stat. 224 (2001).

38. Public Law 107-56, codified at 115 Stat. 272 (2001).

39. Ro Khanna, Walter Jones, and Mark Pocan, "Stop the Unconstitutional War in Yemen," *New York Times*, 10 October 2017, https://www.nytimes.com/2017/10/10/opinion/yemen-war-unconstitutional.html.

40. In the case of the Patriot Act, some say Congress did act to check a president when it replaced the law with the USA Freedom Act of 2015, which ended bulk phone metadata collection. However, some believe that Act changed little, since the data are still stored by phone companies and the NSA can easily acquire them. See Shayana Kadidal, "Surveillance After the USA Freedom Act: How Much Has Changed?," *Huffington Post*, 17 December 2015, https://www.huffingtonpost.com/the-center-for-constitutional-rights/surveillance-after-the-us_b_8827952.html.

41. Mistretta v. United States, 488 U.S. 361, 372 (1989).

42. Curtlyn Kramer, "Vital Stats: Congress Has a Staffing Problem, Too," Brookings Institution, 24 May 2017, https://www.brookings.edu/blog/fixgov/2017/05/24/vital-stats-congress-has-a-staffing-problem-too/.

43. Philip Bump, "The Unprecedented Partisanship of Congress, Explained," *Washington Post*, 13 January 2016, https://www.washingtonpost.com/news/the-fix/wp/2016/01/13/heres-why-president-obama-failed-to-bridge-the-partisan-divide-graphed/?utm_term=.b2374d30eb85.

44. Janet Napolitano, "Exercising Prosecutorial Discretion with Respect to Individuals Who Came to the United States as Children," Department of Homeland Security, 15 June 2012, https://www.dhs.gov/xlibrary/assets/s1-exercising-prosecutorial-discretion-individuals-who-came-to-us-as-children.pdf.

45. Tom Cohen, "Obama administration to stop deporting some young illegal immigrants," *CNN*, 16 June 2012, http://www.cnn.com/2012/06/15/politics/immigration/index.html.

46. For a related controversy over executive overreach and immigration, see United States v. Texas and the legal battles surrounding Obama's Deferred Action for Parents of Americans program. United States v. Texas, 579 U.S. (2016).

47. "Presidential Vetoes," US House of Representatives, 16 August 2017, http://history.house.gov/Institution/Presidential-Vetoes/Presidential-Vetoes/.

48. Philip Rucker and Robert Costa, "Bannon vows a daily fight for 'deconstruction of the administrative state,'" *Washington Post*, 23 February 2017, https://www.washingtonpost.com/politics/top-wh-strategist-vows-a-daily-fight-for-deconstruction-of-the-administrative-state/2017/02/23/03f6b8da-f9ea-11e6-bf01-d47f8cf9b643_story.html?utm_term=.237d65916383.

49. U.S. Const. art. II, § 3.

50. Lincoln also used executive power to suspend the writ of habeas corpus prior to getting congressional approval, again using an emergency justification for an action that potentially infringed on civil liberties. See Bruce A. Ragsdale, "*Ex Parte Merryman* and Debates on Civil Liberties During the Civil War." *Federal Judicial Center*, 2007, https://www.fjc.gov/sites/default/files/trials/merryman.pdf.

51. Zachary Goldfarb, "SNL skit suggests Obama's immigration execu-

tive action is unconstitutional," *Washington Post*, 23 November 2014, https://www.washingtonpost.com/news/wonk/wp/2014/11/23/snl-skit-suggests-obamas-immigration-executive-action-is-unconstitutional/.

4: The Power to Hire and Fire

1. Chris Cillizza, "This is the single most dangerous thing Donald Trump said in his *New York Times* interview," *Washington Post*, 22 November 2016, https://www.washingtonpost.com/news/the-fix/wp/2016/11/22/this-is-the-single-most-dangerous-thing-donald-trump-said-in-his-new-york-times-interview/?utm_term=.2e7c3209fe88.
2. U.S. Const. art. II, § 2, cl. 2.
3. Randall G. Holcombe, "Federal Government Growth Before the New Deal," Foundation for Economic Education, 1 September 1997, https://fee.org/articles/federal-government-growth-before-the-new-deal/.
4. Gilbert King, "The Stalking of the President," Smithsonian.com, 17 January 2012, https://www.smithsonianmag.com/history/the-stalking-of-the-president-20724161/.
5. Robert C. Kennedy, "On This Day: July 23, 1881," *New York Times*, 23 July 2001, https://archive.nytimes.com/www.nytimes.com/learning/general/onthisday/harp/0723.html.
6. Howard Markel, "The Dirty, Painful Death of President James A. Garfield," *PBS News Hour*, 16 September 2016, http://www.pbs.org/newshour/updates/dirty-painful-death-president-james-garfield/.
7. "'A Model Office Seeker,'" *Puck Magazine*, 18 July 1881, http://www.loc.gov/pictures/item/92508892/.
8. "Pendleton Civil Service Reform Act," Ch. 27, 22, Stat. 403.
9. Sean Theriault, "Patronage, the Pendleton Act, and the Power of the People," *The Journal of Politics* 65, no. 1, p. 52, http://onlinelibrary.wiley.com/doi/10.1111/1468-2508.t01-1-00003/full.
10. Jonathan L. Entin, "The Curious Case of the Pompous Postmaster: Myers v. United States," *Case Western Law Review* 65, no. 4 (2015), http://scholarlycommons.law.case.edu/cgi/viewcontent.cgi?article=1007&context=caselrev.
11. Myers v. United States, 272 U.S. 52, 117 (1926).

12. Humphrey's Executor v. United States, 295 U.S. 602, 619 (1935).
13. Humphrey's Executor v. United States, 295 U.S. 602, 619 (1935).
14. Humphrey's Executor v. United States, 295 U.S. 602, 603 (1935). See in particular the distinction the court made between "principal" officers and those who are "quasi-legislative" or "quasi-judicial."
15. As the case explained the holding, "The Federal Trade Commission, in contrast, is an administrative body created by Congress to carry into effect legislative policies embodied in the statute in accordance with the legislative standard therein prescribed, and to perform other specified duties as a legislative or as a judicial aid. Such a body cannot in any proper sense be characterized as an arm or an eye of the executive." Humphrey's Executor v. United States, 295 U.S. 602, 603 (1935).
16. Humphrey's Executor v. United States, 295 U.S. 602, 626-27 (1935).
17. Humphrey's Executor v. United States, 295 U.S. 602, 626-627 (1935).
18. Eliza Wing-yee Lee, "Political Science, Public Administration, and the Rise of the American Administrative State," *Public Administration Review* 55, no. 6 (Nov.–Dec. 1995): 538.
19. Office of Personnel Management, *Data, Analysis & Documentation Federal Employment Reports*, September 2014, https://www.opm.gov/policy-data-oversight/data-analysis-documentation/federal-employment-reports/historical-tables/executive-branch-civilian-employment-since-1940/.
20. "The 50 largest cities in the United States," *Politifact*, 2015, http://www.politifact.com/largestcities/.
21. Federal Communications Commission Created, 47 U.S. Code § 151, 1934.
22. U.S. Const. art. 6, § 3.
23. Amanda Taub and Max Fisher, "As Leaks Multiply, Fears of a 'Deep State' in America," *New York Times*, 16 Feb. 2017, https://www.nytimes.com/2017/02/16/world/americas/deep-state-leaks-trump.html?_r=0.
24. Lisa Rein, "The Plum Book Is Here for Those Angling for Jobs in Trump's Washington," *Washington Post*, 4 December 2016, https://www.washingtonpost.com/news/powerpost/wp/2016/12/04/

the-plum-book-is-here-for-those-angling-for-jobs-in-trumps-washington/?utm_term=.003f5b458d6f.

25. Carroll Kilpatrick, "Nixon Forces Firing of Cox; Richardson, Ruckelshaus Quit; President Abolishes Prosecutor's Office; FBI Seals Records," *Washington Post*, 21 October 1973, A01.

26. Cillizza, "This is the single most dangerous thing Donald Trump said in his *New York Times* interview."

27. Charlie Savage, "George W. Bush Made Retroactive N.S.A. 'Fix' After Hospital Room Showdown," *New York Times*, 20 September 2015, A13, https://www.nytimes.com/2015/09/21/us/politics/george-w-bush-made-retroactive-nsa-fix-after-hospital-room-showdown.html.

28. Savage, "George W. Bush Made Retroactive N.S.A. 'Fix' After Hospital Room Showdown."

29. Jack Goldsmith, interview with Bill Moyers, PBS, 7 September 2007, http://www.pbs.org/moyers/journal/09072007/transcript2.html.

30. "5 U.S.C.—Ethics in Government Act of 1978," https://www.law.cornell.edu/uscode/html/uscode05a/usc_sup_05_5_10_sq3.html.

31. David Johnston, "June 27–July 3; Independent Counsel Law Dies, and Mourners Are Few," *New York Times*, 4 July 1999, http://www.nytimes.com/1999/07/04/weekinreview/june-27-july-3-independent-counsel-law-dies-and-mourners-are-few.html.

32. Morrison v. Olson, 487 U.S. 654 (1988).

33. Morrison v. Olson, 487 U.S. 654, 734 (1988).

34. Humphrey's Executor v. United States, 295 U.S. 602, 626–627 (1935).

35. Whistleblower Protection Act of 1989, Public Law No. 101-12, 101st Cong., 16 March 1989.

36. He did note, however, that Congress could impeach a president over an arbitrary or irresponsible use of the president's firing power. For Madison's view, see "Removal Power of the President, [17 June] 1789," National Archives, 26 November 2017, http://founders.archives.gov/documents/Madison/01-12-02-0143.

37. Stephen M. Kohn, "The Whistle-Blowers of 1777," *New York Times*, 12 June 2011, http://www.nytimes.com/2011/06/13/opinion/13kohn.html?_r=0. See also Kohn, Stephen M., *The Whistleblower's Handbook: A Step-by-Step Guide to Doing What's Right and Protecting Yourself* (Guilford: Lyons Press, 2011).

38. Kohn, "The Whistle-Blowers of 1777." See also Kohn, *The Whistleblower's Handbook*.
39. James Madison, "The Federalist Papers: No. 51," The Avalon Project, 2008, http://avalon.law.yale.edu/18th_century/fed51.asp.

5: The Power to Nominate Supreme Court Justices

1. David Garrow, *Liberty and Sexuality: The Right to Privacy and the Making of Roe v. Wade* (Basingstoke, UK: Macmillan Publishing, 1994), 266.
2. Adam Liptak, "Antonin Scalia, Justice on the Supreme Court, Dies at 79," *New York Times*, 13 February 2016, https://www.nytimes.com/2016/02/14/us/antonin-scalia-death.html.
3. Julie Zauzmer, "Cardinal Donald Wuerl Offers Opening Remarks," *Washington Post*, 20 February 2016, https://www.washingtonpost.com/blogs/liveblog-live/liveblog/updates-funeral-mass-for-scalia/?utm_term=.eb342d5065a6#a3f1483a-74b4-4a22-aa9b-33d3eef25f73.
4. Carl Hulse and Mark Landler, "After Antonin Scalia's Death, Fierce Battle Lines Emerge," *New York Times*, 14 February 2016, https://www.nytimes.com/2016/02/15/us/politics/antonin-scalias-death-cuts-fierce-battle-lines-in-washington.html.
5. Adam Liptak and Matt Flegenheimer, "Neil Gorsuch Confirmed by Senate as Supreme Court Justice," *New York Times*, 7 April 2017, https://www.nytimes.com/2017/04/07/us/politics/neil-gorsuch-supreme-court.html.
6. Russell Wheeler, "Confirming Federal Judges During the Final Two Years of the Obama Administration: Vacancies Up, Nominees Down," Brookings Institution, 18 August 2015, https://www.brookings.edu/blog/fixgov/2015/08/18/confirming-federal-judges-during-the-final-two-years-of-the-obama-administration-vacancies-up-nominees-down/.
7. U.S. Const. art. III.
8. Alexander Hamilton, "The Federalist Papers: No. 78," The Avalon Project, 2008, http://avalon.law.yale.edu/18th_century/fed78.asp.
9. Marbury v. Madison, 5 U.S. 137, 177 (1803).
10. Katzenbach v. McClung, 379 U.S. 294 (1964).

11. Miranda v. Arizona, 384 U.S. 436 (1966).
12. Gideon v. Wainwright, 372 U.S. 335 (1963).
13. Jim Newton, *Justice for All: Earl Warren and the Nation He Made* (New York: Riverhead Books, 2006), 386.
14. Antonin Scalia, *A Matter of Interpretation: Federal Courts and the Law*, ed. Amy Gutmann (Princeton, NJ: Princeton University Press, 1997).
15. Griswold v. Connecticut, 381 U.S. 479, 485–486 (1965).
16. U.S. Const. amend. IV.
17. Griswold v. Connecticut, 381 U.S. 479, 484 (1965).
18. Roe v. Wade, 410 U.S. 113 (1973). See also Lawrence v. Texas, 539 U.S. 558 (2003).
19. Judicial Review Procedure Act 2016, Public Act 2016 No. 50, 17 October 2016 (New Zealand).
20. Hamilton, "The Federalist Papers: No. 78," The Avalon Project, 2008, http://avalon.law.yale.edu/18th_century/fed78.asp.
21. Hamilton, "The Federalist Papers: No. 78."
22. U.S. Const. amend. VIII.
23. Planned Parenthood v. Casey, 505 U.S. 833, 979–1002 (1992) (J. Scalia, dissenting).
24. U.S. Const. amend. XIV, § 1.
25. Linda Greenhouse, "Robert Bork's Tragedy," *New York Times*, 9 January 2013, https://opinionator.blogs.nytimes.com/2013/01/09/robert-borks-tragedy/.
26. Griswold v. Connecticut, 381 U.S. 479, 485–486 (1965).
27. *First Session on the Nomination of Robert H. Bork to be Associate Justice of the Supreme Court of the United States: Hearings before the Committee on the Judiciary*, Senate, 100th Cong. 241 (1987) (quotation of Senator Joe Biden).
28. *First Session on the Nomination of Robert H. Bork to be Associate Justice of the Supreme Court* (quotation of Senator Joe Biden).
29. *First Session on the Nomination of Robert H. Bork to be Associate Justice of the Supreme Court of the United States: Hearings before the Committee on the Judiciary*, Senate, 100th Cong. 753 (1987) (quotation of Senator Patrick Leahy and response from Robert Bork).
30. Nina Totenberg, "Robert Bork's Supreme Court Nomination 'Changed Everything, Maybe Forever,'" NPR, 19 December 2012, www.npr.org/sections/itsallpolitics/2012/12/19/167645600/

robert-borks-supreme-court-nomination-changed-everything-maybe-forever.

31. Michael Joseph Green, *Your Past and the Press* (Lanham: University Press of America, 2004).

32. Green, *Your Past and the Press*.

33. On this issue, Scalia seemed to have Madison on his side, when Madison wrote in 1821: "It must be not in the opinions or intentions of the Body which planned & proposed the Constitution, but in the sense attached to it by the people in their respective State Conventions where it recd. all the Authority which it possesses." Original meaning, not intent, is what matters in interpretation. See James Madison to Thomas Ritchie, 15 September 1821, National Archives, 29 June 2017, http://founders.archives.gov/documents/Madison/04-02-02-0321.

34. Planned Parenthood of Southeastern Pennsylvania v. Casey, 505 U.S. 833, 979–1002 (1992) (J. Scalia, dissenting); Grutter v. Bollinger, 539 U.S. 306 (203) (C. J. Rehnquist, concurring in part and dissenting in part); Obergefell v. Hodges, 576 U.S. (2015).

35. Lawrence v. Texas, 539 U.S. 558, 603 (2003) (J. Scalia, dissenting).

36. Lawrence v. Texas, 539 U.S. 558, 585 (2003).

37. Todd Ruger, "Reagan Aides Foresaw Kennedy Gay-Rights Views that Conservatives Now Lament," *Roll Call*, 26 June 2015, http://www.rollcall.com/news/reagan_aides_foresaw_kennedy_gay_rights_views_that_conservatives_now_lament-242563-1.html.

38. Ruger, "Reagan Aides Foresaw Kennedy Gay-Rights Views that Conservatives Now Lament."

39. Obergefell v. Hodges, 576 U.S. (2015).

40. "The Bork Hearings: An Intellectual Appetite," *New York Times*, 20 September 1987, http://www.nytimes.com/1987/09/20/us/the-bork-hearings-an-intellectual-appetite.html.

41. Kim Eisler, "To the Editor: Eisenhower's 'Mistakes,'" *New York Times*, 28 July 1997, http://www.nytimes.com/1997/07/28/opinion/l-eisenhower-s-mistakes-336475.html?mcubz=1. See also Keith Whittington, *Political Foundations of Judicial Supremacy* (Princeton, NJ: Princeton University Press, 2007), 220.

42. William J. Brennan, "In Defense of Dissents," UC Hastings, 1985, https://repository.uchastings.edu/tobriner/17/.

43. "O'Connor, Sandra Day," Federal Judicial Center, 6 March 2004,

https://web.archive.org/web/20040306042155/http://www.fjc.gov/servlet/tGetInfo?jid=1796.

44. Melanie Arter, "Justice Ginsburg: We Need An All-Female Supreme Court," *CNS News*, 26 November 2012, https://www.cnsnews.com/news/article/justice-ginsburg-we-need-all-female-supreme-court.

45. Jennie Rothenberg Gritz, "Sandra Day O'Connor: 'I Couldn't Get a Job in a Law Firm,'" *The Atlantic*, 28 June 2011, https://www.theatlantic.com/national/archive/2011/06/sandra-day-oconnor-i-couldnt-get-a-job-in-a-law-firm/241166/.

46. Jerry de Jaager, "Justice Scalia Comes Home to the Law School," *The Universtiy of Chicago Law School*, n.d., https://www.law.uchicago.edu/news/justice-scalia-comes-home-law-school.

47. See Jack Balkin, *Living Originalism* (Cambridge, MA: Harvard University Press, 2014). I owe this point to a conversation with Steve Calabresi, who is also an adherent of this kind of originalism.

6: The Commander-in-Chief Power

1. James Madison, *The Writings of James Madison*, vol. 4: 1790–1802, ed. Gaillard Hunt (G. P. Putnam's Sons, 1906), 174, available online at https://tinyurl.com/ycsxjpyq.

2. U.S. Const. art. I, § 2.

3. James Madison to Thomas Jefferson, 2 April 1798, in *The Writings of James Madison*, ed. Gaillard Hunt, vol. 3, art. 1, § 8, cl. 11, doc. 8 (G. P. Putnam's Sons, 1900–1910), available online at http://press-pubs.uchicago.edu/founders/documents/a1_8_11s8.html.

4. "Neutrality Proclamation, 22 April 1793," The National Archives, 2017, https://founders.archives.gov/documents/Washington/05-12-02-0371.

5. John Hart Ely, *War and Responsibility* (Princeton, NJ: Princeton University Press, 1995).

6. Alexander Hamilton, "The Federalist Papers: No. 70," The Avalon Project, 2008, http://avalon.law.yale.edu/18th_century/fed70.asp.

7. Joseph Story, *Commentaries on the Constitution of the United States* (Cambridge: Hilliard, Gray and Company, 1833).

8. Murray Marder, "Nixon 'A-Threat' Clarified," *Washington Post*,

252 • *Notes to Pages 94–96*

9 February 1976, http://jfk.hood.edu/Collection/Weisberg%20 Subject%20Index%20Files/T%20Disk/Tiger%20to%20 Ride%20Miscellaneous/Item%2027.pdf.

9. Marder, "Nixon 'A-Threat' Clarified."

10. Blake Stilwell, "That Time a Drunk Richard Nixon Tried to Nuke North Korea," *Business Insider*, 20 January 2017, http://www.businessinsider.com/drunk-richard-nixon-nuke-north-korea-2017-1.

11. Telecon, Scowcroft/Kissinger, 11 October 1973, reproduced by The National Archives and Records Administration, http://nsarchive2.gwu.edu//NSAEBB/NSAEBB123/Box%2022,%20 File%2010,%20Scowcroft%20-%20Kissinger%20Oct%2011%20 73%205,55%20pm%2089.pdf.

12. William J. Broad and David E. Sanger, "Debate over Trump's Fitness Raises Issue of Checks on Nuclear Power," *New York Times*, 4 August 2016, https://www.nytimes.com/2016/08/05/science/donald-trump-nuclear-codes.html?mcubz=1.

13. Jan Jarboe Russell, *Lady Bird: A Biography of Mrs. Johnson* (Boulder, CO: Taylor Trade Publishing, 2004).

14. Russell, *Lady Bird*, 303.

15. Carl Sferrazza Anthony, *America's First Families: An Inside View of 200 Years of Private Life in the White House* (New York: Touchstone, 2000), 156.

16. James G. Blight, Janet M. Lang, and David A. Welch, *Virtual JFK: Vietnam if Kennedy Had Lived* (Lanham, MD: Rowman and Littlefield, 2010), 34. See also Michael R. Beschloss, *Reaching for Glory: Lyndon Johnson's Secret White House Tapes, 1964–1965* (New York: Simon & Schuster, 2002), 177; Thomas Paterson, Garry J. Clifford, Robert Brigham, Michael Donoghue, and Kenneth Hagan, *American Foreign Relations*, vol. 2: *Since 1895* (Belmont, CA: Wadsworth Publishing, 2014), 337.

17. Dellums v. Bush, 752 F. Supp. 1141 (1990).

18. Authorization for Use of Military Force Against Iraq Resolution, Pub.L. 102–1 (Jan. 14, 1991), https://www.gpo.gov/fdsys/pkg/STATUTE-105/pdf/STATUTE-105-Pg3.pdf.

19. "Judiciary Power and Practice—The War Powers Resolution," *American Foreign Relations* (2017), http://www.americanforeign relations.com/E-N/Judiciary-Power-and-Practice-The-war-powers-resolution.html.

20. 50 U.S.C Ch. 33—"War Powers Resolution," 7 November 1973, https://www.law.cornell.edu/uscode/text/50/chapter-33.
21. That is, unless that president determines that "unavoidable military necessity" requires an additional thirty days to bring about the removal of the armed forces from combat.
22. "Roll Call Vote 102nd Congress—1st Session," 12 January 1991, https://www.senate.gov/legislative/LIS/roll_call_lists/roll_call_vote_cfm.cfm?congress=102&session=1&vote=00002.
23. Dellums v. Bush, 752 F. Supp. 1141, 1146 (1990).
24. Lobel relayed this to me in a conversation.
25. Dellums v. Bush, 752 F. Supp. 1141, 1146 (1990).
26. Campbell v. Clinton, 203 F.3d 19, 45 (D.C. Cir. 2000).
27. Lyle Denniston, "Was the Vietnam War Unconstitutional?," National Constitution Center, 20 September 2017, https://constitutioncenter.org/blog/was-the-vietnam-war-unconstitutional.
28. Charlie Savage, "2 Top Lawyers Lost to Obama in Libya War Policy Debate," *New York Times*, 17 June 2011, http://www.nytimes.com/2011/06/18/world/africa/18powers.html.
29. Zenko, Micah. "The (Not-So) Peaceful Transition of Power: Trump's Drone Strikes Outpace Obama," *Council on Foreign Relations*, 2 March 2017, https://www.cfr.org/blog/not-so-peaceful-transition-power-trumps-drone-strikes-outpace-obama.
30. Scholars like John Yoo argue that "to declare" simply means to announce that a war is happening. However, this would be an anemic power; anyone has the ability to say that a war is happening. "To declare" should rightly be thought of, as Madison did, as the ability to *initiate* a war. For Yoo's argument, see John Yoo, *The Powers of War and Peace: The Constitution and Foreign Affairs after 9/11* (Chicago: University of Chicago Press, 2006).
31. US Const. art. I, § VIII.
32. "Transcript: Vice President on 'Fox News Sunday,'" *Fox News* (published December 22, 2008), http://www.foxnews.com/story/2008/12/22/transcript-vice-president-cheney-on-fox-news-sunday.html.
33. Edward-Isaac Dovere, "Don't Count on the Cabinet to Stop a Trump-Ordered Nuclear Strike," *Politico*, 14 November 2017, https://www.politico.com/magazine/story/2017/11/14/jim-mattis-rex-tillerson-cabinet-stop-trump-nuclear-weapon-war-215824.

34. Garrett M. Graff, "The Madman and the Bomb," *Politico*, 11 August 2017, https://www.politico.com/magazine/story/2017/08/11/donald-trump-nuclear-weapons-richard-nixon-215478.

35. Matthew Fuhrmann and Todd S. Sechser, *Nuclear Weapons and Coercive Diplomacy* (Cambridge: Cambridge University Press, 2017).

36. Scott Sagan, *Moving Targets: Nuclear Strategy and National Security* (Princeton, NJ: Princeton University Press, 1989).

37. David A. Carson, "Jefferson, Congress, and the Question of Leadership in the Tripolitan War," *The Virginia Magazine of History and Biography* 94, no. 4 (October 1986): 413–18, https://www.jstor.org/stable/pdf/4248910.pdf.

38. "An Open Letter to the United Nations Convention on Certain Conventional Weapons," Future of Life Institute, 2017, https://futureoflife.org/autonomous-weapons-open-letter-2017.

39. "The Legality of Drone Warfare," Bureau of Investigative Journalism, n.d., https://www.thebureauinvestigates.com/explainers/legality-of-drone-warfare.

40. "1968—The Year and the War," C-SPAN, 8 September 1993, https://www.c-span.org/video/?50134-1/1968-year-war&showFullAbstract=1.

41. Daniel Yergin, "Fulbright's last frustration: The great dissenter finally found himself a compatible Secretary of State," *New York Times*, 24 November 1974, http://www.nytimes.com/1974/11/24/archives/fulbrights-last-frustration-the-great-dissenter-finally-found.html.

7: Madison and the Creation of the Bill of Rights

1. Thomas Jefferson to James Madison, 20 December 1787, National Archives, 26 November 2017, https://founders.archives.gov/documents/Jefferson/01-12-02-0454.

2. Ralph Louis Ketcham, *James Madison: A Biography* (Charlottesville: University of Virginia Press, 1990), 277. See also: Jack Rakove, *Original Meanings: Politics and Ideas in the Making of the Constitution* (New York: Vintage Books, 1997).

3. George Mason, "Objections to this Constitution of Government," in *The Complete Anti-Federalist Vol. 1*, ed. Herbert J. Stor-

ing and Murray Dry (Chicago: University of Chicago Press, 1981), 11–13.

4. "Virginia 1789 U.S. House of Representatives, District 5," A New Nation Votes, 11 January 2012, https://elections.lib.tufts.edu/catalog/tufts:va.uscongress.5.1789.

5. Rakove, *Original Meanings*. Also see Jack Rakove, "The Bill of Rights," Brownsville, June 2012, https://www.youtube.com/watch?v=R9gG7VToPXc.

6. Thomas Jefferson to James Madison, 20 December 1787, National Archives, 26 November 2017, https://founders.archives.gov/documents/Jefferson/01-12-02-0454.

7. Madison to Jefferson, 17 October 1788 in *The Writings of James Madison, Vol. 5: 1787–1790*, ed. Gaillard Hunt (New York: G. P. Putnam's Sons, 1904), 273, http://press-pubs.uchicago.edu/founders/documents/v1ch14s47.html.

8. U.S. Const. amend. X.

9. NCC Staff, "Five items Congress deleted from Madison's original Bill of Rights," National Constitution Center, 15 December 2016, https://constitutioncenter.org/blog/five-items-congress-deleted-from-madisons-original-bill-of-rights.

10. This doctrine is known as incorporation. The first case came in the nineteenth century with Chicago, Burlington and Quincy Railroad v. City of Chicago (1897), in which the court applied the Fifth Amendment's Just Compensation Clause to the states. Early twentieth-century examples of the doctrine include Gitlow v. New York in 1925, which made state governments protect the freedom of speech, and Palko v. Connecticut, which established that not all, but only the fundamental parts, of the Bill of Rights would be applied to the states.

11. Madison to Jefferson, 17 October 1788, in *The Writings of James Madison, Vol. 5: 1787–1790*, p. 273, http://press-pubs.uchicago.edu/founders/documents/v1ch14s47.html.

12. The Bill of Rights, Library of Congress, n.d., https://www.loc.gov/rr/program/bib/ourdocs/billofrights.html.

13. Pauline Maier, *Ratification: The People Debate the Constitution* (New York: Simon and Schuster, 2011), 458.

14. Thomas Vernon, *The Diary of Thomas Vernon* (Washington, DC: Library of Congress, 1881).

15. "Rhode Island's Ratification," USConstitution.net, 2010, https://www.usconstitution.net/rat_ri.html.

16. Bruce Ackerman and Neal Katyal, "Our Unconventional Founding," *University of Chicago Law Review* 62, no. 2 (Spring 1995), http://chicagounbound.uchicago.edu/cgi/viewcontent.cgi?articl e=4869&context=uclrev.

17. Maier, *Ratification*, 275.

18. James Madison to Thomas Jefferson, 20 May 1798, National Archives, 2017, https://founders.archives.gov/documents/Madison/01-17-02-0090.

19. Rosemarie Zagarri, "The American Revolution and a New National Politics," in *The Oxford Handbook of the American Revolution*, ed. Edward G. Gray and Jane Kamensky (New York: Oxford University Press, 2015), 486.

20. "An Act in Addition to the Act, Entitled 'An Act for the Punishment of Certain Crimes Against the United States,'" 14 July 1798, The Avalon Project, 2008, http://avalon.law.yale.edu/18th_century/sedact.asp.

21. Geoffrey R. Stone, *Perilous Time: Free Speech in Wartime: From the Sedition Act of 1798 to the War on Terrorism* (New York: W. W. Norton, 2005), 63.

22. Chae Chan Ping v. United States, 130 U.S. 581 (1889).

23. This doctrine is known as reverse incorporation: applying the Fourteenth Amendment through the Fifth Amendment. See Bolling v. Sharpe, 347 U.S. 497 (1954).

24. Korematsu v. United States, 323 U.S. 214 (1944).

25. Abrams v. United States, 250 U.S. 616 (1919) (J. Holmes, dissenting).

26. John C. Yoo, "The President's Constitutional Authority to Conduct Military Operations Against Terrorists and Nations Supporting Them," US Department of Justice Memorandum to the Deputy Counsel to the President, 25 September 2001, https://lawfare .s3-us-west-2.amazonaws.com/staging/s3fs-public/uploads/2013/10/Memorandum-from-John-C-Yoo-Sept-25-2001.pdf.

27. Jay Bybee, "Standards of Conduct for Interrogation under 18 U.S.C. sections 2340-2340A," 1 August 2002, https://www.justice.gov/olc/file/886061/download.

28. Jack Rakove, "The Bill of Rights," Brownsville, June 2012, https://www.youtube.com/watch?v=R9gG7VToPXc.

29. Jack Rakove, "The Bill of Rights."

8: The First Amendment and Free Speech

1. John F. Kennedy, "Television and Radio Interview: 'After Two Years—a Conversation With the President,'" 17 December 1962, online by Gerhard Peters and John T. Woolley, The American Presidency Project, http://www.presidency.ucsb.edu/ws/?pid=9060.
2. "Alien and Sedition Acts," Library of Congress, n.d., https://www.loc.gov/rr/program/bib/ourdocs/Alien.html.
3. Andrew Glass, "Former Rep. Matthew Lyon dies, Aug. 1, 1822," *Politico*, 1 August 2017, https://www.politico.com/story/2017/08/01/former-rep-matthews-lyons-dies-aug-1-1822-241147.
4. James Fairfax McLaughlin, *Matthew Lyon, the Hampden of Congress: A Biography* (New York: Wynkoop Hallenbeck Crawford Co., 1900), 373.
5. "Vermont 1798 U.S. House of Representatives, District 1, Ballot 2," A New Nation Votes, 11 January 2012, https://elections.lib.tufts.edu/catalog/tufts:vt.uscongress.runoff.western.1798.
6. "1912 Presidential General Election Results," US Election Atlas, 2016, https://uselectionatlas.org/RESULTS/national.php?year=1912.
7. Eugene V. Debs, "Speech at Canton, Ohio," June 16, 1918, in *Eugene V. Debs Speaks*, ed. Jean Y. Tussey (New York: Pathfinder Press, 1970), 238–74.
8. "The Espionage Act of 1917," 15 June 1917, Digital History, 2016, http://www.digitalhistory.uh.edu/disp_textbook.cfm?smtid=3&psid=3904.
9. "The Sedition Act of 1918," Digital History, 2016, http://www.digitalhistory.uh.edu/disp_textbook.cfm?smtID=3&psid=3903.
10. Eugene V. Debs, "Statement to the Court Upon Being Convicted of Violating the Sedition Act," September 18, 1918, in *Writings of Eugene V. Debs* (St. Petersburg, FL: Red and Black Publishers, 2009) 147.
11. "1920 Presidential Election Results," US Election Atlas, 2016, https://uselectionatlas.org/RESULTS/national.php?year=1920.
12. "Debs Objects to U.S. Constitution," *San Francisco Call*, 13 September 1908, https://cdnc.ucr.edu/cgi-bin/cdnc?a=d&d=SFC19080913.2.28.
13. Debs v. United States, 249 U.S. 211, 215 (1919).
14. Schenck v. United States, 249 U.S. 47, 48, 52 (1919).

15. Alexander Meiklejohn, *Free Speech and Its Relation to Self-Government* (New York: Harper Brothers, 1948).
16. Meiklejohn, *Free Speech and Its Relation to Self-Government.*
17. Meiklejohn, *Free Speech and Its Relation to Self-Government.*
18. Richard Polenberg, *Fighting Faiths: The Abrams Case, the Supreme Court, and Free Speech* (Ithaca, NY: Cornell University Press, 1987), 42.
19. Abrams v. United States, 250 U.S. 616, 620, 623 (1919).
20. Schenck v. United States, 249 U.S. 47, 48, 52 (1919).
21. Abrams v. United States, 250 U.S. 616, 623 (1919).
22. Abrams v. United States, 250 U.S. 616, 628 (1919) (J. Holmes, dissenting).
23. Abrams v. United States, 250 U.S. 616, 630 (1919) (J. Holmes, dissenting).
24. Brandenburg v. Ohio, 394 U.S. 444, 447 (1969).
25. Later, in Virginia v. Black, the court clarified that speech that really constituted a "true threat" could also be banned. See *Virginia v. Black*, 538 U.S 343, 344 (2003).
26. Jessica Schulberg, "Controversial Trump Aide Katharine Gorka Helped End Funding for Group That Fights White Supremacy," Huffington Post, 15 August 2017, http://www.huffingtonpost.com/entry/katharine-gorka-life-after-hate_us_59921356e4b090 96429943b6.
27. John F. Kennedy, "Television and Radio Interview: 'After Two Years—a Conversation With the President,'" 17 December 1962, online by Gerhard Peters and John T. Woolley, The American Presidency Project, http://www.presidency.ucsb.edu/ws/?pid=9060.
28. John F. Kennedy, "Television and Radio Interview: 'After Two Years—Conversation with the President,'" 17 December 1962, online by Gerhard Peters and John T. Woolley, The American Presidency Project, http://www.presidency.ucsb.edu/ws/?pid=9060/.

9: The First Amendment and the Freedom of Religion

1. James Madison to Edward Livingston, 10 July 1822, in *The Writings of James Madison*, ed. Gaillard Hunt, 9 vols. (New York: G. P. Putnam's Sons, 1900–1910), http://press-pubs.uchicago.edu/founders/documents/amendI_religions66.html.

2. Diane Winston, "The History of the National Prayer Breakfast," *Smithsonian*, 2 February 2017, http://www.smithsonianmag.com/history/national-prayer-breakfast-what-does-its-history-reveal-180962017/.

3. Rob Boston, "Doubting Thomas: Prayer Breakfast Theocrats Try to Baptize Jefferson," Americans United for Separation of Church and State, 18 January 2012, https://www.au.org/blogs/wall-of-separation/doubting-thomas-prayer-breakfast-theocrats-try-to-baptize-jefferson.

4. U.S. Const. amend. I.

5. "Memorial and Remonstrance Against Religious Assessments, [ca. 20 June] 1785," National Archives, 26 November 2017, https://founders.archives.gov/documents/Madison/01-08-02-0163.

6. "Memorial and Remonstrance Against Religious Assessments."

7. Leo Pfeffer, *Madison's 'Detached Memoranda': Then and Now*, in *The Virginia Statue for Religious Freedom, Its Evolution and Consequences in American History*, ed. Merrill D. Peterson and Robert C. Vaughan (Cambridge: Cambridge University Press, 1988), 286–87.

8. Vincent Phillip Muñoz, *God and the Founders: Madison, Washington, and Jefferson* (Cambridge: Cambridge University Press, 2009).

9. "Jefferson, Madison, and Jesus on the National Day of Prayer," Baker Institute, 6 May 2010, http://blog.chron.com/bakerblog/2010/05/jefferson-madison-and-jesus-on-the-national-day-of-prayer/.

10. "Presidential Proclamation, 4 March 1815," National Archives, https://founders.archives.gov/documents/Madison/99-01-02-4146.

11. David Greenberg, "Sick to His Stomach," *Slate*, 27 February 2012, http://www.slate.com/articles/news_and_politics/history_lesson/2012/02/how_santorum_misunderstands_kennedy_s_speech_on_religious_freedom_.html.

12. U.S. Const. art. VI, § 3.

13. "Transcript: JFK's Speech on His Religion," NPR, 5 December 2007, https://www.npr.org/templates/story/story.php?storyId=16920600.

14. "Transcript: JFK's Speech on His Religion."

15. Lynch v. Donnelly, 465 US 668, 687 (1984) (O'Connor, J., concurring).

16. Lynch v. Donnelly, 465 US 668, 687 (1984) (O'Connor, J., concurring).
17. "The Johnson Amendment," 26 U.S.C. 501, https://www.law .cornell.edu/uscode/text/26/501.
18. Donald Trump, Presidential Executive Order Promoting Free Speech and Religious Liberty, White House Office of the Press Secretary, 4 May 2017, https://www.whitehouse.gov/the-press-office/2017/05/04/presidential-executive-order-promoting-free-speech-and-religious-liberty.
19. Jay Weiner, "Legislative firestorm erupts over Bradlee Dean's prayer," *Minnesota Post*, 20 May 2011, https://www.minnpost.com/ politics-policy/2011/05/legislative-firestorm-erupts-over-bradlee-deans-prayer.
20. "Memorial and Remonstrance Against Religious Assessments."
21. Martin L. King Jr., "I Have a Dream," Washington, DC, 28 August 1963, https://www.archives.gov/files/press/exhibits/dream-speech.pdf.
22. Town of Greece v. Galloway, 572 U.S. (2014).
23. "Memorial and Remonstrance Against Religious Assessments."
24. "George Washington and His Letter to the Jews of Newport," Touro Synagogue, 2015, http://www.tourosynagogue.org/history -learning/gw-letter.
25. "George Washington and His Letter to the Jews of Newport."

10: The Eighth Amendment and the Ban on Torture

1. Eric Schmitt, "President Backs McCain Measure on Inmate Abuse," *New York Times*, 16 December 2005, http://www.nytimes .com/2005/12/16/politics/president-backs-mccain-measure-on-inmate-abuse.html?_r=0.
2. Jess Bravin, "Waterboarding is Torture, Says International Red Cross," *Wall Street Journal*, 7 August 2014, https://www.wsj.com/ articles/waterboarding-is-torture-says-international-red-cross-1407449858.
3. "Geneva Conventions of 1949 and Additional Protocols, and their Commentaries," International Committee of the Red Cross, n.d., https://ihl-databases.icrc.org/applic/ihl/ihl.nsf/vwTreaties1949.xsp.
4. Wilkerson v. Utah, 99 U.S 130, 135–36 (1878).
5. Neil Lewis, "A Guide to the Memos on Torture," *New York Times*

International, 2005, http://www.nytimes.com/ref/international/24 MEMO-GUIDE.html.

6. Lesley Stahl, "Justice Scalia on the Record," CBS News, 24 April 2008, https://www.cbsnews.com/news/justice-scalia-on-the-record/.

7. "English Bill of Rights 1689," The Avalon Project, 2008, http://avalon.law.yale.edu/17th_century/england.asp.

8. Edward P. Cheyney, "The Court of Star Chamber," *The American Historical Review* 18, no. 4 (July 1913): 727–50, JSTOR, https://www.jstor.org/stable/1834768?seq=1#page_scan_tab_contents.

9. John Rushworth, *Historical Collections*, vol. 2 (1706), 293, https://www.staff.ncl.ac.uk/j.p.boulton/xread/ears.htm.

10. "Charles I, 1640: An Act for the Regulating the Privie Councell and for taking away the court commonly called the Star Chamber," *Statutes of the Realm* 5:1628–80, ed. John Raithby, s.l: Great Britain Record Commission, 1819, 110–12, *British History Online*, http://www.british-history.ac.uk/statutes-realm/vol5/pp110-112.

11. U.S. Const. art. I, § 9, cl. 2.

12. Thomas Babington Macaulay, *The History of England from the Accession of James the Second*, vol. 1 (Philadelphia: J. B. Lippincott, 1879).

13. "English Bill of Rights 1689."

14. Thomas Jefferson, "Thomas Jefferson: Autobiography, 6 Jan.–29 July 1821, 6 January 1821," *Founders Online*, National Archives, last modified April 12, 2018, http://founders.archives.gov/documents/Jefferson/98-01-02-1756. See also James Madison, "Report on Books for Congress, [23 January] 1783," *Founders Online*, National Archives, last modified April 12, 2018, http://founders.archives.gov/documents/Madison/01-06-02-0031.

15. Tim Mak and Shane Harris, "The Most Gruesome Moments in the CIA 'Torture Report,'" *The Daily Beast*, 9 December 2014, http://www.thedailybeast.com/the-most-gruesome-moments-in-the-cia-torture-report.

16. Mak and Harris, "The Most Gruesome Moments in the CIA 'Torture Report.'"

17. Bill Chappell, "Psychologists Behind CIA 'Enhanced Interrogation' Program Settle Detainees' Lawsuit," NPR, 17 August 2017, https://www.npr.org/sections/thetwo-way/2017/08/17/544183178/

psychologists-behind-cia-enhanced-interrogation-program-settle-detainees-lawsuit.

18. Ali Soufan, "I interrogated the top terrorist in US custody. Then the CIA came to town," *The Guardian*, 12 December 2014, https://www.theguardian.com/commentisfree/2014/dec/12/interrogated-terrorist-cia-senate-report.

19. "'Rectal Hydration': Inside the CIA's Interrogation of Khalid Sheikh Mohammed," *NBC News*, 9 December 2014, https://www.nbcnews.com/storyline/cia-torture-report/rectal-hydration-inside-cias-interrogation-khalid-sheikh-mohammed-n265016.

20. Faiz Shakir, "Khalid Sheikh Mohammed Was Waterboarded 183 Times in One Month," *ThinkProgress*, 19 April 2009.

21. "Detainee Treatment Act of 2005," Title X of Division A of the Defense Appropriations Act of Fiscal Year 2006 (Public Law 109-148 of December 30, 2007, Title X; 119 STAT. 2739). For the text, see Office of the Director of National Intelligence, *Legal Reference Book*, https://www.dni.gov/index.php/ic-legal-reference-book/detainee-treatment-act-of-2005.

22. Barack Obama, Executive Order 13491: Ensuring Lawful Detentions, Federal Register 74, No. 16, 27 January 2009, https://www.gpo.gov/fdsys/pkg/FR-2009-01-27/pdf/E9-1885.pdf.

23. "Detainee Treatment Act of 2005."

24. Schmitt, "President Backs McCain Measure on Inmate Abuse."

25. Youngstown v. Sawyer, 343 U.S. 579, 635 (1952) (J. Jackson, concurring).

26. See arguments about value-based reading from Chapter 5.

27. "Convention against Torture and Other Cruel, Inhuman or Degrading Treatment or Punishment," United Nations Human Rights Office of the High Commissioner, 10 December 1984, http://www.ohchr.org/EN/ProfessionalInterest/Pages/CAT.aspx.

28. *Ex Parte Quirin*, 317 U.S. 1 (1942).

29. Boumediene v. Bush, 553 U.S. 723 (2008).

30. Boumediene v. Bush, 553 U.S. 723, 744 (2008).

31. Rochin v. California, 342 U.S. 165, 172 (1952).

32. Jonathan Schell, "When the Gloves Come Off," *The Nation*, 15 October 2008, https://www.thenation.com/article/when-gloves-come/.

33. Nick Gass, "Trump: We have to take out ISIL members' families," *Politico*, 2 December 2015, https://www.politico.com/story/2015/12/trump-kill-isil-families-216343.

11: The Fourteenth and Fifth Amendments and the Guarantee of Equal Protection of the Laws

1. Brown v. Board of Education of Topeka, 347 U.S. 483, 495 (1954).
2. U.S. Const. art. I, § 9.
3. Dred Scott v. Sandford, 60 U.S. 393, 404–405 (1857).
4. Dred Scott v. Sandford, 60 U.S. 393, 404–405 (1857).
5. US Const. amend. XIII, and U.S. Const. amend. XV.
6. U.S. Const. amend. XIV.
7. U.S. Const. amend. XIV, § 1.
8. "On this Day," *New York Times*, 27 March 2001, http://www.nytimes.com/learning/general/onthisday/harp/0327.html.
9. *Controversies in Constitutional Law: Collections of Documents and Articles on Major Questions of American Law*, ed. Paul Finkelman (New York: Garland Publishing, 2000).
10. Scott (Chinese Exclusion) Act, Act of October 1, 1888, c. 1064, 25 Stat. 504.
11. "Chinese Exclusion Act; May 6, 1882," The Avalon Project, 2008, http://avalon.law.yale.edu/19th_century/chinese_exclusion_act.asp.
12. Chae Chan Ping v. United States, 130 U.S. 581, 604–605 (1889).
13. The Separate Car Act, section 2, Act 111, 1890 Louisiana Legislature.
14. Plessy v. Ferguson, 163 U.S. 537 (1896).
15. Executive Order 9066, February 19, 1942, National Archives, https://www.archives.gov/historical-docs/todays-doc/?doddate=219.
16. David G. Savage, "U.S. official cites misconduct in Japanese American internment cases," *Los Angeles Times*, 24 May 2011, http://articles.latimes.com/2011/may/24/nation/la-na-japanese-americans-20110525 .
17. Korematsu v. United States, 323 U.S. 214, 216 (1944).
18. Korematsu v. United States, 323 U.S. 214, 223 (1944).
19. Korematsu v. United States, 323 U.S. 214, 216 (1944)
20. I thank my friend and colleague Jed Shugerman for this point.
21. G. Edward White, "The Unacknowledged Lesson: Earl Warren and the Japanese Relocation Controversy," *Virginia Quarterly Review* (1979), http://www.vqronline.org/essay/unacknowledged-lesson-earl-warren-and-japanese-relocation-controversy.

22. Korematsu v. United States, 323 U.S. 214, 246 (1944) (J. Jackson, dissenting).
23. Madison, "The Federalist Papers: No. 48," The Avalon Project, 2008, http://avalon.law.yale.edu/18th_century/fed48.asp.
24. Brown v. Board of Education of Topeka, 347 U.S. 483, 494–495 (1954).
25. Brown v. Board of Education of Topeka, 347 U.S. 483, 495 (1954).
26. Plyler v. Doe, 457 U.S. 202, 210 (1982).
27. United States v. Windsor, 570 U.S. (2013).
28. "H.R. 3396—Defense of Marriage Act," 104th Congress (1995–1996), https://www.congress.gov/bill/104th-congress/house-bill/3396/text/enr.
29. United States v. Windsor, 570 U.S. (2013).
30. The Civil Liberties Act of 1988 (Pub.L. 100–383).
31. Leslie T. Hatamiya, *Righting a Wrong: Japanese Americans and the Passage of the Civil Liberties Act of 1988* (Redwood City, CA: Stanford University Press, 1993).
32. Donald Trump, Executive Order: Protecting the Nation from Foreign Terrorist Entry into the United States, The White House Office of the Press Secretary, 27 January 2017, https://www.whitehouse.gov/the-press-office/2017/01/27/executive-order-protecting-nation-foreign-terrorist-entry-united-states.
33. Daniel Burke, "Trump says US will prioritize Christian refugees," CNN, 30 January 2017, http://www.cnn.com/2017/01/27/politics/trump-christian-refugees/index.html.
34. Donald Trump, Executive Order: Protecting the Nation from Foreign Terrorist Entry into the United States, The White House Office of the Press Secretary, 6 March 2017, https://www.whitehouse.gov/presidential-actions/executive-order-protecting-nation-foreign-terrorist-entry-united-states-2/.
35. International Refugee Assistance Project v. Trump, 857 F. 3d 554 (4th Cir. 2017), https://assets.documentcloud.org/documents/3733125/5-25-17-4th-Circuit-IRAP.pdf.
36. Greg Stohr, "U.S. Supreme Court Dismisses Remaining Trump Travel Ban Case," *Bloomberg Politics*, 24 October 2017, https://www.bloomberg.com/news/articles/2017-10-24/u-s-supreme-court-dismisses-remaining-trump-travel-ban-case.
37. International Refugee Assistance Project v. Trump, 857 F. 3d 554 (4th Cir. 2017).
38. Bilal Qureshi, "From Wrong to Right: A U.S. Apology for Jap-

anese Internment," NPR, 9 August 2013, https://www.npr.org/sections/codeswitch/2013/08/09/210138278/japanese-internment-redress.

12: How to Stop a President

1. James Madison, "The Federalist Papers: No. 49," The Avalon Project, 2008, http://avalon.law.yale.edu/18th_century/fed49.asp.
2. Madison, "The Federalist Papers: No. 51," The Avalon Project, 2008, http://avalon.law.yale.edu/18th_century/fed51.asp. Madison wrote: "If angels were to govern men, neither external nor internal controls on government would be necessary. In framing a government which is to be administered by men over men, the great difficulty lies in this: you must first enable the government to control the governed; and in the next place oblige it to control itself."
3. Stuart Leibiger, *Founding Friendship: George Washington, James Madison, and the Creation of the American Republic* (Charlottesville: University of Virginia Press, 1999), 104.
4. George Washington, "Undelivered First Inaugural Address: Fragments, 30 April 1789," National Archives, 2017, https://founders.archives.gov/documents/Washington/05-02-02-0130-0002.
5. Washington, "Undelivered First Inaugural Address: Fragments, 30 April 1789."
6. George Washington, "Second Inaugural Address," 4 March 1793, The Avalon Project, 2008, http://avalon.law.yale.edu/18th_century/wash2.asp.
7. Alexander Hamilton, "The Federalist Papers: No. 78," The Avalon Project, 2008, http://avalon.law.yale.edu/18th_century/fed78.asp.
8. Marbury v. Madison, 5 U.S. 137 (1803).
9. For an earlier discussion in which the Court considers the power of judicial review, see Calder v. Bull, 3 U.S. 386, 396 (1798).
10. Richard A. Samuelson, "The Midnight Appointments," The White House Historical Association, 2000, https://www.whitehousehistory.org/the-midnight-appointments.
11. Marbury v. Madison, 5 U.S. 137 (1803).
12. C. Perry Patterson, "James Madison and Judicial Review," *California Law Review* 28, No. 1 (November 1939): 27, http://

scholarship.law.berkeley.edu/cgi/viewcontent.cgi?article=3708&context=californialawreview.

13. "From Thomas Jefferson to William Charles Jarvis, 28 September 1820," National Archives, 26 November 2017, https://founders.archives.gov/documents/Jefferson/98-01-02-1540.

14. Thomas Jefferson to Spencer Roane, 6 September 1819, The National Archives, https://founders.archives.gov/documents/Jefferson/98-01-02-0734.

15. "A Federalist Stronghold: John Marshall's Supreme Court," USHistory.org, 2017, http://www.ushistory.org/us/20e.asp.

16. "An Act to Establish the Judicial Courts of the United States, First Congress. Sess. I. CH 20. 24 September 1789," The Library of Congress, 2017, https://memory.loc.gov/cgi-bin/ampage?collId=llsl&fileName=001/llsl001.db&recNum=196.

17. "Judiciary Act of 1789," Library of Congress, 2017, https://www.loc.gov/rr/program/bib/ourdocs/judiciary.html.

18. Marbury v. Madison, 5 U.S. 137 (1803).

19. "Alien and Sedition Acts," History.com, 2017, http://www.history.com/topics/alien-and-sedition-acts.

20. U.S. Const. amend. X.

21. James Madison, "Virginia Resolution—Alien and Sedition Acts," The Avalon Project, 2008, http://avalon.law.yale.edu/18th_century/virres.asp.

22. U.S. Const. art. VI, cl. 3.

23. "Thomas Jefferson to Spencer Roane, 6 Sept. 1819," in *The Works of Thomas Jefferson, Vol. 12*, ed. Paul Leicester Ford (New York: G. P. Putnam's Sons, 1905), 137. Available online at http://press-pubs.uchicago.edu/founders/documents/a1_8_18s16.html.

24. U.S. Const. art. II, § 1.

13: The Judicial Check on a President

1. "To the Senate and House of Representatives, Third Annual Message: 7 December 1903," The American Presidency Project, www.presidency.ucsb.edu/ws/index.php?pid=29544.

2. Jason Moscovitz, "1996: Chretien extends a 'Shawinigan handshake,'" *CBC News*, 15 February 1996, http://www.webcitation.org/6ESJL9wiO. Clyde H. Farnsworth, "A Scuffle Reopens Canadian Wounds," *New York Times*, 23 February 1996, https://

www.nytimes.com/1996/02/23/world/a-scuffle-reopens-canadi
an-wounds.html.

3. Moscovitz, "1996: Chrétien extends a 'Shawinigan handshake.'"

4. "A Sitting President's Amenability to Indictment and Criminal Prosecution," 16 October 2000, Department of Justice, https://www.justice.gov/file/19351/download. The cited memo is from President Clinton's Department of Justice Office of Legal Counsel (OLC), but the memo summarized and agreed with the position of President Nixon's OLC, which argued that a sitting president could not be indicted.

5. Egil Kroch, "The Break-In that History Forgot," *New York Times*, 30 June 2007, http://www.nytimes.com/2007/06/30/opinion/30krogh.html.

6. Susanna McBee, "Court Battle Set as Nixon Defies Subpoenas," *Washington Post*, 27 July 1973, www.washingtonpost.com/wp-srv/national/longterm/watergate/articles/072773-1.htm.

7. United States v. Nixon, 418 U.S. 683, 707 (1974).

8. United States v. Nixon, 418 U.S. 683, 705 (1974).

9. "A Sitting President's Amenability to Indictment and Criminal Prosecution."

10. The Office of Legal Counsel wrote in an August 5, 1974, memo that a self-pardon would violate the fundamental principle that no one can be the judge in his or her own case. See "Presidential or Legislative Pardon of the President," 5 August 1974, Department of Justice, Office of Legal Counsel, https://www.justice.gov/file/20856/download.

11. U.S. Const. art. 11, §2, cl. 1.

12. Nixon v. Fitzgerald, 457 U.S. 731, 733–738 (1982).

13. Nixon v. Fitzgerald, 457 U.S. 731, 748–749 (1982).

14. "'Clinton v. Starr': A 'Definitive' Account," NPR, 16 February 2010, http://www.npr.org/templates/story/story.php?storyId=123653000.

15. Ronald D. Rotunda, "Indicting the President: President Clinton's Justice Department Says No," Verdict.Justia.com, 14 August 2017, https://verdict.justia.com/2017/08/14/indicting-president-president-clintons-justice-department-says-no.

16. Clinton v. Jones, 520 U.S. 681, 692–710 (1997).

17. Alyssa Mastromonaco, "The Office of Scheduling and Advance," Civics 101, 24 March 2017, https://www.civics101podcast.org/civics-101-episodes/ep18.

14: Federalism

1. James Madison, "Virginia Resolution—Alien and Sedition Acts," The Avalon Project, 2008, avalon.law.yale.edu/18th_century/virres.asp.
2. Thomas Jefferson to James Madison, 26 October 1798, National Archives, 2017, https://founders.archives.gov/documents/Jefferson/01-30-02-0384.
3. U.S. Const. amend. X.
4. "Resolutions Adopted by the Kentucky General Assembly," in *The Papers of Thomas Jefferson, Volume 30: 1 January 1798 to 31 January 1799* (Princeton, NJ: Princeton University Press, 2003), 550–56.
5. "Virginia Resolution—Alien and Sedition Acts," The Avalon Project, 2008, http://avalon.law.yale.edu/18th_century/virres.asp. See also "Resolutions Adopted by the Kentucky General Assembly," in *The Papers of Thomas Jefferson, Volume 30*, 550–56.
6. "Virginia Resolution—Alien and Sedition Acts," The Avalon Project, 2008, http://avalon.law.yale.edu/18th_century/virres.asp.
7. "Resolutions Adopted by the Kentucky General Assembly," in *The Papers of Thomas Jefferson, Vol. 30*, 550–56.
8. *Exposition and Protest, Reported by the Special Committee of the House of Representatives, on the Tariff, Read and Ordered to be Printed, Dec. 19th 1828* (Columbia, SC: D. W. Sims, 1829).
9. "Resolutions Adopted by the Kentucky General Assembly," 550–56.
10. John C. Calhoun, "Original Draft of the South Carolina Exposition, prepared for the Special Committee on the Tariff," in *Reports and Public Letters of John C. Calhoun*, ed. Richard K. Crallé (New York: D. Appleton & Co., 1864), 41.
11. In an 1830 letter, Madison wrote: "I have made no secret of my surprize and sorrow at the proceedings in S Carolina, which are understood to assert a right to annul the Acts of Congress within the State, and even to secede from the Union itself." See James Madison to N. P. Trist, February 15, 1830, in *The Writings of James Madison, Volume 9. 1819–1836*, ed. Gaillard Hunt (New York: G. P. Putnam's Sons, 1910), 357. Available at the Online Library of Liberty, http://lf-oll.s3.amazonaws.com/titles/1940/1356.09_Bk.pdf.
12. "Jefferson's Fair Copy: The Kentucky Resolutions," in *The Papers of Thomas Jefferson, Vol. 30: 1 January 1798 to 31 January*

1799 (Princeton, NJ: Princeton University Press, 2003), 543–49, https://jeffersonpapers.princeton.edu/selected-documents/jefferson's-fair-copy.

13. James Madison, "Notes on Nullification," in *The Writings of James Madison, Volume 9. 1819–1836*, ed. Gaillard Hunt (New York: G. P. Putnam's Sons, 1910), 586.

14. James Madison, "On Nullification: December 1834," *Founders Early Access*, 2017, http://rotunda.upress.virginia.edu/founders/default.xqy?keys=FOEA-print-02-02-02-3065.

15. Michael Klarman, *From Jim Crow to Civil Rights: The Supreme Court and the Struggle for Racial Equality* (Oxford, UK: Oxford University Press), 2006.

16. Jens Manuel Krogstad, Jeffrey S. Passel, and D'Vera Cohn, "5 Facts about Illegal Immigration in the U.S.," Pew Research Center, 27 April 2017, http://www.pewresearch.org/fact-tank/2017/04/27/5-facts-about-illegal-immigration-in-the-u-s/.

17. "The Effects of Immigration on the United States Economy," Wharton Budget Model, 27 June 2016, http://www.budget model.wharton.upenn.edu/issues/2016/1/27/the-effects-of-immigration-on-the-united-states-economy.

18. Richard Perez-Pena, "Contrary to Trump's Claims, Immigrants Are Less Likely to Commit Crimes," *New York Times*, 26 January 2017, https://www.nytimes.com/2017/01/26/us/trump-illegal-immigrants-crime.html?mcubz=1&_r=0.

19. Patrick Jonsson, "Trump's Bid to Federalize Cops Faces Roadblock: Cops," *Christian Science Monitor*, 29 March 2017, https://www.csmonitor.com/USA/Justice/2017/0329/Trump-s-bid-to-federalize-cops-faces-roadblock-cops.

20. Scott Herhold, "Appellate Justice Miguel Marquez to become Santa Clara County COO," *Mercury News*, 3 August 2016, http://www.mercurynews.com/2016/08/03/appellate-justice-miguel-marquez-to-become-santa-clara-county-coo/.

21. Simon Maloy, "Mass deportation is coming: Trump's Homeland Security Department lays out game plan to expel large numbers of immigrants," *Salon*, 21 February 2017, https://www.salon.com/2017/02/21/mass-deportation-is-coming-trumps-dhs-lays-out-game-plan-to-expel-large-numbers-of-immigrants/.

22. "Secure Communities: Overview," Immigration and Customs Enforcement, 2017, https://www.ice.gov/secure-communities.

23. Donald Trump, Executive Order: Enhancing Public Safety in the

Interior of the United States. The White House Office of the Press Secretary, 25 January 2017, https://www.whitehouse.gov/the-press-office/2017/01/25/presidential-executive-order-enhancing-public-safety-interior-united/.

24. James Queally, "ICE agents make arrests at courthouses, sparking backlash from attorneys and state supreme court," *LA Times*, 16 March 2017, http://www.latimes.com/local/lanow/la-me-ln-ice-courthouse-arrests-20170315-story.html.

25. Drew Schwartz, "Motel 6 Is Turning Undocumented Immigrants In to ICE, Attorneys Believe," *Vice*, 13 September 2017, https://www.vice.com/en_us/article/xwg87n/motel-6-is-turning-undocumented-immigrants-in-to-ice-attorneys-believe-vgtrn.

26. "Race and Ethnicity in Santa Clara County, California," in Statistical Atlas, 2017, https://statisticalatlas.com/county/California/Santa-Clara-County/Race-and-Ethnicity.

27. Eric Kurhi, "Surprise Findings for Santa Clara, Alameda counties regarding ICE requests to detain immigrants," *Mercury News*, 21 March 2017, http://www.mercurynews.com/2017/03/21/santa-clara-alameda-counties-on-ice-shame-list-of-those-not-detaining-immigrants/.

28. Printz v. United States, 521 U.S. 898, 905–918 (1997).

29. South Dakota v. Dole, 483 U.S. 203, 211 (1987).

30. County of Santa Clara v. Trump, 3:17-cv-00574 (N.D. Cal.), https://www.clearinghouse.net/detail.php?id=15622.

31. Kyle John Day, *The Southern Manifesto: Massive Resistance and the Fight to Preserve Segregation* (Jackson: University Press of Mississippi, 2015).

32. U.S. Const. amend. X.

33. George Washington, "Second Inaugural Address," 4 March 1793, The Avalon Project, 2008, http://avalon.law.yale.edu/18th_century/wash2.asp.

15: The Congressional Check and Impeachment

1. Alexander Hamilton, "The Federalist Papers: No. 65," The Avalon Project, http://avalon.law.yale.edu/18th_century/fed65.asp.

2. Another process of removal is outlined in the Twenty-Fifth Amendment, which allows a vote of the majority of the cabinet with the approval of the vice president to temporarily remove

a president, followed by a congressional vote to determine full removal. The procedure is unlikely to be invoked except in the case of severe physical or mental illness because it relies on the votes of members of the president's own cabinet whom he or she has appointed. See U.S. Const., Amend. XXV.

3. George Washington, "Second Inaugural Address," 4 March 1793, The Avalon Project, 2008, http://avalon.law.yale.edu/18th_century/wash2.asp.

4. U.S. Const. art. I, § 2, cl. 5, and art. I, § 3, cl. 6 and 7.

5. "The 1957 Pulitzer Prize Winner in Biography or Autobiography: *Profiles in Courage*, by John F. Kennedy (Harper)," The Pulitzer Prizes, 2017, www.pulitzer.org/winners/john-f-kennedy.

6. John F. Kennedy, *Profiles in Courage* (New York: Harper Perennial Modern Classics, 2006).

7. Under *Myers*, as we saw in Chapter 4, the president can fire executive officers of the cabinet at will.

8. U.S. Const. art. II, § 4.

9. Kenneth C. Davis, "The History of American Impeachment," *Smithsonian*, 12 June 2017, https://www.smithsonianmag.com/history/what-you-need-know-about-impeachment-180963645/.

10. Noah Feldman, "James Madison Didn't Want to Normalize Impeachment," *Bloomberg View*, 7 November 2017, https://www.bloomberg.com/view/articles/2017-11-07/james-madison-didn-t-want-to-normalize-impeachment.

11. H. Lowell Brown, *High Crimes and Misdemeanors in Presidential Impeachment* (London: Palgrave MacMillan, 2010).

12. Hamilton, "The Federalist Papers: No. 65," The Avalon Project, 2008, avalon.law.yale.edu/18th_century/fed65.asp.

13. Hamilton, "The Federalist Papers: No. 65," 7 March 1788, The Avalon Project, 2008, http://avalon.law.yale.edu/18th_century/fed65.asp.

14. U.S. Const. art. I.

15. "President Andrew Johnson Impeached," History.com, 2010, http://www.history.com/this-day-in-history/president-andrew-johnson-impeached.

16. Hans Trefousse, *The Radical Republicans* (New York: Knopf Doubleday, 2014).

17. "The Civil Rights Bill of 1866," History, Art & Archives, United States House of Representatives, 9 April 1866, history.house.gov/Historical-Highlights/1851-1900/The-Civil-Rights-Bill-of-1866/.

18. "Congress and Civil Rights," Digital History, 2003, http://www.digitalhistory.uh.edu/exhibits/reconstruction/section4/section4_congress.html.
19. "King Andy and the Radicals: The Impeachment of Andrew Johnson," Constitutional Rights Foundation, 2017, www.crf-usa.org/impeachment/impeachment-of-andrew-johnson.html.
20. Paul H. Bergeron, *The Papers of Andrew Johnson*, vol. 10, *February–July 1866* (Knoxville: University of Tennessee Press, 1992), 41–48.
21. Bergeron, *The Papers of Andrew Johnson: February–July 1866*, 48.
22. Bergeron, *The Papers of Andrew Johnson: February–July 1866*, 48.
23. Paul H. Bergeron, *The Papers of Andrew Johnson*, vol. 11, *August 1866–January 1867* (Knoxville, University of Tennessee Press, 1994), 180.
24. "The Impeachment of Andrew Johnson (1868) President of the United States," *United States Senate*, 2017, https://www.senate.gov/artandhistory/history/common/briefing/Impeachment_Johnson.htm.
25. Frederick Douglass, "A Treacherous President Stood in the Way," *The Atlantic*, December 1866, https://www.theatlantic.com/politics/archive/2017/08/a-treacherous-president-stood-in-the-way/537066/.
26. Johnson also undermined civil rights in other ways, such as by vetoing the Civil Rights Act of 1866, the Military Reconstruction Act of 1867, and the Freedmen's Bureau Bill of 1866.
27. Patrick Barkham, "Clinton Impeachment Timeline," *The Guardian*, 18 November 1998, https://www.theguardian.com/world/1998/nov/18/clinton.usa.
28. Andrew Glass, "Bill Clinton's impeachment trial ends, Feb. 12, 1999," *Politico*, 12 February 2009, https://www.politico.com/story/2009/02/bill-clintons-impeachment-trial-ends-feb-12-1999-018734.
29. Alison Mitchell, "The President's Acquittal: The Overview; Clinton Acquitted Decisively: No Majority For Either Charge," *New York Times*, 13 February 1999, http://www.nytimes.com/1999/02/13/us/president-s-acquittal-overview-clinton-acquitted-decisively-no-majority-for.html.
30. For a more scholarly take on this issue, see Keith Whittington, for example, https://niskanencenter.org/blog/possibly-impeachable-offenses/.

31. Ann Coulter, *High Crimes and Misdemeanors: The Case Against Bill Clinton* (Washington, DC: Regnery Publishing, 2002).

32. "Motion of No Confidence," *Parliament.UK*, n.d., https://www.parliament.uk/site-information/glossary/motion-of-no-confidence/.

33. U.S. Const. art. I, § 9, cl. 3

34. Charles L. Black Jr., *Impeachment: A Handbook* (New Haven, CT: Yale University Press, 1974), 37–41.

35. U.S. Const. art. I, § 3, cl. 7.

36. James MacGregor Burns and Susan Dunn, *George Washington* (New York: Times Books, 2013).

37. Thomas Jefferson to George Logan, 12 November 1816, National Archives, 2017, https://founders.archives.gov/documents/Jefferson/03-10-02-0390.

38. Ralph Ketcham, *James Madison: A Biography* (Charlottesville: University of Virginia Press, 1990), 640.

39. Elinor Evans, "Bribes, Gifts, and Scandal: 7 Stories of Corruption That Shocked Britain," *BBC History Extra*, 14 March 2017, http://www.historyextra.com/article/bbc-history-magazine/bribes-scandal-stories-corruption-shocked-britain.

40. U.S. Const. art. I, § 9, cl. 8. The Title of Nobility Clause of the Constitution states: "No Title of Nobility shall be granted by the United States: And no Person holding any Office of Profit or Trust under them, shall, without the Consent of the Congress, accept of any present, Emolument, Office, or Title, of any kind whatever, from any King, Prince, or foreign State."

41. On foreign emoluments, see U.S. Const. art. I, § 9, cl. 8. On domestic emoluments, see U.S. Const. art. II, § 1, cl. 7, which states: "The President shall, at stated Times, receive for his Services, a Compensation, which shall neither be increased nor diminished during the Period for which he shall have been elected, and he shall not receive within that Period any other Emolument from the United States, or any of them."

42. Lily Rothman, "The History Behind Donald Trump's Refusing a Presidential Salary," *Time*, 15 November 2016, http://time.com/4570858/donald-trump-salary-president-history/.

43. "Second Inaugural Address of George Washington, 4 March 1793," The Avalon Project, 2008, http://avalon.law.yale.edu/18th_century/wash2.asp.

44. Jennifer Wang, "Why Trump Won't Use a Blind Trust and What His Predecessors Did with Their Assets," *Forbes*, 15 November 2016, https://www.forbes.com/sites/jenniferwang/2016/11/15/why-trump-wont-use-a-blind-trust-and-what-his-predecessors-did-with-their-assets/#311dc0f729c0.

45. Walter Einenkel, "When Jimmy Carter was president, he gave up his self-built peanut farm and then was investigated," *Daily Kos*, 8 December 2016, https://www.dailykos.com/stories/2016/12/8/1608781/-When-Jimmy-Carter-was-president-he-gave-up-his-self-built-peanut-farm-and-then-was-investigated.

46. Elizabeth Drew, *Washington Journal: Reporting Watergate and Richard Nixon's Downfall* (New York: The Overlook Press, 2014), Chapter 20.

Conclusion

1. U.S. Const. art. II, § 1.

Index